GOLD

C1 Advanced

NEW EDITION

CONTENTS

Introduction p. 4

2

CONTENTS

Introduction to the Gold Advanced Exam Maximiser

The **Gold Advanced Exam Maximiser** is specially designed to maximise your chances of success in the C1 Advanced examination.

The **Exam Maximiser** will help you prepare for the C1 Advanced exam by offering you:

- **further practice and revision** of all the important vocabulary, grammar and skills (reading, writing, listening and speaking) that you study in the **Gold Advanced Coursebook**.
- **more information** about the kinds of questions you will have to answer in the C1 Advanced exam.
- **guidance** with the strategies and techniques you should use to tackle exam tasks.
- **exam-style exercises** so that you can practise using the techniques.
- **regular extra Use of English** sections to help you practise the language and strategies you have learnt.
- **details of common mistakes** at this level and how to avoid them.
- **a complete practice exam** which you can use for preparation just before you sit for the exam. This means that you will know exactly what to expect in each paper and there are no unpleasant surprises.

How can I use the Gold Advanced Exam Maximiser?

The **Exam Maximiser** is very flexible and can be used by students in a variety of situations and in a variety of ways. Here are some typical situations:

> **1** You are doing a C1 Advanced course with other students, probably over an academic year. You are all planning to take the exam at the same time.

You are using the **Gold Advanced Coursebook** in class. Sometimes you will also do the related exercises or even a whole unit from the **Exam Maximiser** in class; your teacher will also ask you to do exercises from it at home as well. You will use the entire **Exam Maximiser** or you will use it selectively, depending on your needs and the time available.

> **2** You have already done a C1 Advanced course and you are now doing an intensive course to prepare for the exam.

Since you have already worked through the **Gold Advanced Coursebook** or perhaps another C1 Advanced Coursebook, you will use the **Exam Maximiser** in class. This, together with practice tests such as

Pearson's **Practice Tests Plus: Cambridge Advanced 2 New Edition** (2014) will give you a concentrated and highly focused short exam course.

> **3** You have a very short time in which to prepare for the C1 Advanced exam.

Your level of English is already nearing C1 Advanced exam standard, although you have not been following a coursebook. You now need specific exam skills. You will use the **Exam Maximiser** independently, because you need practice in the exam tasks and strategies for approaching them.

> **4** You are re-taking the C1 Advanced exam as unfortunately you were not successful in your first attempt.

You may need to retake the exam because you were not sufficiently familiar with the exam requirements. You will not need to follow a coursebook, but you will use the **Exam Maximiser** to develop your exam techniques and build up your confidence.

> **5** You are preparing for the C1 Advanced exam on your own.

Maybe you are not attending a C1 Advanced class, but wish to take the exam and prepare for it independently. You will get the practice and preparation by using the **Exam Maximiser** by itself. You can give yourself additional practice by using practice tests such as Pearson's **Practice Tests Plus: Cambridge Advanced 2 New Edition** (2014) just before taking the exam.

What is in the Gold Advanced Exam Maximiser?

Each unit has **grammar**, **vocabulary**, **listening**, **speaking** and **writing** sections. These are linked to the topics of the Gold Advanced Coursebook, and provide further practice in relevant skills and exam tasks. There are **Use of English** sections in exam format after every two units which provide more practice in the tasks and are based on the topic areas of the two units.

At the back of the book, there is a short section giving examples of **common language errors** and short activities to help you avoid making them. There is also a section on **exam strategies** for the **writing** and **speaking** papers.

Once you have worked through all the units, you will be ready to try the **Practice test** at the back of the book.

Exam overview

There are four papers in the C1 Advanced exam:

Reading and Use of English	1 hour 30 minutes (40 percent of marks)
Writing	1 hour 30 minutes (20 percent of marks)
Listening	40 minutes (approx.) (20 percent of marks)
Speaking	15 minutes (20 percent of marks)

The **C1 Advanced** is at Cambridge/ALTE level 4, set at C1 level on the Common European Framework of Reference. Candidates achieving a Grade A receive a certificate stating they demonstrated ability at C2 level. Candidates who perform below C1 level receive a certificate stating they demonstrated ability at B2 level.

Paper	Formats	Task focus
Reading and Use of English: eight parts, 56 questions	**Part 1**: multiple-choice cloze: choosing which word from a choice of four fits in each of eight gaps in a text	**Part 1**: use of vocabulary, e.g. idioms, collocations, fixed phrases, phrasal verbs, complementation
	Part 2: open cloze: writing the missing word in each of eight gaps in a text	**Part 2**: awareness and control of grammar with some vocabulary
	Part 3: word formation: changing the form of a given word to fit eight gaps in a text	**Part 3**: vocabulary, in particular the use of the correct form of a given word
	Part 4: key word transformation: completing six new sentences so they have a similar meaning to those given	**Part 4**: use of grammatical and lexical structures
	Part 5: answering six multiple-choice questions on one long text	**Part 5**: reading for detailed understanding of a text, opinion, attitude, tone, purpose, main idea
	Part 6: reading four short texts to match questions or statements	**Part 6**: comparing and contrasting opinions and attitudes across four short texts
	Part 7: choosing which paragraphs fit into gaps in a text	**Part 7**: reading to understand text structure, coherence and cohesion
	Part 8: deciding which section of a single text or which text out of several contains given information or ideas	**Part 8**: reading to locate relevant ideas and information in a single text or several texts
Writing Part 1: one compulsory task **Writing Part 2**: one task from a choice of three	**Part 1**: using given information which provides context and ideas for an essay of 220–260 words	**Part 1**: writing an essay based on two points from three given points. Candidates evaluate the points and express their own opinions, with reasons
	Part 2: producing one piece of writing of 220–260 words from a choice of three which may include a letter, review, proposal or report	**Part 2**: writing for a specific reader using appropriate layout and register, and a variety of functions
Listening: four parts, 30 questions	**Part 1**: three short unrelated extracts, each with two multiple-choice questions	**Part 1**: understanding gist, feeling, attitude, opinion, speaker purpose, etc.
	Part 2: monologue with a sentence-completion task	**Part 2**: understanding and recording specific information
	Part 3: interview with one or more speakers and six multiple-choice questions	**Part 3**: understanding attitude and opinion of one or more speakers
	Part 4: five short monologues on a theme to match to one of eight options in two tasks	**Part 4**: understanding gist, attitude, main points, etc.
Speaking: four parts	**Part 1**: general conversation	**Part 1**: general social language
	Part 2: comparing two out of three pictures and answering two further questions	**Part 2**: comparing, speculating and expressing opinions
	Part 3: conversation between candidates based on a question and written prompts. Candidates then negotiate towards a decision.	**Part 3**: giving and asking for opinions, explaining, negotiating, etc.
	Part 4: discussion on topics related to Part 3	**Part 4**: expressing and justifying opinions and ideas

Where we live

Speaking
Interview (Part 1) ▶ CB page 6

1 ▶ 01 **Listen to the questions an examiner asks. Match the examiner's questions (1–6) with the answers (A–E). There is one extra question for which there is no answer.**

A   That's a difficult one. Probably working in America? I've got to finish my studies first and then I'd like to travel and work my way across the USA.

B   That's easy – I use social networking sites. I'm on Facebook a lot and, of course, I text and email my best mates regularly and we meet up a lot, too.

C   Actually, most of the time I tend to stay in my country. We've got some lovely seaside towns and, of course, we have the mountains, too.

D   Let's think … Most probably I'll be doing an assignment. Now I come to think of it, I've got one to finish for my history course and the deadline is Monday.

E   Yes, I used to play a lot of tennis when I was at secondary school. I belonged to a tennis club then, too. But I gave it up when I left and went to university. I didn't have enough time, I'm afraid.

Use of English
Multiple-choice cloze (Part 1) ▶ CB page 7

1 **Match 1–6 with A–F to make collocations.**

1	be	A	development
2	high	B	success
3	personal	C	in a position to do something
4	live	D	alone
5	signify	E	salary
6	a mark of	F	a change

2 Read the article. For questions 1–8, decide which answer (A, B, C or D) best fits each gap.

Going it **alone?**

Many young people nowadays want to **(0)** _A. settle_ down by themselves and live alone. Some social commentators regard this as a negative trend, indicating that there has been a **(1)** .... of accepted social norms and society is changing.

Owning a home has long been something young people have **(2)** .... to. However, many find it hard to get a **(3)** .... on the property ladder and continue to live with their family or share with friends. Those earning high salaries are in a better **(4)** .... to invest in a property and live alone because they can **(5)** .... it.

So what is the attraction of living alone? Clearly, a person can be independent and choose a lifestyle that **(6)** .... them. Some feel it gives them the **(7)** .... to develop themselves personally and professionally. It also seems that living alone has become a **(8)** .... of success.

The question is, does this trend really mean that we are all becoming less sociable, or simply more willing to stand on our own two feet?

0	**A** settle	**B** place	**C** put	**D** sit
1	**A** breakdown	**B** turndown	**C** let-down	**D** comedown
2	**A** fantasised	**B** hoped	**C** aspired	**D** wished
3	**A** leg	**B** hand	**C** arm	**D** foot
4	**A** condition	**B** position	**C** circumstance	**D** situation
5	**A** afford	**B** pay	**C** spend	**D** provide
6	**A** fits	**B** suits	**C** matches	**D** applies
7	**A** extent	**B** range	**C** gap	**D** space
8	**A** mark	**B** brand	**C** label	**D** symptom

Grammar
Verbs in perfect and continuous forms
▶ CB page 8

1 Choose the correct alternative in each sentence.

1 We've painted the kitchen and _it's taking such a long time/ we're glad it's over_.

2 By this time next Tuesday _I'll have lived/I've lived_ here for a month.

3 When it got to six o'clock, _it had been raining/it had rained_ for ten hours.

4 I've been doing this research for hours and _I still haven't finished/ it was hard work_.

5 Looking back, I've realised why _I made/I've been making_ that one mistake last year.

6 We've only studied together for a short time but _I've known/ I've been knowing_ him for several years.

2 Put the verbs in the box in the correct category. One verb fits two categories.

agree believe belong care deny feel have hear like own prefer smell taste understand want

1 Verbs of feeling
2 Verbs of knowing or thinking
3 Verbs of possession
4 Verbs of communicating
5 Verbs of sensing

3 Decide if the verbs in Activity 2 are stative (S), dynamic (D) or can be both (B).

4 Decide if one or both sentences are possible in each item. Tick (✓) the sentences that are correct.

1 **A** I'm not liking living here.
  B I don't like living here.

2 **A** She has a baby.
  B She's having a baby.

3 **A** I feel quite ill.
  B I'm feeling quite ill.

4 **A** My stomach hurts.
  B My stomach is hurting.

5 **A** I need a new place to live.
  B I'm needing a new place to live.

6 **A** Who does this car belong to?
  B Who is this car belonging to?

5 Complete the sentences with the present simple or present continuous form of the verb in brackets.

1 I .... (smell) something burning. Did you leave the oven on?

2 He .... (prefer) to sit at the back and waste time to doing some real work.

3 I .... (see) Carol at the meeting tomorrow – I could ask her then.

4 I'm sorry, I've got to go. My friend .... (arrive) at the airport this afternoon!

5 He .... (think) of buying a new flat but he can't really afford it.

6 This ice cream .... (taste) salty but I quite like it!

Vocabulary
Compound words ▶ CB page 12

1 **Complete the sentences with the compound words in the box.**

cut-price   drop-down   high-rise   long-standing   mass-produced
run-down   sun-soaked   theatre-goer   wind-swept

1   I live on the twentieth floor of a .... tower block in the city centre, and it's great.
2   The town's become quite .... and people no longer want to live there.
3   I had a .... arrangement with a friend to meet on Saturday.
4   I bought lots of .... tickets for the cinema just because they were cheap.
5   The brochure said the resort was .... and hot but actually it was .... and cold.
6   I've been a keen .... for ages, and I love all types of plays.
7   I hate filling in online forms with .... menus.
8   I rarely buy .... clothes – I prefer designer items.

Reading
Multiple choice (Part 5) ▶ CB page 10

1 **Read the article on the right. What is the writer's main purpose?**

1   to persuade other people to live in Spain
2   to describe the process of becoming a happy expat

2 **Read the article again. For questions 1–6, choose the answer (A, B, C or D) which you think fits best according to the text.**

1   What is most unexpected for the writer?
   A the early arrival of a plane that is usually late
   B something she subconsciously includes in a message
   C a difficult question she is asked by her family
   D the respect other travellers give her
2   Feeling comfortable in another country isn't easy if
   A you are not accepted by the local people.   **C** you are out of touch with your family.
   B you are always moving on.   **D** you have some official problems.
3   The writer compares her accommodation in Madrid and Patagonia to focus on
   A expenses.   **B** practicalities.   **C** health problems.   **D** ethical issues.
4   What does the writer say about feeling at home in Madrid?
   A It didn't happen quickly.
   B It depended on finding a good place to live.
   C It was a result of becoming proficient in Spanish.
   D It required an acceptance of a slower lifestyle.
5   According to the writer, which aspect of Spanish culture gives both traditional and modern experiences?
   A sport   **B** food   **C** shopping   **D** nightlife
6   The writer believes that expats are often
   A disappointed by their new life.   **C** anxious about their decision to move.
   B insecure in the first few months.   **D** unlucky in their choice of destination.

About the exam:

In Reading and Use of English Part 5, you read a text and then answer six multiple-choice questions about it. Each question gives you four options to choose from. Only one is correct.

Strategy:

- Read the text and the title quickly to get an idea of what it is about. Then read the questions but do not look at the options yet as this can be confusing.
- Find the section of text that the question relates to and read it carefully. Think of the answer without referring to the options. Find information to support your answer.
- Look at the options and choose the one that is closest to your idea.
- Make sure that there is evidence for your answer in the text and that it is not just a plausible answer you think is right.
- Remember that the correct option will not be phrased in the same way as in the text.

HOME | **NEWS** | TRAVEL   search 🔍

Madrid, my home sweet home

It took a long time, but expat Isabel Eva Bohrer is finally ready to call Madrid her home.

'Back home!' Whenever I board and disembark a plane, I make a point of texting my family about the status of my travels. The Iberia flight from Munich, where I grew up, to Madrid, where I had been living for two years, had been on time. 'That's a surprise,' I thought – the Spanish airline is notorious for its delays and strikes. Yet when I hit the 'Send' button of my phone, I was caught even more profoundly by surprise. For the first time, I had referred to Madrid as my home.

As expats, we are bound to reflect on the notion of home at one point or another. Where is home? For many expats, the concept isn't black or white. Home involves numerous grey areas, including family and friends, memories, language, religion, lifestyle, culture and more. Having lived abroad in the United States, Argentina, Chile, Brazil, Switzerland and France, among others, I knew what it was like *not* to feel at home. In the United States, not having a Social Security Number made me an outsider, causing numerous inconveniences, such as not being able to get a phone contract with certain providers. In Brazil, not speaking the language perfectly had made me uneasy as I sensed that people talked behind my back.

In Spain, my blonde hair and fair skin clearly mark me as not a native. And yet, over the course of two years, I have managed to feel at home in the Spanish capital. My unpretentious apartment in the barrio de Salamanca – as opposed to the waterproof tent I had lived in while working on an organic farm in Argentine Patagonia – allowed me to unload my baggage, both physically and mentally. Instead of having to gather wood for the night's fires, as I had done when hiking in the South American mountains, I could settle down and focus on my professional goals as a writer.

But the feeling of home transcends the mere fact of having a somewhat permanent place to live. It is a mental sensation of equilibrium that is achieved over time. For me, feeling at home in Madrid has been a slow progressing relationship. The city initially made my acquaintance as a child: I had attended several summer camps to improve my language skills. At age 16, I completed an internship at an architecture firm in the north of the city. And at age 22, the capital and I hit a home run: I came back for good, moving into my current *piso* (apartment). Slowly but surely, I learnt to live the Spanish lifestyle. Dealing with *cantamañanas* (literally translated as 'those who sing tomorrow') is the quotidian routine here.

As a natural optimist, I continue to believe in all the positive aspects of living in Madrid. If sports ignite your spirit, Spaniards will welcome you to cheer along – the third-straight crowning of the Spanish football team at Euro 2012 was unprecedented. Unparalleled, too, is the nightlife, which will enthral flamenco lovers and clubbing addicts alike. At 8 a.m. you can watch the sun rise with *chocolate con churros*. In fact, the culinary joys never seem to sleep in Spain. There are tapas bars open at all hours, too many to enumerate. For the best *bacalao* (cod fish) in town, try Casa Labra, and the Bar Los Caracoles near the Rastro flea market for some Spanish *escargot*.

From the azure sky, my glance returned to the SMS on my phone: 'Glad to hear you arrived safely,' my family had texted back. Though they referred to that particular Munich–Madrid flight, I read the message as a more universal interpretation of the expat lifestyle. As expats, we undergo a period of ambiguity, in which we always feel like those who have just arrived. But if you give your new destination a chance, it can eventually become your home.

3 **Match the adjectives from the article (1–6) with their meanings (A–F).**

1	notorious	A	never happened before
2	numerous	B	famous for something negative
3	unpretentious	C	impossible to match or equal
4	quotidian	D	a large number of
5	unprecedented	E	down to earth, simple
6	unparalleled	F	everyday

4 **Complete the sentences with the underlined words in the article.**

1 Paul is a nice guy but he's got a load of .... I don't think he's got over losing his second wife yet.

2 I was .... grateful for your help.

3 The dancers are superb and they .... the audiences every night.

4 Coffee has started to give me indigestion problems and I will have to give it up ....

5 You need to phrase the letter carefully so that there's no possibility of .... at all.

6 The .... that the film's leading actor was sitting somewhere in the audience was exciting.

1

Task 1

For questions 1–5, choose from the list (A–H) what each speaker values most about living alone.

A the chance to relax
B the lack of responsibility to others
C the absence of noise
D the ability to learn new skills
E the freedom to speak their mind
F the opportunity to think clearly
G the possibility of developing new interests
H the wide choice of friends to spend time with

Speaker 1	1
Speaker 2	2
Speaker 3	3
Speaker 4	4
Speaker 5	5

Task 2

For questions 6–10, choose from the list (A–H) what problem each speaker identifies about living alone.

A not having a family
B feeling bored
C getting practical help
D not eating well
E having to do housework
F needing to meet new people
G not being able to ask for advice
H managing financially

Speaker 1	6
Speaker 1	7
Speaker 3	8
Speaker 4	9
Speaker 5	10

Listening

Multiple matching (Part 4)
▶ CB page 9

1 ▶ 02 You will hear five short extracts in which people are talking about living alone. While you listen, you must complete both tasks.

Vocabulary

Expressions with *space* and *room*
▶ CB page 9

1 There is a mistake in three of the sentences. Find the mistakes and correct them.

1 I've got so many books I'm running out of room on the bookshelf.
2 The concert was so popular that by the time I arrived there was standing space only.
3 I love cities with lots of open room in them.
4 If the train is crowded, it's polite to make space for as many people to get on as possible.
5 I need to find a quiet space in the library to study.
6 In my report my tutor said there was space for improvement in my work.
7 The evidence was so clear that there was little room for doubt about his guilt.
8 I hate it when people in the cinema try to spill over into my space – it's very uncomfortable!

Grammar

Conjunctions ▶ CB page 13

1 Join the pairs of sentences using the conjunctions in brackets.

Example:

I will come next week. I will not come unless Sally comes too. (*provided*)

I will come next week, provided that Sally comes too.

1 They're looking for a place to live. They haven't found it. (*as yet*)
2 Telling people to recycle everything doesn't work. Making laws doesn't work either. (*nor*)
3 People in the city use public transport. People in the countryside don't. (*whereas*)
4 Planning cities carefully has a positive effect on the future. Saving energy does too. (*as*)
5 The local council can't solve the parking problem. Residents will have to do it. (*as*)
6 No one will stop using their cars. Public transport is so unreliable. (*as long as*)

Writing
Essay (Part 1) ▶ CB page 14

1 **Look at the exam task and the two plans. Then read the sample answer and decide which plan the writer has followed.**

Your class has been watching a panel discussion about how the problem of lack of housing in towns and cities can be solved. You have made the notes below.

> **How housing problems in cities and towns can be solved**
> - renovate empty properties
> - extend the suburbs
> - build high-rise blocks

> **Some opinions expressed in the discussion**
> 'We shouldn't use up any more countryside because we've lost enough green space over the years as it is.'
> 'There's no point building more new houses when there are so many empty places with no one in them.'
> 'High-rise buildings are terrible places to live and people can feel really isolated in them.'

Write an essay for your tutor discussing **two** of the solutions in your notes. You should **explain which solution is better**, **giving reasons** to support your opinion. You may, if you wish, make use of the opinions expressed in the documentary but you should use your own words as far as possible.

Write your **essay** in **220–260** words in an appropriate style.

Plan 1
- **Introduction:** explain the housing problems in your area and summarise the three approaches to solving them
- **Paragraph 1:** say why extending suburbs would not be a good idea
- **Paragraph 2:** say why building high-rise blocks would not be a good idea
- **Conclusion:** say why renovating properties would be the best answer

Plan 2
- **Introduction:** describe the problem briefly and say what might happen if nothing is done
- **Paragraph 1:** say why renovation is a good idea but give a drawback, too
- **Paragraph 2:** say why high-rise blocks could be good in spite of previous problems
- **Conclusion:** say why both would be preferable to losing countryside and give final opinion

Most of us are all too well aware that there is a real shortage of affordable housing in towns and cities today. Properties in central locations are extremely expensive and whether you are planning to rent or buy, the prices are increasing all the time. The government and local councils need to take steps to address this issue otherwise many people will be forced to commute long distances to work.

One answer might be to renovate the thousands of existing properties that currently stand empty. This would cost far less than building completely new homes and it would improve the appearance of some neighbourhoods that have become relatively run-down. One obstacle to this, however, is the fact that the owners of some of these empty or even derelict properties are often impossible to trace. A possible solution might be the imposition of compulsory purchase orders on properties like these.

Another option could be to use the limited space available to construct modern, high-rise buildings that could house large numbers of families, rather than single dwellings. The original tower blocks that became popular in the last century failed their occupants in many ways. They had many design faults and did not cater well for the large number of people who lived in them. However, modern, well-designed buildings that include a range of facilities on site, surrounded by landscaped gardens and plenty of green space, could prove successful.

In conclusion, I must point out that there is no easy solution to this problem. Much depends on the amount of money available to invest. In my opinion, renovation is the most obvious solution and the less we encroach on the countryside, the better.

2 **Read the sample answer again and find words with a similar meaning to the words below.**

1 problem	3 now	5 difficulty
2 if not	4 quite	6 invade

3 **Do the exam task in Activity 1.**

2 The art of conversation

Speaking
Long turn (Part 2) ▶ CB page 16

About the exam:

In the Speaking test Part 2, you will be asked to talk on your own for about a minute. You will be given three pictures relating to a topic and asked to choose two of them to talk about. You will always have to do three things: compare the pictures and answer two questions. The questions are written above the pictures, so you can see them while you're speaking.

Strategy:

*   Choose which two pictures you want to talk about and tell the examiner.
*   When you compare the pictures, talk about their main focus (e.g. places, the people, feelings, reactions) and any other relevant points. Do not give a detailed description of each picture. Use phrases like *both pictures show …* and *in both situations … .*
*   Remember to address the three different parts of the task and try to speak for the full minute.

1 ▶ **03 Look at the exam task. Read a candidate's answer and think of possible words or phrases that could fill the gaps. Then listen and check your answers.**

> Look at the pictures. They show people who have to communicate well in their job. Compare two of the pictures and say why the people need to communicate well while doing these jobs and what skills they need to be able to do this.

OK, I'm going to look at these two pictures – the one of the teacher and the one of the politician; at least I'm **(1)** .... he's a politician because it looks as if he's at an important press conference. Both pictures show people who need to communicate well in their jobs. In **(2)** .... , both of them have to get across important information but for different reasons. The teacher is trying to explain something to young students in a science class who may be hearing about something for the first time, whereas the politician is talking to a whole group of experienced journalists and photographers; I **(3)** .... it could be just before an election and he's trying to explain his position, or he could be just meeting the press after something important has happened and he has to brief them about this.

The teacher has to communicate very well to be certain that the children understand the point of the experiment and also I **(4)** .... saying that he must make sure that the children are enjoying the lesson – that's really important for effective learning. In this picture they look as if they're having a good time. The politician, on the other hand, has to appear confident, convincing and persuasive. He has to convince the journalists about what he is saying. I don't **(5)** .... that politicians don't always tell the whole truth but as **(6)** .... , they need to be quite good actors!

Grammar
Review of narrative tenses
▶ CB page 17

1 Choose the correct alternative to complete the sentences.

1 It was just last week that I *had gone/went* to visit an old friend who I *didn't see/hadn't seen* for years.

2 He *left/had left* the room without saying anything and I *didn't speak/wasn't speaking* to him again.

3 *I've been working on/I'd worked on* this essay for the last two hours, so I'm tired now.

4 I *had/have* only just met her when she was *changing/changed* her job and soon afterwards she *left/was leaving*.

5 I *was born/was being born* during a thunderstorm, and I love stormy weather now.

6 After I *was reading/had read* her email, I was *sending/sent* her a private message to give her advice.

7 Although I was enjoying the meal, I *had already decided/was deciding* I didn't want to go back to the restaurant again.

8 When I *had arrived/arrived*, everyone *had talked/was talking* at once and it was impossible to hear what they *were saying/had been saying*.

9 I *had turned/turned* all the lights off before I *left/was leaving* the house.

10 The hotel I *had booked/was booking* in advance for my holiday was very disappointing, so I *had checked out/checked out* after only one night.

2 Complete the sentences with the correct form of the verbs in brackets.

1 I .... (born) in a small town in the country but I .... (move) to the town when I was only three.

2 I .... (never met) such interesting people until I .... (go) to Sam's party last Saturday.

3 I ....(plan) to visit my mother at the weekend, and just as I .... (book) a train ticket she .... (call) me.

4 From an early age, I .... (find) it difficult to speak in front of a lot of people.

5 My friend .... (turn up) just at the exact moment I .... (think) about calling her.

6 I .... (work) in the same place for years when unexpectedly I .... (lose) my job.

7 I made sure when I visited my grandmother that I .... her some flowers. (take)

8 It was sad to find that someone I .... (know) for years .... (cannot help) me when I asked.

Listening
Multiple choice (Part 1)
▶ CB page 18

1 ▶ 04 You will hear three different extracts. For questions 1–6, choose the answer (A, B or C) which fits best according to what you hear. There are two questions for each extract.

Extract 1
You hear part of a discussion between two people who attended a marketing conference.

1 What is the man doing?
   A giving his opinion of the conference
   B explaining why he attended the conference
   C describing his reaction to speakers at the conference

2 What do the speakers agree about the conference?
   A It was a waste of time.
   B It was better than expected.
   C It exhibited some interesting new products.

Extract 2
You hear part of a radio discussion about the art of conversation.

3 How does the man feel about conversation?
   A embarrassed about talking to strangers
   B confused about the use of technology
   C concerned about people not talking to each other

4 What do the speakers both think about the art of conversation?
   A It is important to talk face to face.
   B Twitter can be a useful means of communication.
   C People need to be taught how to conduct conversations.

Extract 3
You hear part of a radio discussion between two speech therapists.

5 How does the woman feel about being a speech therapist?
   A stressed by what she has to do
   B worried about the amount of work involved
   C concerned that people don't understand her job

6 What do both speakers think is important in their job?
   A being able to speak clearly
   B working as part of a team
   C having had good training

Reading
Gapped text (Part 7) ▶ CB page 20

About the exam:
In Reading and Use of English Part 7, you read a text with six missing paragraphs. You choose the correct paragraph to fill each gap from a jumbled list. There is one extra paragraph you do not need.

Strategy:
- Read the text quickly, ignoring the gaps, to get a good idea of what it is about.
- Try to guess the sort of information that might be missing.
- Scan the jumbled list of options.
- Use clues in the paragraphs before and after the gaps to help you choose the ones that fit.
- Make sure that the completed text makes sense and is logical.

1 Read the article on page 15 and choose the best title.

1 Learn how to talk to animals
2 Most effective forms of animal communication
3 The art of conversation in the natural world

2 Six paragraphs have been removed from the article. Choose from the paragraphs A–G the one which fits each gap (1–6). There is one extra paragraph which you do not need to use.

3 Match the words from the article and paragraphs (1–8) with their meanings (A–H).

1	converge	A	come together
2	squeamish	B	together, speak at the same time
3	unperturbed (by)		
4	liken (to)	C	easily upset, shocked
5	akin (to)	D	reproduce, copy
6	emulate	E	not concerned, worried
7	in unison	F	meeting
8	encounter	G	compare
		H	similar, comparable

A In the course of this research, she had a close encounter with a bull elephant, wandered over Arctic ice floes to discover how polar bears converge from hundreds of miles apart, and allowed herself to be stung all over by fire ants.

B At the other end of the zoological scale, she listened in on an ant conversation. 'Suppose you disturb an ants' nest, the soldier ants will rush out and crawl up your leg, but you won't feel anything at first until suddenly, in unison, they bite you. The reason is that they are calling to each other: "One, two, three . . . bite now!"'

C 'As they passed, I could hear them and others unseen in the distance singing to one another – more a feeling in my chest than in my ears,' she says. 'It was brief, but it was one of the most fantastic moments of my life. I still see it as I go to sleep. I know it will never happen to me again.'

D While the squeamish would choose a different adjective, Uhlenbroek is obviously unperturbed by encounters such as this. Her research shows how animals have a hidden world of complex and sophisticated communication. They sing in frequencies humans cannot hear, detect colours our eyes cannot see and send messages by smell and vibrations.

E We see this again with whales who use complex sound systems to talk to each other over vast distances in order to find a mate. Charlotte recalls her extraordinary chance encounter off Australia's Pacific coast and explains why thinking of it saddens her. She explains about the way they use sound and what it means for their chances of survival.

F As a result of this, Uhlenbroek also believes animals have something to tell us, if only we'd listen. 'They are very undemanding company,' she says. Humans are forever thinking about other things, wondering 'if ...,' but with animals, it's very straightforward, very tranquil.

G Such 'reading' of their language is akin to listening to a crowd of football supporters. The numbers and health of the group are clear from the breadth and strength of the howls. 'If football fans had bad colds, they wouldn't be able to shout quite as strongly, would they?' says Uhlenbroek. The subtler messages, however, she likens to listening to the harmonies of an orchestra.

Charlotte Uhlenbroek was floating in the Pacific Ocean in a thick mist when what she describes as 'a wall of whale' rose alongside her. It was a 40-ton humpback and her calf, which swam by so close that she could reach out and touch the youngster.

1 ____

'Like those whales, every creature on the planet has to communicate to survive,' she says. 'The most basic instincts – to feed, to defend and to breed – all rely on communication. We communicate or we die, almost instantly.' Charlotte spent a fascinating two years discovering the sophisticated ways in which animals talk to each other.

2 ____

'This last experiment was particularly interesting,' she says. 'We decided to see how they reacted when I sprayed myself with a pheromone that is known to attract males and females in both the human and animal world. Within moments, thousands and thousands of fire ants had come from nowhere and were all over me. It was absolutely amazing.'

3 ____

She remembers an American grey wolf which rubbed vigorously against her. 'It was exchanging scents,' she says, 'an invitation to become part of her group. I was most flattered.' She also managed to communicate with them using special calls. Analysis showed their responses to be highly orchestrated. They informed her who and how many they were, and their status: how healthy they were and whether they were an active, strong or weak group.

4 ____

She had less success communicating with an elephant because it is impossible for a human to emulate this animal's voice: it's just too deep. Because of their trunk, they have a built-in resonator that produces ultra-low-frequency rumbles. The sound waves can carry for great distances underground. 'They can recognise as many as 100 individual calls and, from a mile away, detect which family members are in the vicinity.'

5 ____

Dolphins, on the other hand, use a 'signature whistle' to identify themselves and they also know the individual calls of all the other dolphins in the area. Bernard Walton tells us, 'We recorded them saying, effectively, "Hi Fred, it's Charlie here," and Fred replying, "Hi Charlie, I'll just call Frank over to join us." Most animal signals are fairly fixed, but this is really sophisticated brainpower.'

6 ____

Apparently, they broadcast along a channel about 3,000ft down, which carries most sound frequencies better than any other, and over a range of 135 million square kilometres. But this channel also carries the sound of ship engines, which is just about at the same frequency and is escalating.

So the whales are now having to 'shout' to make themselves heard. And they cannot shout much louder. If the whales can't communicate, they can't breed. If they can't breed, they die. We can hear them singing now . . . but for how much longer?

Use of English
Word formation (Part 3)
▶ CB page 19

About the exam:

In Reading and Use of English Part 3, you read a text with a gap in some of the lines. You must change the word in capitals at the end of these lines so they fit the gap in the same line.

Strategy:

- Read the whole text so that you know what it is about.
- Look at each sentence in detail.
- Think about what kind of word you need and whether you need a negative prefix or a suffix.
- Read the sentence again to check whether you need a plural form.
- Check your spelling, as it must be correct.

1 Read the article. For questions 1–8, use the word given in capitals at the end of some of the lines to form a word that fits in the gap in the same line.

Can you spot fake followers?

Some Twitter users have thousands of followers. Clearly, they must be
(0) _fascinating_ people. But are they really? **FASCINATE**
Some of their followers are pretty
(1) .... ; in fact, they don't **RESPOND**
seem remotely interested in any of the
(2) .... made by the person they're **CONTRIBUTE**
following. And that's a real giveaway: these followers don't exist. They've been added to the person's account by companies selling fake followers to anyone hoping to boost their
(3) .... **REPUTE**
An apparently high number of followers like this gives the very **(4)** .... impression **LEAD**
that the person has social influence. However, people such as artists or aspiring musicians who are less concerned about this might still
not find the idea **(5)** .... Having **APPEAL**
thousands of followers could possibly lead to offers of work and enhance their image as a
(6) .... commodity. Although it's not **DESIRE**
(7) .... to sell followers, and it can be **LEGAL**
an **(8)** .... marketing tool, somehow **EFFECT**
it feels wrong. If your followers are fake, they don't care about you – and they certainly don't read your comments. So why bother?

2

Vocabulary
Communication collocations
▶ CB page 22

1 Match 1–6 with A–F to make collocations. Use the words in brackets to help you.

1 small   **A** presentation (business)
2 gossip   **B** debate (university)
3 intellectual   **C** idea (politics)
4 professional   **D** wi-fi connection (internet)
5 controversial   **E** column (newspaper)
6 dodgy   **F** talk (party)

2 Choose the correct answer (A, B or C) to complete each sentence.

1 It's important to be able to .... small talk in social situations.
   A make   **B** deliver   **C** give
2 It can be hard to .... a conversation going if no one will add anything else.
   A continue   **B** hold   **C** keep
3 The politician .... a great speech at the conference.
   A said   **B** delivered   **C** led
4 It's great to meet friends and .... a chat with them.
   A get   **B** make   **C** have
5 Universities often run clubs where they .... debates on important issues.
   A hold   **B** do   **C** give
6 Some people are too nervous to .... presentations in front of large audiences.
   A have   **B** hold   **C** make

3 Complete the sentences with the words in the box.

deep   husky   monotonous   soft   soothing   squeaky

1 She has such a .... voice I find it difficult to hear what she's saying.
2 She speaks in a high .... voice – like a mouse!
3 His voice is very .... and low – he's easy to recognise!
4 Whenever I get a cold, I get a sore throat and my voice sounds quite ....
5 When you're having a conversation it's not a good idea if your voice is .... because variation of pitch makes you sound interesting.
6 Singing to a baby in a .... voice often calms them and helps them go to sleep.

Grammar
Defining and non-defining relative clauses ▶ CB page 23

1 Choose the correct alternative in each sentence. In some sentences more than one answer may be possible.

1 I don't talk to people *that/who/which* I don't know.
2 I had a long chat to the man, *who/that/what* gave me his contact details afterwards.
3 Tourist guides *who/that/when* speak several languages are the best.
4 It's good raconteurs *that/which/what* I like talking to.
5 The man *whose/who's/whom* with Emma is her boss.
6 It was late *when/that/which* I saw the man outside my house.
7 Peter, *who's/whose/whom* father works in television, is also a good presenter.
8 The debate, *that/which/what* I only joined in on towards the end, was very stimulating.

2 Decide if the relative clauses in Activity 1 are defining (D) or non-defining (ND).

3 Find and correct the mistakes in the sentences.

1 Something what I enjoy is watching chat shows on TV.
2 He studies with postgraduate students, among who he seems to excel.
3 I'm going on an IT course, that should be very interesting.
4 Celebrities whom are often used to sell products in advertising campaigns make a lot of money.
5 The lecturer who's talks are always really informative is leaving the university.
6 The woman, that was rather well dressed, was talking too loudly on her mobile.

4 Decide if the relative clauses in the article are defining or non-defining and add six commas.

Whose class is it?
In class, children who are often reluctant to discuss things in groups say it's because the groups have been organised by the teacher. Because of this, these lessons which are often unsuccessful may not be repeated. However, teachers who involve the children in the reason for the grouping find that their lessons are often more successful. So what is their explanation? Groups which have been organised by the children themselves tend to be based on friendships. So what happens is that children who on the whole like to get on with their friends may find it hard to disagree with each other. They may also agree with what their friends have said without actually thinking about it critically. What's important is to listen to everyone in the class whose opinions are equally valuable. It may also be a good idea to avoid seating children directly opposite each other which avoids confrontation.

Writing
Proposal (Part 2) ▶ CB page 24

About the exam:
In Writing Part 2, you choose one of three questions to answer. One may be a proposal. In a proposal, you need to outline existing problems or requirements and make recommendations supported by reasons.

Strategy:
- Divide your proposal into relevant sections and give each one a clear heading.
- Begin with an introduction setting out the purpose of the proposal and your intentions.
- Finish with recommendations and a summary sentence.
- Use impersonal language throughout but give your opinion at the end.

1 **Look at the exam task and the sample answer. Which of the statements below is correct?**

1 The aim of the proposal is to improve foreign students' language in order to pass exams.

2 The aim of the proposal is to help foreign students mix with other students at the university.

A group of foreign students will soon be arriving to attend a degree course at your university. Their listening and reading skills in your language are proficient. However, they have had little practice in speaking. You have been invited to submit a proposal outlining the reasons for setting up a programme to help them develop their speaking skills and explaining what would be involved. A decision will then be made on what sort of programme to set up.

Write your **proposal** in **220–260** words in an appropriate style.

2 **Read the sample answer again and answer the questions.**

1 Has the writer given a clear indication of what the proposal includes?

2 Has the writer used an impersonal style throughout?

3 Has the writer used appropriate headings for the sections of the proposal?

4 Has the writer given recommendations?

5 Has the writer given their opinion clearly?

3 **Match items 1–5 in Activity 2 with phrases A–E below.**

A My suggestion would be to … ; I would urge the university to …

B It is thought that … ; A survey would indicate that …

C Issues to be addressed; Points for inclusion

D I intend to … ; I shall then give examples of …

E It is my considered opinion that … ; In my view, …

4 **Do the exam task. Remember to plan your proposal first.**

You have seen this announcement on a noticeboard at your college.

> Your college principal has decided to invest in state-of-the-art technology to help both tutors and students in the college.

You have been invited to write a proposal outlining the need for state-of-the-art technology, suggesting and explaining how it would help tutors and learners in the college. A decision will then be made on what equipment should be bought.
Write your **proposal** in **220–260** words in an appropriate style.

A speaking programme for foreign students

Introduction
In this proposal I shall give reasons for designing a special programme to help foreign students at our university to become more proficient in their oral language skills.

Reasons for developing a programme
Foreign students coming to our college to study need to have a high level of proficiency in our language. Most of these students have passed the relevant language examinations and encounter few problems. They have often, however, had little opportunity to use the language for speaking. Although their current skills help them with their studies, they need to integrate into the general student population and speaking the language fluently would help this.

A possible speaking programme
A speaking programme should encourage foreign students to interact with native speakers. The programme should have a systematic element which ensures regular sessions outside their academic study time, as well as the provision of opportunities to socialise with native speakers on a less organised basis.

Recommendations
My recommendations for setting up a programme would be:
- A member of staff should be appointed to run the scheme.
- A series of classroom-based discussion sessions should be scheduled.
- Foreign students and general students should be invited to a series of organised social events such as cinema trips, walks and parties.

I strongly believe that a programme like this would benefit the foreign students and allow them to get maximum profit from their time here.

Multiple-choice cloze (Part 1)

For questions 1–8, read the text below and decide which answer (A, B, C or D) best fits each gap. There is an example at the beginning (0).

To sell or not to sell?

You may think selling your house is easy but everyone wants to get the **(0)** ....*C, best*........ deal. Unfortunately, the housing market is **(1)** .... to highs and lows, which could prevent your **(2)** .... the price you want. However, displaying your house at its best could persuade **(3)** .... buyers that your house is worth more than a similar one nearby. Here are some simple steps you can take that might **(4)** .... a sale.

De-clutter and throw away superfluous stuff. It may have sentimental value for you but to a buyer it's junk. Tidy shelves and work surfaces. **(5)** .... most buyers will renovate a house as soon as they move in, it is worth **(6)** .... up the place by painting, replacing worn carpets and so on. The look you want is neat but lived in – comfortable and cosy but suggesting that there is still **(7)** .... for a purchaser to put their own **(8)** .... on the house. At the moment it's your home and you love it but the trick is to make buyers love it, too.

0	A nicest	B biggest	C best	D richest
1	A liable	B subject	C possible	D likely
2	A succeeding	B winning	C achieving	D managing
3	A developing	B unrealised	C potential	D capable
4	A secure	B fix	C verify	D stick
5	A But	B Despite	C However	D Although
6	A doing	B getting	C making	D working
7	A space	B room	C place	D capacity
8	A idea	B brand	C character	D stamp

Open cloze (Part 2)

For questions 9–16, read the text below and think of the word which best fits each gap. Use only one word in each gap. There is an example at the beginning (0).

Communication gone too far?

We're keen to keep in touch with friends at **(0)** ....*all*.... hours of the day or night – and tweeting has become a mainstream form of communication. But **(9)** .... it really appropriate in all situations?

Many tweeters have a strange urge to post their reactions to things as quickly as possible, to avoid being thought of as lagging behind. But **(10)** .... if in a theatre, people tweet during the performance itself, thereby ruining it for those around them? It's hard to imagine a live theatrical experience as anything **(11)** .... than devalued when the faces of half the audience can be seen in the glow of their phone screens, typing **(12)** .... of following the play. The success of a performance requires the audience to **(13)** .... attention.

Some U.S. theatres have **(14)** .... matters into their own hands by designating some sections that are well away **(15)** .... the others as 'tweet seats'. Nevertheless, when even a small part of the audience is inattentive, doing something **(16)** .... composing a thought in a tweet, it affects the whole atmosphere.

Word formation (Part 3)

For questions 17–24, read the text below. Use the word given in capitals at the end of some of the lines to form a word that fits in the gap in the same line. There is an example at the beginning (0).

My favourite place

My favourite place may surprise you as it's not obviously **(0)** _appealing_. I'm sure most people gravitate towards the **(17)** .... palaces of Venice or the natural beauty of Sydney but I am **(18)** .... drawn to a remote valley in Iceland. It was created thousands of years ago by a violent natural catastrophe when a volcanic **(19)** .... under a glacier caused a flood that created a huge canyon. The **(20)** .... walls of rock on either side now protect this valley from the **(21)** .... of the ferocious Arctic winds. Over the years a forest has grown up in what is an **(22)** .... area of calm. I find it has its own soothing atmosphere which others may find **(23)** .... or even threatening. However, it draws me back time after time. I camp there and the peace and quiet helps me get my monotonous everyday life into perspective. It also enables me to appreciate the formidable power and **(24)** .... force of nature!

APPEAL

HISTORY

INSTINCT

ERUPT

TOWER

STRONG

EXPECT

PLEASE

ESCAPE

Key word transformation (Part 4)

For questions 25–30, complete the second sentence so that it has a similar meaning to the first sentence, using the word given. Do not change the word given. You must use between three and six words, including the word given. Here is an example (0).

Example

0   It's six years since I moved here.

BEEN

I _have been living here for_ six years.

25   John gave me the incentive to go to college.

ENCOURAGED

It .... to go to college.

26   I can't get another thing on my desk – my study is incredibly cluttered!

ROOM

My study is incredibly cluttered, and so there is .... on my desk!

27   I only missed him after he left the party.

UNTIL

I .... after he had left the party.

28   She didn't listen to my idea at all and refused to consider it.

DISMISSIVE

She .... my idea and refused to consider it.

29   I wanted to buy Jo a special watch but when I arrived there were none left in the shop.

OUT

I wanted to buy Jo a special watch but the shop .... time I arrived.

30   The man at the party was unknown to me.

NOT

I .... the man at the party was.

3 Ages and stages

Reading
Cross-text multiple matching (Part 6) ▶ CB page 28

1 Read four reviews of a book about child psychology. For questions 1–4, choose from the reviewers (A–D). The reviewers may be chosen more than once.

Which reviewer

has a different view to Reviewer A regarding the accuracy of Barnes' claims about how babies interpret the world?   **1** ☐

shares Reviewer D's thoughts about some rather obvious conclusions drawn by psychologists?   **2** ☐

has a similar opinion to Reviewer B about the way the book compares the baby and adult mind?   **3** ☐

has a different view to the others about whether the book is comprehensive enough?   **4** ☐

2 Choose the correct meaning (A or B) for each word from the texts.

Text A
1 *underrated*   A not well explained   B not appreciated enough
2 *innate*   A that you are born with   B complicated

Text B
3 *conversely*   A on the other hand   B additionally
4 *crammed with*   A full of   B experimenting on

Text C
5 *acute*   A unusual   B sharp
6 *insights*   A overview   B clear understanding

Text D
7 *sympathetic to* A feeling pity for   B approving of
8 *innovative*   A original   B logical

Parents Monthly 23

Learning how children think

Four reviewers comment on scientist Annie Barnes' book, called *Learning how children think.*

A In her latest book, Annie Barnes covers all of the theories related to the development of human consciousness and concludes that the minds of babies have been significantly underrated. She suggests that, far from being simple, babies' brains have a special kind of consciousness; they have an innate ability to develop theories about how the world works. She claims a baby's mind can evaluate theories about everyday happenings and not just simply live through them. One of the book's most intriguing suggestions, based on well-documented research, is that, while it's important for adults to be able to imagine unfulfilled or potential outcomes in different situations, it is actually in such so-called 'thought experiments' that babies excel.

B Barnes' clear and readable style is aimed at the general reader and she makes a useful comparison to help understand the difference between the consciousness of a baby and that of an adult: the lantern and the spotlight. A baby has a 'lantern' consciousness which is wider and more diffuse than an adult's; this is because it is set to absorb as much as possible from new experiences. Conversely, adults learn to 'spot', or focus, in order to function efficiently in the world. Barnes' descriptions of her working life hint at labs crammed with infants pulling levers and pushing buttons while white-coated scientists follow their eye movements and scan their brains. Yet she also thinks of babies as scientists; she describes them as 'learning machines', constantly experimenting on the world and analysing their results with enthusiasm. The basis of child learning seems to be no different from the more conscious and deliberate approach of adults, and this thorough and well-informed book provides detailed examples.

C One fascinating chapter in Barnes' book concerns morality. Children seem to have an acute sense of fairness; they know how others feel and can act on that knowledge. In one experiment concerning food described in the book, babies were left with researchers who indicated clearly that they loved the vegetable broccoli but hated crackers. Whatever their own preferences, the toddlers gave the broccoli lovers their 'preferred' food rather than the crackers. It seems we are born with a sense of otherness, which experience later knocks out of us. This, however, is hardly revolutionary – as most parents of teenagers are already well aware. One issue Barnes could have addressed is the potential downside to the willingness of young minds to imagine and believe. She only sees this as an advantage. If people in authority say fire hurts, the child believes. However, this does not negate Barnes' other findings. Her aim is to describe how infant mentality develops and what we can learn from it; this she does, and in analysing how a child's mind grows, she provides insights into the human mind in general.

D Barnes clearly enjoys being around small children and is sympathetic to the deeper philosophical implications of their way of thinking. Her book is absorbing and educative, despite sometimes feeling as if she is spending too much time simply confirming what parents and pre-school teachers have long known. There is a well-founded fear that developmental psychologists risk 'reading-in', that is, thinking that small children understand the world intentionally and consciously, as adults do. The experiments reported by Barnes are generally well designed and sensitive to the danger of misinterpretation. Nevertheless, she sometimes seems to go too far, as when claiming that babies recognise the actions they copy and reproduce. Barnes helpfully says children are like the research and development department of a company; what she means is that they are creative and innovative, though not always correct. She suggests that adults are more like the production and marketing section, focusing on a project and following it through to its logical conclusion. It's a neat comparison in what is an in-depth volume.

Vocabulary
Stages of life ▶ CB page 26

1 **Which word or phrase in each group is the odd one out? Why?**

1	over the hill	no spring chicken	elderly	infant
2	adolescent	youth	child	teenage
3	aging	growing up	developing	maturing
4	childish	childlike	juvenile	immature
5	adult	grown-up	pensioner	middle-aged

2 **Complete the sentences with the correct form of the word in brackets.**

1 It's the .... (*innocent*) of children that is so appealing.

2 Teenagers develop .... (*mature*) through experience and guidance.

3 Even adults can exhibit .... (*infant*) behaviour sometimes!

4 It's sad when an old person develops .... (*senile*) and loses their mental faculties.

5 Many older people manage to retain their .... (*youth*) looks nowadays.

6 The elderly man had a twinkle in his eye and a .... (*boy*) charm that was appealing.

Grammar
Future forms ▶ CB page 27

1 **Find and correct the mistakes with future forms in the sentences.**

1 By the end of the week I'll be finishing this project.

2 Hurry up – the performance is going start in two minutes!

3 I'm sure he'll be winning the competition.

4 I can't concentrate, so I will have stopped work now.

5 This time next week I'll fly to the USA.

6 Hopefully, they'll be announcing the results by lunchtime.

2 **Complete the second sentence so that it has a similar meaning to the first sentence, using the word given. Use between three and six words.**

1 Before he put forward the proposal, I'm sure he took the comments of local residents on board. **WILL**

Before he put forward the proposal, I'm sure he .... of local residents on board.

2 I expect I'll leave home before I'm twenty. **TIME**

I expect I will .... I'm twenty.

3 I know that I'll find the right job soon. **MATTER**

I know it .... before I find the right job.

4 They confidently expect the broadcast to go ahead at 6 p.m. **SURE**

They .... go ahead at 6 p.m.

5 I'm sure he'll get a promotion very soon. **LONG**

I'm sure it .... he gets a promotion.

6 I have decided to make a definite plan for my future career. **AM**

What .... is make a definite plan for my future career.

Introductory *it* ▶ CB page 30

3 **Match the first half of the sentences (1–6) with the second (A–F). Add *it* in the correct place.**

1 I get pretty angry

2 The politician made it clear

3 Most teenagers think

4 I can't stand

5 I find exciting

6 Don't worry if you don't get on at first;

A is the older generation that doesn't understand them!

B that was important to look after older people.

C will be better later.

D when I make new friends.

E when families have big arguments.

F when you leave all up to me to make up after a fight!

4 **Find and correct the mistakes with the use or omission of *it* in the sentences.**

1 He made obvious to everyone that he didn't like her.

2 I cannot bear it to see children unhappy.

3 Children owe to their parents to look after them in their old age.

4 Was great to meet his sister last week.

5 One day may be you who needs help from other people.

6 I think is important for all generations to get along with each other.

5 **Rewrite the sentences using the introductory *it*.**

Example:

That relationships often break down is sad.

It's sad that relationships often break down.

1 To think how different generations could help each other is heartwarming.

2 Experiencing good relationships is so important in life.

3 To understand another person can be very difficult.

4 Getting on with siblings can sometimes be tough.

5 Having a role model is important for teenagers.

6 Making up with a friend after a quarrel can be emotional.

Speaking
Collaborative task and discussion (Parts 3 and 4) ▶ CB page 31

About the exam:

In Speaking Part 3, you discuss a question with your partner for two minutes. You have several points to consider during your discussion, which are related to the question. The question and related points will be given to you as a mind map. After two minutes, the examiner will stop your discussion and ask a question where you need to make some kind of decision. You have another minute to discuss this.

Strategy:

• Spend time discussing each point. Spend more time on those you know more about or are interested in. You do not need to discuss all the points.

• Make sure you share the speaking time and that it is a discussion and not a series of long turns. Involve your partner and react to what he or she says.

• You do not need to agree on your decision.

1 **Look at the exam task and the extracts from a discussion between two candidates. Which points are they talking about? Do you agree with them?**

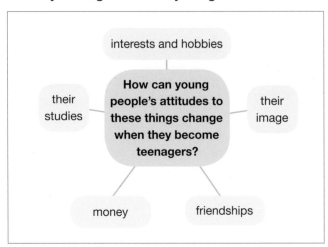

interests and hobbies

their studies

How can young people's attitudes to these things change when they become teenagers?

their image

money

friendships

Extract 1

M: Well, if we look at studies, I think this is something where teens' attitudes can be very different to children's, don't you think?

F: Oh, yes. When you're younger, learning is often a lot of fun but when you're older, it gets a load more serious.

M: That is so true! We're under much more pressure to succeed and I think the enjoyment factor can disappear sometimes.

Extract 2

F: It's true that your attitude changes but it's hard to nail down how.

M: I agree but I think it's to do with different levels and types of relationships.

F: You mean, like, you have a wide social circle but there are people who are important to you for different reasons?

M: Exactly. For support, for advice, because they're cool, sometimes simply because you want your social network to be bigger than someone else's!

Extract 3

F: That's an interesting one. I don't think kids think about it a lot – unless it's just to buy snacks and stuff.

M: You've got a point but I think that's only part of it. Kids are getting much more into clothes, accessories, gadgets and so on, aren't they?

F: Yeah, but who usually buys them?

A: I see what you mean!

2 **Read the extracts in Activity 1 again. Underline phrases the candidates use to expand on what the other candidate says.**

3 ▶ **05 Read the decision question for this task. Which of the prompts from Part 3 do you think the candidates will choose? Listen and see if you were right.**

Now you have about a minute to decide which of these things you think will become the most important to young people when they leave full-time education.

4 **Listen again and complete the phrases.**

1 I don't like to .... it but …

2 I think it's .... to be money.

3 Yes, there's ...., but …

4 I .... think it's money.

5 We'll have to .... here, then.

6 .... say both money *and* friendships.

Use of English
Multiple-choice cloze (Part 1) ▶ CB page 32

1 Read the blog post. For questions 1–8, decide which answer (A, B, C or D) best fits each gap.

What is the secret of longevity?

The person who comes up with the answer as to how to **(0)** ..A, live.... a long and happy life will make a fortune. Until that happens, scientists, life coaches and fitness fanatics are all free to put forward their own pet theories.

Leaving **(1)** .... the wackiest ideas, their suggestions all seem equally plausible and could well play an important **(2)** .... in uncovering the truth about longevity. Follow this diet, exercise, **(3)** .... yourself with people who love you, sleep long hours – these are all **(4)** .... things to do, and indeed could **(5)** .... to a longer life span.

But something gets in the way of our doing them, and trying to follow advice and failing creates stress, which has a really negative impact on our **(6)** .... of well-being. People are put off by things that challenge them, and this includes the apparent impossibility of **(7)** .... a perfect lifestyle. To many it seems an unattainable goal that is out of **(8)** ....

Maybe the secret of longevity is simple – moderation in everything.

	A	B	C	D
0	live	survive	exist	maintain
1	behind	alone	aside	away
2	function	responsibility	task	role
3	involve	connect	surround	relate
4	sensitive	emotional	sensible	sensational
5	lead	produce	result	make
6	awareness	sense	impression	consciousness
7	achieving	compiling	arriving	determining
8	touch	contact	range	reach

Listening
Multiple choice (Part 3) ▶ CB page 33

About the exam:

In Listening Part 3, you hear an interview involving two or more people. There are six multiple-choice questions, each with four options. You hear the interview twice.

Strategy:
- Read the questions to get an idea of the topic.
- The first time you listen, underline key words and mark possible answers.
- Make sure the option you choose actually answers the question.

---

1 ▶ 06 You will hear an interview with a man called Jon Simmons and a woman called Clare Harries, who both work as life coaches. For questions 1–6, choose the answer (A, B, C or D) which fits best according to what you hear.

1 Jon feels that the job of a life coach is
  A similar to being a therapist.
  B focused on future possibilities.
  C based on individual experiences.
  D more complicated than people realise.

2 Clare says she became a life coach because
  A it involved something she enjoyed doing.
  B it enabled her to re-evaluate her own issues.
  C it was a logical extension of her other interests.
  D it was necessary to replace the lack of family support.

3 What surprises Clare about the kind of people who seek her expertise?
  A They are open to informal advice.
  B They are only looking for better jobs.
  C They are upset by rapid changes in society.
  D They are often working within a large organisation.

4 What does Jon think is most important to understand about relationships?
  A They should be developed slowly and carefully.
  B They have to reflect an individual's moral attitude.
  C They start with the individual's attitude to him or herself.
  D They fail if people around an individual are critical of them.

5 Jon and Clare both think the most important message to get over to clients is
  A control negative thinking.
  B take positive action at all times.
  C decide what really makes you really happy.
  D make good use of your particular skills.

6 What do Jon and Clare both feel is the most rewarding part of their job?
  A understanding more about themselves
  B improving the lives of large numbers of people
  C creating a relationship with another person
  D watching another person develop their confidence

Writing
Report (Part 2) ▶ CB page 34

About the exam:
In Writing Part 2 you may have the choice of writing a report. The purpose of a report is to give information and make recommendations using an impersonal style.

Strategy:
- Use headings for the different sections of your report. This makes it easier for the target reader and also ensures that you organise and present your information clearly.
- Use an impersonal style. The use of the passive is quite common in report writing.
- Make sure you give both an introduction where you outline the aim of the report and a conclusion where you summarise the main points.

1 Look at the exam task and the two plans. Which plan do you think is best?

> The Principal of your college wants to give more assistance to new students. You have agreed to write a report describing the problems that new students at the college often encounter and recommending ways to help them.
>
> Write your **report** in **220–260 words** in an appropriate style.

Plan A
- **Paragraph 1:** Say how the problems new students face can affect how well they do at college and describe these problems.
- **Paragraph 2:** Give examples from your own experience and say how they affected you.
- **Paragraph 3:** Summarise the opinions of a teacher you interviewed.
- **Paragraph 4:** Give a conclusion about what is the best thing to do to avoid the problems.

Plan B
- **Paragraph 1:** Say why you're writing the report.
- **Paragraph 2:** Give examples of some difficulties for new students: finding their way around, who to go to for information, socialising, etc.
- **Paragraph 3:** Make some suggestions to help: an information leaflet, a buddy system, a day visit, etc.
- **Paragraph 4:** Give a short summary of how your ideas might help.

2 Look at another exam task and tick (✓) the things you have to do in the report.

> The education authority in your area wants to assess how useful the current provisions at schools and colleges are for equipping students with skills to deal with working life after they leave full-time education. You have agreed to write a report describing and evaluating the current provisions and recommending improvements.
>
> Write your **report** in **220–260 words** in an appropriate style.

1 Give clear examples of what you were taught and how you profited from this.
2 Give an overview of what schools in your area do to help their students prepare for working life.
3 Explain how and why this preparation benefits or does not benefit the students.
4 Say whose fault this is and explain your criticisms.
5 Make some suggestions about how the preparation could be improved.
6 Give a detailed programme of sessions that you think would be good.

3 Read the sentences and put a cross (✗) next to the ones that would not be appropriate to include in the report.

1 In this report I am planning to describe what schools do at the moment to prepare their students for when they leave.
2 Having said that, there are disadvantages to allocating a significant amount of time to life skills classes like these. Here are a few of them.
3 There is currently little focus on teaching students how to deal with their finances effectively.
4 My recommendations would include providing more opportunities for students at school to visit different workplaces.
5 I think you've got to get more trained staff in to give extra classes in finance and cookery and things like that.
6 Should these recommendations be implemented, students will be better able to deal with a range of problems they may encounter after leaving school.

4 Do one of the exam tasks on this page. Make notes and write your report. Remember to:
- use an impersonal style.
- use clear headings.
- address all the points in the task.

Listening
Sentence completion (Part 2) ▶ CB page 38

About the exam:
In Listening Part 2, you complete gaps in eight sentences. The answers come in the same order as the sentences. You must write the exact word(s) you hear in each gap, although the sentence itself may be a paraphrase.

Strategy:
- Read the instructions so that you understand the context and who is speaking.
- Read the sentences. Think about what kind of word you will need to write.
- Listen and complete the sentences. On the second listening, check your answers.
- Make sure your answers are grammatically correct and there are no spelling mistakes.

1 ▶ 07 **You will hear a ballet dancer called Susie Watson giving a presentation to students about her life. For questions 1–8, complete the sentences.**

A dancer's life

Susie describes studying accountancy as a sort of **(1)** .... while she was at vocational school.

After finishing her dance training, Susie found the difficulty of getting a **(2)** .... surprising.

Susie feels that it's **(3)** .... for her to try to develop a perfect technique.

Susie uses the word **(4)** .... to describe how she regards the attitude of dancers towards recovering from injury.

Susie thinks that the amount of time dancers spend in a **(5)** .... might surprise many people.

Susie has not found improving her **(6)** .... quick or easy.

Susie worries that she might neglect **(7)** .... when she rehearses dance steps.

According to Susie, it's **(8)** .... that marks out a successful dancer.

2 **Listen again and write the exact words used for the underlined phrases.**

1 My parents wanted me to have <u>an alternative option</u>.
2 Luckily I <u>kept going</u>.
3 Young dancers at ballet school imagine that'll <u>guarantee them a career</u>.
4 As with any job, you <u>have to work your way up</u>.
5 Not everyone is <u>suited to</u> the life of a dancer.
6 This means we have to be <u>at our very best</u>.

Grammar
verb patterns: -ing/infinitive ▶ CB page 39

1 Complete the article with the correct form of the verbs in the box.

---

act become break do feel fulfil get over make
overcome polish produce put try understand

⏱ TIME IN   DO IT NOW OR PUT IT OFF UNTIL LATER?

People often find that success eludes them. But how often is this their own fault? One thing that we are all good at **(1)** .... is procrastinating. Shakespeare's Hamlet is a prime example of someone who failed **(2)** .... and, in fact, was rendered incapable of action by his need **(3)** .... things off – in other words, to procrastinate. And because this is such a universal failing, it may be that it is that very quality that endears him to us all. But it's not a good thing – we should force ourselves **(4)** .... it. Procrastinators are less wealthy, less healthy and regret their inability **(5)** .... quick decisions. So why are so many of us like this? What is it that prevents us from **(6)** .... our true potential? Are we attempting **(7)** .... perfectionists, claiming that we need time **(8)** .... our work – or even that we can only do our best work under pressure? The latter is untrue, as work done at the last minute contains more mistakes than that done on time. Our procrastinating behaviour inconveniences others and leaves us **(9)** .... flustered and guilty. Social scientists are struggling **(10)** .... the causes of this malaise and from that knowledge work out strategies **(11)** .... it. There are various suggestions they have come up with for those having trouble getting things done. They say we should consider **(12)** .... a task down into manageable chunks so that it seems less daunting and keep on **(13)** .... to accept why we are delaying in the first place: is it fear, wishing **(14)** .... something perfect or boredom with the task? Apparently, knowing the reason means we can deal with it. As for me, I'm off to have a rest and think about it all!

2 Find and correct the mistakes with verb patterns in the sentences. There are mistakes in six of the sentences.

1 My coach encouraged me to try out for the first team.

2 It was the idea of getting a high-powered job that made me going to university.

3 Many people have tried explain the secret of success but they fail to pin it down.

4 My parents helped me overcoming financial difficulties when I was trying to get my foot on the property ladder.

5 I really feel there is nothing to prevent me from fulfil my potential.

6 I have to force myself to getting up in the mornings but once I'm up, there's no stopping me!

7 People who avoid taking risks will never be high achievers.

8 It's people who dare trying new things that inspire others to do the same.

Vocabulary
verb/noun collocations ▶ CB page 40

1 Choose the incorrect verb in each sentence.

1 It takes a great deal of effort to *realise/fulfil/obtain* your potential.

2 It's a good idea to *set/aim/achieve* targets if you want to be successful.

3 Many people find it hard to *overcome/face/beat* setbacks in life.

4 People are often nervous about *grasping/taking/seizing* control in difficult situations.

5 Good businesspeople are able to *take/seize/get* every opportunity that comes their way.

6 Try to *trust/rely on/accept* your intuition – you're usually right!

7 I often *bring/get/take* inspiration from autobiographies I've read about successful people.

8 It's very satisfying to *win/settle/break* an argument.

2 Replace the underlined phrases in the sentences with phrases A–F.

A doubt my ability
B find inspiration
C overcome setbacks
D seek popularity
E take advantage of
F to accept praise

1 It's hard to <u>recover</u> when something goes wrong.

2 Where do you <u>get your ideas from</u>?

3 Try to <u>grasp</u> every opportunity that comes your way.

4 People often fail because they <u>want to be liked</u>.

5 Modest people find it embarrassing and awkward <u>when people say they are good</u>.

6 <u>I'm not sure that I am able</u> to do it.

Use of English
Key word transformation (Part 4)
▶ CB page 41

About the exam:
In the Reading and Use of English paper, Part 4, there are six unrelated sentences. For each one, you complete a new sentence that has a similar meaning. You use a word given in capitals for each sentence, which you must not change. You are given the beginning and end of each new sentence and you can only write between three and six words in the gap.

Strategy:
- Read the sentence carefully and think about its exact meaning.
- Think about other ways of expressing the meaning, using the key word.
- Don't change the key word.
- Write between three and six words, including the word given.
- Contractions (e.g. *didn't*) count as two words.

1 Complete the second sentence so that it has a similar meaning to the first sentence, using the word given. Do not change the word given. You must use between three and six words, including the word given.

0 It's impossible that you saw John last night – he's in the USA!

HAVE

John's in the USA, so *you can't have seen* him last night.

1 I am confident that he will be successful in his career.

CHANCES

I am confident .... in his career.

2 If you feel stressed, breathing slowly should calm you down.

MAKE

Breathing slowly .... if you feel stressed.

3 I am really bad at remembering people's names when I meet them.

MEMORY

I .... people's names when I meet them.

4 He lost his job because he was inefficient.

GROUNDS

He lost his job .... his inefficiency.

5 I'm sorry that I didn't help him.

REGRET

I .... him.

6 I couldn't go away for the weekend because I didn't have enough money.

PREVENTED

I was .... for the weekend by lack of money.

Reading
Multiple choice (Part 5)
▶ CB page 42

1 Read the article quickly and choose the best option (A, B or C) to complete the title.

1 nurture talent early on

2 practice, not talent

3 headhunt high performers

2 Read the article again. For questions 1–6, choose the answer (A, B, C or D) which you think fits best according to the text.

1 The writer is concerned that motivational speeches do not

  A carry conviction.

  B give useful advice.

  C interest the audience.

  D respect the listeners.

2 The writer believes we should learn more about

  A the factors behind motivation.

  B the ways people's commitment to tasks can be developed.

  C the importance of workers' different principles.

  D the similarities between practices in business and education.

3 Research suggests that successful people

  A do not need to work hard.

  B have an innate talent.

  C benefit from personal training.

  D can learn very quickly.

4 In paragraph 4, the writer poses several direct questions in order to

  A make readers consider their own experiences.

  B invite comment.

  C emphasise his point.

  D consider different situations.

5 According to the writer, employers need to

  A encourage ambition in their employees.

  B ensure employees know their place in a company.

  C record the development of each employee.

  D reward good performance of their employees.

6 The writer uses the phrase *a rank-and-yank appraisal system* to refer to

  A insufficient investment in personal development.

  B promotion that is too rapid.

  C an acceptance of poor performers at high levels.

  D changing the recruiting strategy of a company.

Sections | **Issues** | Settings | *Monday 19* | search

Secret to success:

ost of us have been on the receiving end of an inspirational speech. Usually it is delivered by a former Olympian at a company conference and is all about the big M: motivation. It is sometimes eloquently delivered and often fun to listen to but most people leave the room wondering how thirty minutes of biographical information about a rowing champion is going to help them back in the office. Nobody would dispute that motivation is a key driver of performance but this knowledge does not help many of us understand where it comes from. Listening to a sportsperson speaking about their own personal journey may be uplifting but how is it going to leave a lasting and usable legacy in terms of how you approach your job? It is almost insulting to think it could.

It is not <u>anecdotes</u> we need, so much as a science of performance, underlying principles that help unlock the question of why some people work hard and excel while others don't; why some are committed to what they are doing while others exist in a state of semi-detachment. It is a question with

<u>ramifications</u> not just for business but for education. And, fortunately, the answers are beginning to emerge. To see how, we need to take a step back and ask a deeper question: where does excellence come from?

For a long time, it was thought that the answer hinged, in large part, upon talent. Hard work may be important but if you don't have the ability, you are never going to become top class. It is the notion that high-level performers have excellence encoded in their DNA. It turns out that this point of view is mistaken. Dozens of studies have found that high flyers across all disciplines learn no faster than those who reach lower levels of <u>attainment</u> – hour after hour, they improve at almost identical rates. The difference is simply that high achievers practise for more hours. Further research has shown that when students seem to possess a particular gift, it is often because they have been given extra tuition at home.

The question of talent versus practice/ experience would not matter much if it was merely theoretical. But it is much more than that. It influences the way we think and feel, and the way we engage with our world. And it determines our motivation. To see how, consider an employee who believes success is all about talent – this is known as the 'fixed mindset'. Why would they bother to work hard? If they have the right genes, won't they just cruise to the top? And if they lack talent, well, why bother at all? And who can blame someone for having this

kind of attitude, given the underlying premise? If, on the other hand, they really believe that practice trumps talent – the 'growth mindset' – they will persevere. They will see failure as an opportunity to adapt and grow. And if they are right, they will eventually excel. What we decide about the nature of talent, then, could scarcely be more important.

So, how to create a growth mindset within an organisation? Interventions that have presented participants with the powerful evidence of how excellence derived from perseverance – which explains the possibility of personal transformation – have had a dramatic impact on motivation and performance. When this is allied with clearly identifiable pathways from shop floor to top floor, so that employees can see the route ahead, these results are strengthened further.

Businesses that focus on recruiting external 'talent' with 'the right stuff' on the other hand, and who neglect the cultivation of existing personnel, foster the fixed mindset. A rank-and-yank appraisal system is also damaging because it suggests that the abilities of those ranked the lowest cannot be developed. In short, an <u>ethos</u> constructed upon the <u>potential</u> for personal transformation is the underlying psychological principle driving high performance. It is an <u>insight</u> that is not merely deeply relevant to business but to any organisation interested in unlocking human potential.

3 Look at the phrases *fixed mindset* and *growth mindset* in paragraph 4 of the article. Which speaker below shows a 'fixed mindset' and which shows a 'growth mindset'?

1 'I'm in the right job. There's no point pushing for promotion because I'd be out of my depth.'

2 'I've never tackled anything like that before but I guess I can learn as I go along.'

4 Match the underlined words in the article with their synonyms (1–6).

1 consequences
2 capability
3 philosophy
4 personal stories
5 understanding
6 achievement

Grammar
modal verbs ▶ CB page 44

1 **Choose the correct alternative to complete the sentences.**

1 I'm sorry. I *should have done/could do* better in that race – I *must have been/should have been* too nervous.

2 I *mustn't have practised/needn't have practised* so hard – all the other competitors weren't very good, so I *could have won/might win* easily.

3 What do you think you *must have done/could have done* differently when you first took up the sport so that you *might improve/might have improved* more quickly?

4 What *must you do/did you have to do* when you were younger to develop your skill to this level?

5 I was so lucky with my coach – he made me believe I *need to/could have* a great career, and that belief *should be good/must be good* for any athlete.

6 If I hadn't worked so hard, I *need not have been/might not have been* chosen for the team.

Speaking
Collaborative task and discussion (Parts 3 and 4) ▶ CB page 45

1 **▶08 Look at the exam task and listen to two candidates doing the first part of the task. Which two points do they discuss?**

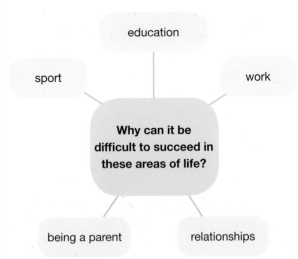

Here are some areas of life where people want to be successful and a question for you to discuss.

- education
- sport
- work
- **Why can it be difficult to succeed in these areas of life?**
- being a parent
- relationships

Talk to each other about why it can be difficult to succeed in these areas of life.

Now you have about a minute to decide which two areas you think it is most rewarding to succeed in.

2 **Listen again and complete the sentences.**

1 That's very ....

2 It's .... compatibility, really.

3 .... that a lot of relationships fail because …

4 .... succeeding in education?

5 That .... you don't concentrate enough on your work.

6 A(n) .... is my brother.

3 **Match the sentences in Activity 2 (1–6) with their functions (A–F).**

A giving an example
B making a suggestion
C giving an opinion
D giving a consequence
E giving a generalisation
F expressing agreement

Writing
Essay (Part 1) ▶ CB page 46

1 **Look at the exam task and the two introductory paragraphs on page 31. Which is more appropriate to begin the essay?**

Your class has attended a panel discussion on how schools can help students develop skills important for their future lives. You have made the notes below.

Ways schools can help students develop important life skills
- encourage more competitive sports
- have off-site team-building days
- introduce home-making and parenting classes

Some opinions expressed in the discussion
'Too much competition can have a negative effect on some students.'
'Team-building activities can be fun and kids learn things without realising!'
'Cooking and looking after children should really be taught by parents, not schools.'

Write an essay for your tutor discussing **two** of the suggestions in your notes. You should **explain which suggestion is better for schools to help students**, **giving reasons** to support your opinion.

You may, if you wish, make use of the opinions expressed in the discussion but you should use your own words as far as possible.

Write your **essay** in **220–260** words in an appropriate style.

A Schools teach us a lot of information and help us pass exams. What else should they teach us? When I was at school, I learnt a lot about maths and science and famous writers but when I left school, I didn't know much about how to look after my money or even how to cook basic meals. Perhaps schools should teach us more things like that.

B It is generally accepted that education should not only focus on developing students' academic knowledge or preparing them for examinations. It is important to broaden the scope of education at schools to include preparing students for life in general after they leave school. However, it is not necessarily easy to find the best ways of doing this.

2 **Read the candidate's essay below and tick (✓) the things the candidate *hasn't* done.**

1 discussed two of the suggestions in the exam task
2 given pros and cons of both suggestions
3 chosen which suggestion is better
4 given reasons for his opinions
5 used a direct question to emphasise a point
6 used both simple sentences and more complex ones
7 used impersonal constructions
8 used between 220 and 260 words

3 **Do the exam task.**

Your class has listened to a discussion about the roles of different people in influencing a person's aspirations and character development. You have made the notes below.

> **People that can influence someone's aspirations and character development**
> - celebrities
> - family members
> - peers

> **Some opinions expressed in the discussion**
> 'Young people see the fame and money that celebrities have, sometimes without having a particular talent, and think Yes, I'd like that!'
> 'Most people feel guilty about letting their family down if they don't do well.'
> 'Everyone wants to fit in and be accepted by their peers, so they change their behaviour accordingly.'

Write an essay for your tutor discussing **two** of the types of people in your notes. You should **explain which types of people have more influence**, **giving reasons** to support your opinion.

You may, if you wish, make use of the opinions expressed in the discussion but you should use your own words as far as possible. Write your **essay** in **220–260** words in an appropriate style.

One way schools try to help their students is by exposing them to competition as early as possible. It is believed that by participating in competitive sports or quizzes, students will learn how to face the demands of a working life that revolves around competition. This can benefit many students. They learn how to cope with and learn from defeat and grow in confidence, seeing how perseverance can achieve results. However, this is not necessarily the case for all students. There are many who fail and are humiliated by their failure. Where is the lesson in this?

In my opinion, a far better way to help young people is to encourage team-building activities. These can take the form of working in groups in lessons or even going on special training days to outdoor activity centres. What is important is for them to learn to work together in an enjoyable way.

In our lives there will be many times when we need to co-operate in order to achieve things. Developing the ability to work with other people, rather than against them is, to my mind, a very important life skill indeed.

Multiple-choice cloze (Part 1)

For questions 1–8, read the text below and decide which answer (A, B, C or D) best fits each gap. There is an example at the beginning (0).

A success story – or is it?

Success, like beauty, lies in the **(0)** ....._A eye_..... of the beholder. How one person chooses to define it can be very different from how others perceive it. For some people, it's earning a fortune, **(1)** .... for others it's working in a voluntary position helping those less fortunate. It's also relative rather than **(2)** .... because the person who **(3)** .... a new skill has achieved success in their terms just as much as the self-made millionaire.

Ironically, there may also be an underlying contradiction in the term. **(4)** ...., an actress who has a glamorous life and seems to have everything she wants may actually be troubled by the loss of her **(5)** .... life as paparazzi invade her personal **(6)** ....

It also has something to do with the length of time success **(7)** .... Many young people are happy with short-term fame but **(8)** .... it's true that reaching that one goal might be comparatively straightforward, maintaining that success is often much harder. And surely, it's long-term success that is ultimately the most satisfying and also the most enviable?

```
0  A eye         B look       C sight       D view
1  A as          B while      C so          D since
2  A total       B whole      C complete    D absolute
3  A wins        B earns      C gets        D masters
4  A After all   B At first   C At once     D Apart from
5  A secret      B private    C individual  D separate
6  A zone        B area       C space       D place
7  A goes        B holds      C keeps       D lasts
8  A despite     B even       C although    D however
```

Open cloze (Part 2)

For questions 9–16, read the text below and think of the word which best fits each gap. Use only one word in each gap. There is an example at the beginning (0).

The unhappiness of phones

Some people claim we would all feel much happier if, instead **(0)** ...._of_........ constantly checking for emails and texts, we turned off our smartphones completely and concentrated **(9)** .... those people physically present. Such messages are a big distraction and **(10)** .... people may be unaware of it, they can cause stress and unhappiness. Thinking about **(11)** .... instead of concentrating makes us less productive at work and can also lead to our having unsatisfying and incomplete personal relationships. If we are **(12)** .... careful, we will lose the knack of enjoying the warmth of human company, preferring to **(13)** .... our attention taken by messages from those far away. Some people say the art of forming real relationships and keeping them going seems to be **(14)** .... threat from the march of technology. The good news, however, is that **(15)** .... small changes to the way in which we use our phones can be very effective and that it is not **(16)** .... late to recognise the danger and do something about it. After all, we all want to be happy!

32

Word formation (Part 3)

For questions 17–24, read the text below. Use the word given in capitals at the end of some of the lines to form a word that fits in the gap in the same line. There is an example at the beginning (0).

The route to perfection

Can there be perfection without pain for those who are **(0)** successful **SUCCESS**
in the world of dance? Achieving excellence depends on many different things, including physique and luck. However, it is **(17)** .... that **DISPUTE**
those who dance professionally must also follow a **(18)** .... training **RIGOUR**
regime, combining this with complete **(19)** .... to their art – and this **DEDICATE**
can certainly be painful. Dancers have to be as strong as **(20)** .... **ENDURE**
athletes but they also have to combine fitness with elegance and **(21)** .... It's said that giving a **MUSIC**
professional dance performance is not **(22)** .... to playing a football **SIMILAR**
match as dancers have to combine periods of sustained activity with short bursts of **(23)** .... energy, while **EXPLODE**
also being able to recover quickly. In the past dancers trained mostly by going through **(24)** .... routines **REPEAT**
but in the modern world, with its high standards of fitness, they use additional techniques such as gym routines to gain muscle strength and stamina. Their ultimate aim is perfection, and this doesn't come easily.

Key word transformation (Part 4)

For questions 25–30, complete the second sentence so that it has a similar meaning to the first sentence, using the word given. Do not change the word given. You must use between three and six words, including the word given. Here is an example (0).

Example

0   Jane was advised to work harder by her maths teacher.
RECOMMENDED
The maths teacher recommended that Jane should work harder.

25   This was Peter's biggest challenge to date.
FACED
Peter .... challenge before.

26   I wish I had tried harder when I was at school!
REGRET
I really .... when I was at school!

27   I wish people wouldn't talk during the performance – it makes me really uptight!
NERVES
It really .... people talk during a performance!

28   He is so ambitious – he's determined that he'll be successful in the company.
MARK
He is determined .... in the company.

29   Can you suggest a way of turning dreams into reality for ambitious people?
TRUE
Can you suggest how .... for ambitious people?

30   I don't want to participate in the project.
RATHER
I .... part in the project.

5 The feel-good factor

Use of English
Open cloze (Part 2) ▶ CB page 48

1 Read the article. For questions 1–8, think of the word which best fits each gap. Use only one word for each gap.

○ ○ ○

HOME | NEWS | **HAPPINESS**   search 🔍

Can meditation be a secret weapon?

☯

Recent research has come **(0)** up with some interesting findings about our approach to finding happiness. It seems that **(1)** .... from being an absolute, happiness is a skill that can be learnt, and the level achieved depends largely on the time and effort people **(2)** .... prepared to invest in it. So **(3)** .... does anyone go about this? Allegedly, meditation plays a role. The left side of the brain is associated **(4)** .... happiness while the right side is more negative. Brain scans performed on those **(5)** .... meditate frequently demonstrated raised levels of positivity in the left side, while the more negative right side was kept **(6)** .... check. This raises key questions. Can only regular meditators be happy? It seems **(7)** ...., as levels of positivity were seen to be higher even in infrequent meditators. So the good news might be that a minor modification to our perception of things **(8)** .... us could lead to a big change in our sense of well-being. It's certainly food for thought!

2 Look at the gapped words in the article and match them with descriptions A–F.

A   a negative
B   a dependent preposition
C   a relative pronoun
D   a verb
E   a preposition
F   a fixed prepositional phrase

3 Read the article again. Which sentence best summarises the writer's main point?

1   Meditation is the only way to create a feeling of happiness.
2   We can change our level of happiness by altering our mindset.
3   Happiness is only achievable with a lot of effort.

About the exam:
In Reading and Use of English Part 2, you read a text with eight gaps. The missing words may test grammar words (e.g. verb forms, referents), use of connectors (e.g. *however*, *although*) or vocabulary (e.g. phrasal verbs, collocations).

Strategy:
- Read the title and the whole text so that you understand what it is about.
- Read the whole sentence with the gap, to look for clues as to what kind of word you need.
- Check the words before and after each gap and look for grammatical collocations.
- Read the whole text through once you have completed it to make sure you have not missed any connectors, plurals or negatives.

Speaking
Long turn (Part 2) ▶ CB page 49

1 ▶ 09 **Look at the task and the pictures. Which two pictures would you choose? Listen to a candidate doing the task. Did she choose the same ones?**

> Look at the pictures. They show people experiencing special moments. Compare two of the pictures and say why these moments might be special for the people and how memorable these moments might be.

2 **Complete the candidate's answer. Then listen again and check your answers.**

I'd like to talk about these two pictures. In my opinion the people in both pictures are experiencing a feel-good moment. It's special for all of them but, obviously, for different reasons. The people are in contrasting locations, too. One looks as **(1)** .... it's in a cold place, in a lovely mountainous area, whereas the other is obviously hot. In both pictures the place **(2)** .... be very quiet but in the second I **(3)** .... the woman herself must stay quiet so as not to disturb the animals. The woman in the first picture is **(4)** .... with people we can't see, but from the way she looks, I'd **(5)** .... she's feeling proud about achieving something difficult. She certainly looks pretty pleased with herself. And this is just a(n) **(6)** .... but this **(7)** .... be the first time she's ever done anything so physically difficult, so it would be a very special moment for her. In the second picture the woman **(8)** .... very happy and excited. I **(9)** .... she's always wanted to go on a safari like this. I can't be **(10)** .... but I imagine this is probably a special moment for her because she's never seen such amazing animals close up before.

Listening
Multiple choice (Part 3) ▶ CB page 50

1 ▶ 10 **You will hear an interview with Janet Wilson and Dave Edwards, who are both stand-up comedians. For questions 1–6, choose the answer (A, B, C or D) which fits best according to what you hear.**

1 Janet's interest in stand-up comedy started because
   A she was dissatisfied with normal performing roles.
   B she enjoyed writing her own jokes and scripts.
   C she knew it would fulfil her desire for a challenge.
   D she felt it linked to her primary interest in acting.

2 How did Janet's parents react to her career?
   A They hesitated about supporting her.
   B They wished she had been more studious.
   C They were pleased she was doing something she loved.
   D They were concerned about the insecurity of it.

3 How does Dave feel when he's performing?
   A frustrated by an unresponsive audience
   B privileged to be able to make people happy
   C tired by the effort of keeping people amused
   D concerned when an audience doesn't like him

4 According to Dave, a successful comedian must
   A be a charismatic presence on stage.
   B win lots of prestigious awards.
   C be able to ignore unhelpful criticism.
   D feel confident about growing as a performer.

5 What do Janet and Dave both think about the future of stand-up comedy?
   A It will be increasingly competitive.
   B Success may be harder to come by.
   C The kind of material used could change.
   D Comedians may have to become more professional.

6 When talking about her own future, Janet accepts/ realises she should
   A be prepared for setbacks in her career.
   B do some other work for financial reasons.
   C develop a better stage presence.
   D turn down offers to develop other skills.

Grammar
substitution and ellipsis ▶ CB page 51

1 Replace the underlined words in the article with the words in the box.

doing that   it   one   that (×2)   them   they (×2)

More than just a pet

Two of my friends recently adopted a dog. By **(1)** <u>adopting a dog</u> they have given me an insight into how animals can promote well-being. **(2)** <u>My friends</u> were happy enough before they brought Buster home but rarely have I seen anything bring so much joy into a home as he has.

It's unsurprising that greater health and happiness can come from caring for a pet. One research study tracked people working in stressful jobs who adopted cats or dogs; caring for **(3)** <u>the cats or dogs</u> lowered the person's blood pressure more effectively than medicine. People who own dogs tend to get more exercise than people without **(4)** <u>a dog</u>, and **(5)** <u>exercise</u> is a guaranteed way of boosting your health and happiness.

Having said **(6)** <u>exercise is a guaranteed way to boost health and happiness</u>, I would never suggest that families with young children should get a puppy or any similar pet; not because **(7)** <u>getting a puppy</u> is problematic in itself, but parents nowadays lead such busy lives that looking after a young animal is the last thing **(8)** <u>parents</u> want to worry about. But families can still benefit from the love of animals by adopting lower-maintenance pets such as fish or by helping out with other people's animals.

2 There is one word missing in each conversation. Add it in the right place.

1   **A:** Are you going to buy that car?
    B: No, I can't afford at the moment.
2   **A:** Do you think the trains will be busy this evening?
    B: I expect because it's always busy on a Friday.
3   **A:** People seem happier these days!
    B: Do you think? I hadn't noticed!
4   **A:** I'm going to Rome in the summer for a short holiday.
    B: Really? So I! Maybe we'll be there at the same time.
5   **A:** Please tell Sue that I'll be late for the meeting.
    B: Of course I. What time will you get here?

Reading
Multiple matching (Part 8) ▶ CB page 52

About the exam:
In Reading and Use of English Part 8, you match questions or statements to paragraphs or sections of a text.

Strategy:
- Read the text(s) quickly to get a general idea of the topic.
- Read through the questions and underline key words and phrases that may help you.
- Scan the text(s) to find parts with a similar meaning to what you have underlined. Remember that the words will not be the same.

1 Read the article on page 37. Which writer, A, B, C or D does NOT relate a concrete personal experience to exemplify a point of view?

2 Read the article again. For questions 1–10, choose from the sections A–D. You may choose any of the sections more than once.

Which writer

Describes the consequences of anticipated wealth or income?	1
Mentions an inherited trait?	2
Condemns some people's use of money to manipulate others?	3
Mentions different interpretations of a particular term?	4
Believes that experts do not tell us anything new?	5
Refers to physical reactions to events?	6
Refers to money left outside the family?	7
Reinforces a point by using a comparison between two family members?	8
Mentions the need for money to alleviate certain problems?	9
Comments that age has brought better understanding of a person's opinions?	10

Secret of a happy life –
in our genes or in our pockets?

Four readers comment on the importance of wealth.

A

Most of us tend to assume that having a good income which enables us to maintain a certain standard of living, with excess to use on luxuries for ourselves, is desirable. But does it make us happy? Experience tells me no. My uncle had an exceptionally high-powered job and he profited financially from it, but in no way would I describe him as a happy person – he was one of the grumpiest people I've ever met. He hoarded his money, spent the minimum necessary on himself, nothing on helping others, and after his death willed the whole fortune to an animal charity. In direct contrast, my uncle on my mother's side was generous to a fault with the money he earned from a similarly well-paid job. He too was single, but his view on the world was positive and his house was full of singing and laughter. I guess what I'm trying to say is that happiness may be partly in a person's genes, and partly in whatever life throws at them. Those of us with the gene will find something happy in life.

B

I have to admit that people who seriously debate the contribution that income can make to a person's overall feeling of well-being, and conclude that material possessions and having the wherewithal to buy them is *not* an indicator of happiness, really get under my skin. Of course everyone knows that all the wealth in the world can't make someone like or love you, or pay for miraculous cures for medical problems. And we've all met people who get really stressed because they need to work so hard to sustain the lifestyle that money has brought them. They certainly aren't particularly happy. We don't need surveys and scientific projects to tell us that, surely? But equally, we don't need anyone to tell us that having enough money to maintain good health or at least pay for the treatments and care we need when we are suffering is clearly very important. It's a fact of life. Whatever fancy language psychologists may use to tell us that money doesn't make us happy, a lack of money can definitely make life hard!

C

My grandmother used to say 'money is the root of all evil', which I couldn't really get my head round when I was a child. Now, however, I can see what she meant, although I think the saying exaggerates the point, as all sayings do. I'd just like to point out how devastating the expectation of money can be on a family. I was brought up to believe that in life you reap what you sow – i.e. you work, you earn, you live – what you

earn is yours. I want my parents to use their money while they're alive, not to leave it to me when they die. That is why I get upset when I see people who plan their lives around an expected inheritance, and the ruptures this can create within a family are horrifying. My best friend's father took his own brother to court because he thought the division of the inheritance from their parents was unfair. It caused such a rift in the family that they haven't spoken for ten years. What is that all about? And the way that controlling people use money to bribe family members to act in certain ways, threatening to disinherit them if they act otherwise – it's simply beyond my understanding.

D

In my opinion happiness, or being happy, isn't a state of mind, I think it's the wrong choice of word. For me the word *happiness* conjures up more a series of moments when – to be a little poetic – your heart lifts or feels full. To give a couple of examples, it's like when you watch a friend get married and you almost cry because it makes you feel so good, or when you get the best possible results in a test and you want to punch the air and shout 'Yes!' So, when you get these surveys or questionnaires and experts commenting about whether money brings happiness or things like that I feel that they're considering the wrong question. Isn't it more about contentment or comfort? And it's all relative anyway, as far as I'm concerned. Some people, whether they're billionaires with considerable inherited wealth, or those surviving on very little money, will always find things that will make them feel good.

3 **Find words and phrases in the article that match meanings 1–8.**

1 collected/cluttered (section A)
2 almost too liberal with money (Section A)
3 the funds/finances (Section B)
4 irritate (Section B)
5 at the same time (Section B)
6 understand something complex (Section C)
7 a division/gap (Section C)
8 needs to be seen in context (Section D)

Grammar

hypothetical meaning ▶ CB page 54

1 Complete the sentences with the correct form of the verb in brackets.

1 I wish I .... (*own*) a pet – I'd probably feel happier.

2 If only they .... (*give*) me the chance to organise the party next week – I'd be good at it.

3 It's high time people .... (*start*) appreciating the good things in life.

4 I wish I .... (*go*) to see that comedian in the theatre last week – the reviews were great.

5 If only I .... (*not get*) involved with the project!

6 I wish I .... (*can improve*) my dancing technique but it's hard.

7 I'd rather my brother .... (*not play*) his music so loudly in the evenings.

8 It's high time we .... (*leave*), otherwise we'll be late for the party.

2 Complete the second sentence so that it has a similar meaning to the first sentence, using the word given. Do not change the word given. You must use between three and six words, including the word given.

1 I think you have waited long enough to make your decision. **HIGH**
It .... your decision.

2 I regret changing my job last year. **WISH**
I .... my job last year.

3 I wish I had been more polite to my boss when I spoke to her. **ONLY**
If .... politely to my boss.

4 Getting up early every morning is so difficult and I hate it! **PREFER**
I .... later every morning!

5 I prefer to decide everything myself instead of asking Paul. **RATHER**
I .... the decisions myself instead of asking Paul.

6 I made a mistake with my choice of course to study. **WISH**
I .... different course to study.

Vocabulary

prefix *mis-* and false opposites ▶ CB page 55

1 Replace the underlined words with the correct form of the words in the box. Use the prefix *mis-*.

behave fortune interpret give lead trust print understand

1 That young boy is always <u>behaving badly</u> – he needs to be taught some manners.

2 She's had a lot of <u>bad luck</u> recently – she deserves better.

3 I <u>didn't understand exactly</u> what she wanted, so I bought the wrong thing.

4 I <u>don't trust</u> that salesman – I don't think he always tells the truth.

5 Some advertising doesn't tell the whole truth – in fact, it quite often <u>deceives</u> people.

6 It's often possible to <u>not understand the correct meaning of</u> a person's body language.

7 Books in digital form often have <u>printing mistakes</u> in them.

8 I had <u>a lot of doubts</u> about whether it was a good idea to write to him.

sentence adverbs ▶ CB page 56

2 Complete the sentences with the adverbs in the box.

happily hopefully oddly enough sadly understandably unfortunately

1 ...., the couple meet again years later and the love affair continues.

2 ...., no one sees the murder although it happens in a very public place.

3 ...., there will be another series next year but nothing has been announced so far.

4 ...., the victim is scared of walking down that street again.

5 ...., I haven't seen the sequel, so I can't comment on it.

6 ...., the dog has to be put down at the end of the film.

Writing
Review (Part 2) ▶ CB page 56

About the exam:
In Writing Part 2, you choose between several options. One of these options may be a review of a book, film, new product, theatrical performance or something else that you have experience of. You write between 220 and 260 words.

Strategy:
- Include some information about what you are reviewing but don't include a lot of detail about one element of it.
- Give your reactions, whether positive, negative or both, and include recommendations for the readers.
- Use an informal style to engage readers.

1 Look at the exam task and the sample answer. Then decide which paragraph-opening sentence (A–E) best fits each gap.

You see this announcement on a website.

> ### What makes you laugh?
> When we're feeling a bit low, watching something funny on TV can lift our spirits. We'd like to post some reviews of TV series that give us a good giggle.
>
> Send us a review of a TV series which you think will cheer us all up, giving reasons for your choice.

Write your **review** in **220–260** words in an appropriate style.

A The script is witty and the characterisations are superb.

B The series is based on the works of P.G. Wodehouse, of Jeeves and Wooster fame.

C It happens to all of us.

D It is refreshing to watch a comedy series where the jokes are innocent but extremely funny.

E *Blandings* is an unlikely source of amusement for me.

2 Read the sample answer again and answer the questions.

1 How does the writer engage the reader in the first paragraph?
2 How does the writer use a possible negative point to make a positive one?
3 What factual information does the writer give?
4 List the adjectives used in the review.
5 How does the writer persuade us to watch the series?

(1) .... One moment you can be feeling really depressed and fed up with life and then something comes on the television which makes you giggle and by the end of the programme you find that you're smiling rather than scowling. That is exactly what I found when I watched the series *Blandings* on television last week.

(2) .... I usually shy away from slapstick comedy but *Blandings* manages to use this as well as other different types of humour in a way that seems to work brilliantly. I am glad I switched on.

(3) .... It is set in 1929 and it revolves around the lives of an aristocratic but hugely eccentric family who reside at a wonderful minor stately home called *Blandings Castle*. Timothy Spall plays the forgetful but lovable lord of the manor and the very talented Jennifer Saunders is his sharp-voiced sister who wants him to face up to his duties as a pillar of the local community. Unfortunately, this is a role he detests.

(4) .... However, what makes it so amusing is the way it pokes mild fun at a bygone age where money, title and class ruled society. We see the British at their best and at their worst, and it is an excellent example of how the British can laugh at themselves.

(5) .... I can thoroughly recommend the series to anyone who is feeling a little gloomy and I can almost guarantee that you won't be able to resist a smile. Channel 2, 7 p.m. on Sundays. You won't regret it.

3 Read the exam task again and think about the questions below. Then plan and write your review.

1 What is the series? Is it old or recent? Why did you start watching it?
2 What is the situation? Who are the actors?
3 What makes this series special in your opinion?
4 Who would you recommend it to?

6 Living with the past

Use of English
Word formation (Part 3) ▶ CB page 58

1 Write the correct form of the words below.

1 accurate (adj) .... (n)
2 portray (v) .... (n)
3 speculate (v) .... (n)
4 exhibition (n) .... (v)
5 injury (n) .... (pl n)
6 identify (v) .... (n)

2 Read the article. For questions 1–8, use the word given in capitals at the end of some of the lines to form a word that fits in the gap in the same line.

The discovery of a lost King

You wouldn't expect to find a dead king under a city car park, yet, **(0)** _astonishingly_, this was where archaeologists found Richard III, an English king who was killed in 1485. — ASTONISH

Richard has always been a **(1)** .... figure, which is not surprising when he was — CONTROVERSY
(2) .... as a villain and murderer in the play by Shakespeare. The accuracy — MORTAL
of this portrayal is **(3)** .... but the fact that Richard was killed at the Battle of — DEBATE
Bosworth Field is **(4)** .... — DISPUTE

After the battle, the exact whereabouts of his body was a mystery for centuries, but when archaeologists came across a skeleton in a car park in Leicester, speculation was rife about whether this could be the bodily **(5)** .... of the lost king. The skeleton exhibited — REMAIN
similar injuries to those recorded at the battle, and so scientists carried out carbon dating, which placed the skeleton in the fifteenth century. After that, **(6)** .... of DNA — ANALYSE
from the king's living **(7)** .... put the identification of the skeleton beyond — DESCEND
doubt – the evidence was **(8)** .... The missing king of England had been found. — CONCLUDE

3 Find the words from Activity 1 in the article and check your answers.

Listening
Multiple choice (Part 1) ▶ CB page 59

1 ▶ 11 You will hear three different extracts. For questions 1–6, choose the answer (A, B or C) which fits best according to what you hear. There are two questions for each extract.

Extract 1

You hear part of a discussion about keeping mementos and things from the past.

1 The man feels that keeping things from the past is

  A helpful for people to establish their sense of identity.

  B necessary to preserve certain things for posterity.

  C a way of making good use of old things.

2 What do both speakers think about the past?

  A Some things are only significant for those directly involved.

  B People need to feel a link to their ancestors.

  C It's essential to help older relatives retain their memories.

Extract 2

You hear part of a radio discussion about the role of museums in modern life.

3 What is the woman doing?

 A explaining why museums are not financially viable today

 B describing what is involved in running a museum

 C outlining reasons why museums are irrelevant nowadays

4 The speakers both think that museums

 A can be expensive to maintain.

 B have potential for educational use.

 C are popular with certain types of people.

Extract 3

You hear two people talking about a historical film they have seen.

5 How does the man feel about the film?

 A annoyed about the way it was marketed

 B bored because of the lack of a clear narrative

 C frustrated by the pace of the film

6 The speakers agree that historical films

 A are a good way to teach children about the past.

 B often include incorrect information for dramatic effect.

 C make history more interesting for many people.

Grammar
comparing ▶ CB page 60

1 **Complete the sentences with the words in the box.**

as by far far far more like most much
much less   quite

1 I'm .... interested in history lessons now that the teacher shows us films.

2 He's very good-looking, just .... his father.

3 History lessons are nothing like as boring nowadays .... they were when I was at school!

4 .... the best old castle I have seen on holiday was in Wales.

5 People are .... more involved with researching their family tree now that so .... information is on the net.

6 I think people find out .... as much from the internet as they do from books.

7 It's .... interesting doing family research on your own than with other people.

8 I found out the .... fascinating information about my family by talking to my grandmother.

Speaking
Long turn (Part 2) ▶ CB page 61

1 **Look at the exam task and the pictures. Put a cross (X) next to the things that the candidate should *not* do.**

1 Give a detailed description of two pictures.

2 Comment on all three pictures.

3 Talk about the similarities between the pictures.

4 Choose the best way to record events.

5 Relate personally to the pictures.

6 Ask his/her partner's opinion.

7 Try to address all parts of the task.

> Look at the pictures. They show people recording events and information for the future. Compare two of the pictures and say why these records might be important to people in the future and how accurate the recording needs to be.

2 ▶ 12 Listen to a candidate doing the task. Tick (✓) the things in Activity 1 that he does.

Reading
Multiple choice (Part 5)
▶ CB page 62

1 Read the article. What is the writer's main purpose?

1 to review a documentary
2 to explain the problems of hoarders
3 to explore a family problem
4 to warn people of the dangers of hoarding

2 Read the article again. For questions 1–6, choose the answer (A, B, C or D) which you think fits best according to the text.

1 When he was younger, the writer believed his father's collection of strange old things
   A was amusing to look at.
   B should be taken seriously.
   C bordered on the obsessive.
   D was understandable at his age.

2 After watching the documentary, the writer was
   A certain his father had a severe health problem.
   B confused by his father's symptoms.
   C aware his father's situation wasn't as bad as some.
   D worried his father was in a dangerous environment.

3 The writer mentions Jasmine's new job to
   A indicate possible psychological effects of her upbringing.
   B show she survived childhood difficulties and became successful.
   C compare types of environment people live in today.
   D emphasise that Jasmine's priorities are not influenced by her mother.

4 When helping Vasoulla, Jasmine had to
   A remove some of Vasoulla's possessions secretly.
   B make Vasoulla see the funny side of the situation.
   C ask an expert to diagnose Vasoulla's condition.
   D force Vasoulla to part with some possessions.

5 During the documentary, Vasoulla
   A managed to recover from her obsession.
   B overcame her frustration with her messy house.
   C recognised the value of Jasmine's help.
   D found important things she had long forgotten.

6 What has the writer learnt about his father?
   A He wanted to preserve things to remember the past.
   B He was concerned about wastage.
   C He hoped to make money from his possessions.
   D He was determined to make life easier for his family.

3 Find adjectives in the article that match meanings 1–8.

1 old and rotting (Paragraph 1)
2 not dangerous (Paragraph 2)
3 impossible to go through (Paragraph 2)
4 depressing (Paragraph 4)
5 untroubled (Paragraph 5)
6 lasting for a short time (Paragraph 5)
7 very angry (Paragraph 6)
8 mad (Paragraph 6)

4 Complete the sentences with the adjectives in Activity 3.

1 The cheese had been in the fridge far too long and it had gone ....
2 There had been a landslide because of the heavy rain and the road was ....
3 I was .... when my neighbour built an extension to his house that completely blocked the sunlight into our garden.
4 The beauty of flowers is .... but it is worth waiting to see each year.
5 I was .... by the teacher's criticisms because I knew I could do better.
6 My brother had this .... idea to swim across the Atlantic but we talked him out of it.

5 Choose the correct answer (A or B) for each sentence.

1 The writer uses the phrase *multi-storey storage facility* (line 28) to
   A show how big Vasoulla's house is.
   B emphasise the strength of her obsession.

2 The phrase *commandeered by clutter* (line 35) suggests that
   A Vasoulla is not in control.
   B Vasoulla needs more work surfaces.

3 The phrase *flotsam and jetsam* (line 80) is used to suggest that
   A what Vasoulla has collected is not systematic.
   B Vasoulla is becoming overwhelmed by her junk.

MY HOARDER MUM AND ME

I'd always considered my father to be something of a hoarder. Our family home was flanked by a pair of garages but neither was used for anything as prosaic as parking cars. Instead, they both bulged, ceiling to floor, with a bizarre and ever-growing menagerie of stuff: old windsurfing magazines, broken kettles, mouldy carpets, two dozen or more used stick-deodorants. At the time, I thought my father's stockpiling of apparently redundant objects was funny, a harmless eccentricity shared by middle-aged men nesting in garages and sheds across the land.

Years later, when Obsessive Compulsive Disorder became a recognised medical condition, I started to wonder if those overflowing garages might have been bad for his health. Watching the moving documentary *My Hoarder Mum and Me* put my father's relatively benign symptoms into context. In it, Vasoulla, a lifelong hoarder and mother of TV presenter Jasmine Harman, invited a film crew into her home, or rather, her multi-storey storage facility. Every room in Vasoulla's house contained more stuff than space. The staircases were almost impassable and in the kitchen, Vasoulla had problems chopping vegetables because every flat surface had already been commandeered by clutter. The house would have looked tidier if it had been struck by a tornado.

To her credit, Vasoulla realised that she had a serious problem, not least because her hoarding had been going on – and getting worse – for years. Her grown-up sons remembered thinking it normal for dinner to be served in a bedroom; it was the only room that could accommodate the whole family. The hoarding had evidently been especially hard on Jasmine. 'All the way through my life I've felt that my mum's stuff was more important than me,' she reflected quietly. Any Freudian analysts watching will have been scribbling in their notebooks when Jasmine told us she now presents a TV property series that helps people to find their ideal homes. In contrast to Vasoulla, Jasmine 'vacuums everything, sofas, chairs, even the kitchen worktops.'

Over the course of the documentary, which followed the family over several months, Jasmine coaxed and cajoled Vasoulla to jettison at least some of her junk. It was a slow, painful process – Vasoulla had been known to buy back her own possessions just hours after donating them to charity. In need of professional help, Jasmine consulted a Dr Mataix-Cols, who told her hoarding was considered a form of OCD but did not get the attention and research grants it deserved because it wasn't yet recognised as a condition in its own right. The author of another book about hoarding had even more dispiriting news for Jasmine. 'Give up,' she was told, 'because hoarders never stop hoarding.'

Unperturbed by these gloomy prognoses, Jasmine helped Vasoulla sift through the flotsam and jetsam. It was impossible not to share Jasmine's frustration with her mother's attachment to even her most ephemeral possessions ('Can I throw away a copy of the *Financial Times* from 2010?'). Yet by the end, you also shared Jasmine's triumph as the carpets of three of her mother's rooms were reintroduced to the light of day for the first time in years. It would be an overstatement to say that Vasoulla had conquered her obsession. But she was touchingly appreciative of what Jasmine had done for her and vowed to continue their house-clearing project. 'It feels good to see the table again,' she said.

After hearing Vasoulla's extraordinary story, I realised that my father isn't a hoarder at all. It isn't objects he prizes. It's their usefulness. Like many of his generation, who grew up in post-war austerity, my father likes to squeeze every drop of value from everything he owns, even if it means storing it for decades to do so. The windsurfing magazines will come in handy if he gets back into windsurfing; the carpet could do for a third garage. He even had a brilliant scheme for his collection of used deodorants. Incensed that you could never reach the final ten percent of the deodorant because of its plastic casing, he decided to heat and transfer the residue from each into an empty casing, thereby creating one new, reconstituted deodorant. At the time, my brother and I thought he was potty. But now I see that my father was actually decades ahead of the curve. He wasn't hoarding our family's discarded possessions; he was recycling them.

Vocabulary

adjective/noun collocations
▶ CB page 62

1 Choose the correct alternative in each sentence.

1 She went on a tailor-made *trip/flight* last year to the USA.

2 I'm very interested in my ancestors – I've started creating my family *base/tree*.

3 Genealogy tourism is a fast-growing *sector/fashion* of the travel industry.

4 One TV programme about genealogy was a *runaway/running* success.

5 People are especially interested in *sociable/social* history.

6 It's easy to trace your family *roots/basis* using technology.

prefixes and suffixes ▶ CB page 64

2 Complete the sentences by adding the prefixes in the box to the adjectives in brackets.

im- in- ir- un-

1 Finding the remains of the old castle was a(n) .... (*credible*) experience.

2 Trying to work on an archaeological dig is completely .... (*practical*) because of the mud.

3 It's .... (*responsible*) to promote building programmes on land of historical importance.

4 Trying to find all one's ancestors is completely .... (*realistic*) – so much information has been lost over time.

3 Complete the second sentence so that it has a similar meaning to the first sentence. Replace the underlined words and use suffixes.

1 Most mistakes in archaeology <u>can be forgiven</u>.
Most mistakes in archaeology ....

2 The publishing house <u>has produced</u> a lot of historical books.
The publishing house .... in the area of historical books.

3 His suggestion <u>shows great imagination</u>.
His suggestion ....

4 His attitude towards the development of the site <u>keeps changing</u>.
His attitude towards the development of the site is ....

5 The quality of the old documents <u>varies</u>.
The quality of the old documents is ....

6 <u>It's quite hard to get access</u> to the building.
The building is not ....

Grammar

modifying adverbs ▶ CB page 65

1 Match 1–6 with A–F to make collocations. Sometimes more than one answer is possible.

1	bitterly	A	sure/awesome
2	absolutely	B	perfect/finished
3	pretty	C	tired/unreliable
4	practically	D	false/believable
5	entirely	E	perfect/impossible
6	completely	F	disappointed/upset

2 Choose the correct answers (A, B or C) to complete the article.

What do we know about Shakespeare?

People feel it's **(1)** .... important to learn as much as possible about important figures in history, and for English people there are **(2)** .... more important figures than Shakespeare. However, **(3)** .... little is known about him and so any concrete information that can be discovered is **(4)** .... important. In Stratford-on-Avon, Shakespeare's birthplace and the town where he is buried, a dig took place in the grounds of New Place, the house he owned in his later life. This dig exposed evidence that provides **(5)** .... important information about how Shakespeare's house looked when he lived there, and the make-up of his household. Archaeologists found pottery and animal remains in the dig; these are **(6)** .... key evidence to prove that the household was **(7)** .... important in the town. It seems that Shakespeare's daughter Susanna entertained royalty in the house in 1643. I found the whole project **(8)** .... captivating and I hope archaeologists are on the brink of finding out much more about Shakespeare's life that they can be **(9)** .... sure of. I will be **(10)** .... disappointed if they don't!

	A	B	C
1	extremely	slightly	entirely
2	many	little	few
3	fairly	remarkably	quite
4	unbelievably	absolutely	utterly
5	totally	completely	vitally
6	greatly	really	entirely
7	quite	practically	entirely
8	somewhat	practically	completely
9	seriously	absolutely	practically
10	bitterly	perfectly	completely

Writing
Essay (Part 1) ▶ CB page 66

1 Look at the exam task. Tick (✓) the things that you have to do.

1 Write about three points.
2 Include all the ideas expressed in the documentary.
3 Avoid using words directly from the question.
4 Write less than 200 words.

> Your class has watched a documentary about the difficulties of knowing the truth about historical events. You have made the notes below.
>
> > **Why it is difficult to know the truth about historical events**
> > - evidence
> > - popular culture
> > - politics
>
> > **Some opinions expressed in the documentary**
> > 'One way is to look at official records – they can't lie, can they?'
> > 'Stories get passed down through generations but who knows if they're true or just exaggerated?'
> > 'Politicians can interpret history and use it to their own advantage!'
>
> Write an essay for your tutor discussing **two** of the points in your notes. You should **explain which you think has the most influence** on how historical events are described, **giving reasons** to support your opinion.
>
> You may, if you wish, make use of the opinions expressed in the discussion but you should use your own words as far as possible.
>
> Write your **essay** in **220–260** words in an appropriate style.

2 The phrases in italics in the sentences below can be used to give an impersonal introduction to a fact or opinion. Complete them with the words in the box.

believe   claimed   common   considered   generally   undeniably   well-known

1 *It is a* .... *fact that* politicians bury information that they do not wish us to know.
2 *It is often* .... *that* past records have been altered or destroyed.
3 *There are several viewpoints that need to be* .... Whereas it is important to encourage patriotism, it is also …
4 *Many people* .... *that* everything they read in history books is true.
5 *It is* .... *knowledge* that in times of war, propaganda is often used as a weapon.
6 *The issue of* political misinformation *is* .... *important and needs to be addressed.*
7 *It is* .... *believed that* legends have a basis in fact.

3 Note down the following.

1 a historical event that has turned out to have been misrepresented in history books
2 an example of a historical figure or event that is retold in legend, folk music, etc.
3 examples of types of records used to determine what happened in the past

4 Do the exam task in Activity 1. Remember to:
- organise your work into paragraphs that deal with separate points.
- include both an introduction and a conclusion.
- use examples and give reasons for your opinions.
- use impersonal phrases where appropriate.

Multiple-choice cloze (Part 1)

For questions 1–8, read the text below and decide which answer (A, B, C or D) best fits each gap. There is an example at the beginning (0).

The sweet smell of success

As a child I was captivated by the idea of being a baker – it was the **(0)** ...*A, aroma*.. of bread and cakes! In the event it didn't happen but now I do sell sweets online. That wasn't intentional – after college I'd been **(1)** .... down for every job I'd applied for, so starting my own business was my last option. I did a lot of research, looking for a **(2)** .... market, an unexploited area I could make my own. I earmarked the sweets sector, and persuaded a friend with marketing experience to come into **(3)** .... with me. I intended this to be a temporary arrangement until I **(4)** .... for a real career but after a while I found I enjoyed the flexibility and decided to develop it into a **(5)** .... viable business. It was a scary proposition, and it was hard **(6)** .... with initial feelings of doubt. I was turning my **(7)** .... on security, taking financial risks, but I was in charge, **(8)** .... the shots. It's been hard work, but the future's looking sweet.

0	**A** aroma	**B** stench	**C** scent	**D** odour
1	**A** got	**B** turned	**C** put	**D** taken
2	**A** part	**B** corner	**C** section	**D** niche
3	**A** contract	**B** partnership	**C** alliance	**D** collaboration
4	**A** picked	**B** decided	**C** chose	**D** opted
5	**A** totally	**B** rather	**C** slightly	**D** quite
6	**A** making	**B** getting	**C** coping	**D** being
7	**A** back	**B** shoulder	**C** head	**D** body
8	**A** risking	**B** telling	**C** calling	**D** giving

Open cloze (Part 2)

For questions 9–16, read the text below and think of the word which best fits each gap. Use only one word in each gap. There is an example at the beginning (0).

Do I really feel good about that?

I've always been a sucker for **(0)** ......*a*...... slick marketing campaign – I fall for **(9)** .... every time. Marketing people have got me completely sussed – they understand my mindset, how to push my buttons. You see, buying something new **(10)** .... me feel happy. The problem **(11)** ...., that kind of euphoria only lasts for a moment. After that comes guilt and more often than **(12)** .... I return the item I've been so pleased with for a refund. So I get locked into an unending spiral of spend followed by **(13)** .... is popularly called 'buyer's regret'.

I've been checking out options that might help me curb my buying impulses. I'm learning to spread purchases **(14)** .... much as I can – instead of going on one big spending spree, I try to limit **(15)** .... to one purchase per shopping trip. I can't give up my credit card completely, but now it's earmarked **(16)** .... luxury items alone. I'm on the right road to balancing my books, and that's success in my mind.

Word formation (Part 3)

For questions 17–24, read the text below. Use the word given in capitals at the end of some of the lines to form a word that fits in the gap in the same line. There is an example at the beginning (0).

Facing up to things

One of the biggest issues many of us face in the modern world is that of **(0)** procrastination. We're all experts at putting off things that we're **(17)** .... or afraid to deal with head on.

PROCRASTINATE

WILL

It also appears that whenever we come up with **(18)** .... reasons for not meeting a deadline or leaving a job **(19)** ...., we're not the only ones guilty of this. It's been said that nearly a quarter of the world's population follow the same pattern of **(20)** ....

IMAGINE

FINISH

BEHAVE

Sadly, although we might like to think it, we're not all **(21)** .... who are able to produce excellent work under pressure – this is a well-used excuse. In addition, there may be consequences arising from this mistaken point of view, though we probably regard them as **(22)** .... and unimportant.

PERFECT

SIGNIFY

Nevertheless, putting things off can lead to some quite startling **(23)** .... such as stress, poor health and lack of success at work. It can also cause those around us great **(24)** ...., so is something we should all be aware of.

COMPLICATE

CONVENIENT

Key word transformation (Part 4)

For questions 25–30, complete the second sentence so that it has a similar meaning to the first sentence, using the word given. Do not change the word given. You must use between three and six words, including the word given. Here is an example (0).

Example

0 I don't have any free time, so I can't come to the theatre with you.

WOULD

If I had some free time, I would come to the theatre with you.

25 Many people resent having to work so hard.

WISH

Many people .... to work so hard.

26 What the archaeologists discovered when they opened the tomb was amazing.

MADE

The .... when they opened the tomb was amazing.

27 People are more interested in history than you might expect.

LESS

You .... interested in history.

28 For me, imagining what life must have been like then is not possible.

QUITE

I find it .... what life must have been like then.

29 It's difficult for a poorly performing company to make a profit.

TURN

If a company is performing poorly, it's difficult .... one.

30 For me, the failure of the company was incredibly disappointing.

BITTERLY

I .... the failure of the company.

7 The hard sell

Grammar
review of conditionals ▶ CB page 70

1 Complete the first, second and third conditional sentences with the correct form of the verb in brackets.

1 If I hadn't gone shopping that day, I .... (*not buy*) that dress.

2 If a sales assistant is good at their job, they .... (*help*) you find what you want.

3 If I .... (*want*) to buy a new car, I would have to save very hard!

4 If I .... (*go*) shopping tomorrow, I will try to find a new outfit for the party.

5 If children .... (*be*) taken shopping, they always get bored.

6 If shopping were all done online, it .... (*be*) much easier.

2 Choose the correct alternatives to complete the mixed conditional sentences.

1 If I *hadn't bought/didn't buy* my new sports car, I *wouldn't feel/wouldn't have felt* so happy right now.

2 The boy *would have contacted/had contacted* you already if he *were/would have been* serious about you now.

3 If the company *had done/did* better market research in the past they *would understand/would have understood* their market better today.

4 I *would be/have been* a better teacher today if I *had had/would have* more training at the start.

5 If I *hadn't bought/didn't buy* that expensive jewellery last month, I *would be able/would have been able* to afford that holiday now.

6 If you *had thought/thought* about it more carefully before you accepted the job, you *wouldn't be working/hadn't been working* there now.

Vocabulary
collocations: sales and marketing ▶ CB page 71

1 Match words from Box A and Box B to make collocations.

A   customer   junk   marketing   online   product   retail

B   feedback   mail   manager   park   placement   shopping

2 Choose the correct alternative in each sentence.

1 It'd be great to work in the *retail/selling* sector – I love shopping!

2 It's important for salespeople to *make/achieve* high sales figures.

3 Companies like to establish a solid customer *base/ground*.

4 Some successful brands manage to build up a *trusting/loyal* clientele who never shop anywhere else.

5 Salespeople are set sales *targets/aims* to reach every month.

6 Advertising *techniques/campaigns* on television can be annoying when they seem to be exaggerating the truth.

Listening
Multiple choice (Part 3)
▶ CB page 72

1 ▶ 13 You will hear two young entrepreneurs, Emily Johnson and James Harris, talking about starting their own marketing business at a young age. For questions 1–6, choose the answer (A, B, C or D) which fits best according to what you hear.

1 What does Emily say about starting her own business?

A It was something she had always planned for.

B She followed the advice of a friend.

C She wanted to choose the work she did.

D It was a logical extension of her interest in design.

2 Emily thinks that at the beginning of her career she was helped most by her

A university course.

B unpaid work experience.

C own natural talent.

D determination to succeed.

3 How did James feel when he started his business?

A anxious about the chance he was taking

B confident about his approach to business

C excited by the uncertainty of the project

D keen to learn as much as he could

4 What does James think is the hardest thing for young entrepreneurs?

A overcoming the reputation that young people have

B getting their peers to take them seriously

C building up a large enough client base

D becoming known among established businesses

5 Emily says that what she enjoys most about running her own business is

A feeling that her work is leading to her own success.

B being able to make her own decisions.

C seeing her advertisements in public.

D helping others to achieve their aims.

6 What do Emily and James both think is the most important advice for young entrepreneurs?

A Don't let anything discourage you.

B Develop your own identity and brand.

C Don't expect to be able to have a social life.

D Be sure your business is something worth doing.

Use of English
Multiple-choice cloze (Part 1)
▶ CB page 73

1 Read the article. For questions 1–8, decide which answer (A, B, C or D) best fits each gap.

58 | It's all about technique

Selling a new product is a complex business, especially when the product could be **(0)** A classed as a luxury, and many people are involved in the process of introducing it to the market. Once the work of designing and manufacturing the product has been completed, it's **(1)** .... the salespeople to sell it and, hopefully, **(2)** .... the company a fortune! Two words are key in a marketing **(3)** ....: *buzz* and *hype*. Each of these has an important part to play. *Buzz* is what salespeople want to create through **(4)** .... of mouth – potential customers talking about the new product, creating a demand for it, building a sense of excitement about the **(5)** .... and generating a positive market **(6)** .... *Hype*, advertising created by the company itself, is the sales **(7)** .... the company puts out to promote its wares. Which is more effective? People are inclined to distrust the hard sell and recommendation from loyal customers is likely to carry greater **(8)** .... among consumers.

0	A classed	B clarified		C grouped		D graded
1	A in for	B back through		C down by		D up to
2	A create	B make		C turn		D keep
3	A campaign	B movement		C project		D drive
4	A saying	B expression		C word		D phrase
5	A opening	B start		C initiation		D launch
6	A reply	B acknowledgement	C answer		D response
7	A fact	B pitch		C argument		D information
8	A value	B appreciation		C acceptance	D weight

Vocabulary
collocations with *go* ▶ CB page 73

1 Complete the sentences with the words in the box.

bald bankrupt deaf downhill mad mouldy sour viral

1 If milk is left in a warm room, it goes ....

2 When bread gets too old, it goes ....

3 When men get old, they often lose their hair and go ....

4 Videos online often go .... and get millions of hits.

5 In a recession, unfortunately, many companies go ....

6 His general health is declining – he's really going ....

7 Dishonesty makes me angry – I go .... when people tell lies.

8 Older people often go a bit .... and have to turn the TV up very loud!

Reading
Gapped text (Part 7) ▶ CB page 74

1 Read the article on page 51 quickly and choose the best option to complete the title.

1 depend on online advertising

2 try to change our habits

3 prioritise experience and ethics

2 Read the article again. Six paragraphs have been removed from the article. Choose from the paragraphs A–G the one which fits each gap (1–6). There is one extra paragraph which you do not need to use.

3 The phrases in italics in the sentences below are from the article. Complete them using the words in the box.

beneficial comes incentives knock-on tap
king

1 In this age of online shopping *the customer is truly* ....

2 We've put money aside for emergencies but I don't think we'll need *to* .... *into* it just yet.

3 In the end, the success of a business venture .... *down to* the dedication and investment put into it.

4 The company *offers* .... to workers who want to take on extra responsibility.

5 This is a decision that is going to have a lot of .... *effects* for quite a long time.

6 We shall no doubt come to a *mutually* .... arrangement from which we can both profit.

4 Match the underlined words in the article and paragraphs with their meanings (1–7).

1 piece of clothing

2 belief

3 too much of something

4 strongly desire

5 something that is ugly

6 putting life back into something

7 having original and imaginative ideas about the future

A So how will these changing attitudes to buying and selling affect retail and our High Streets? Well, it's quite simple. Be good at what you do. Be good in the way you do business. Otherwise you won't survive. Today the customer is truly king. We can shop where we want, when we want, whatever time of day we want and pretty much at whatever budget we want.

B And we should follow this approach and be building the same business model for smaller businesses with the focus on giving shoppers something different. Shops which offer an interesting range of items, grounded in good practice, and sharing space in a mutually beneficial way: co-creating.

C That was the year I was invited to lead the government's review into <u>reinvigorating</u> Britain's High Streets, which were becoming like ghost towns. During my work, I met many of the retail giants to discuss how we could rebuild a sustainable future for our High Streets.

D These are the type of companies led by forward-thinking CEOs like Uniqlo, which have redefined the selling of fashion basics by putting brilliant fashion design at affordable prices into a store over five floors with a lifewear concept, interactive mirrors, rooftop event spaces. Then there's an outdoor clothing brand that actually encourages its customers to extend the life of their garments by operating a <u>garment</u> repair service.

E I believe we have reached a place where digital plays an everyday important and continuing part of our lives but we now seek more experiences to compensate for our digital <u>overload</u>. Indeed, 38 percent of the millennial generation would rather spend on an experience or something 'interesting' rather than just buying more 'stuff'.

F Many of them and the politicians were particularly in thrall to Green. 'You have to understand,' one captain of retail industry said to me, when we met to discuss retail concerns, 'He's made millions. The man knows what he's doing.' No recommendations were to be made until we had heard what the big man had to say.

G But the worst part of all this is, it could have been saved. It could have been a brilliant retail business. But to do so would have required vision, investment, creative entrepreneurship and a real understanding of people, their lives and aspirations, plus a big dose of Moral Capitalism. Instead the business model preferred was asset stripping, streamlining processes, cost-cutting and squeezing suppliers.

To Survive on the High Street ...

Another big chain store, BHS, is closing down. I'm not surprised but I'm saddened. The loss of one of Britain's best known stores will have devastating effects on our struggling High Streets, and in turn the local communities who will be living with these big empty <u>eyesores</u>.

[1]

And, as we have seen, it was disastrous for the company. This news takes me back to 2011. Woolworths had collapsed and closed up. I was visiting High Streets up and down the country seeing the knock-on effects of not only the recession, but internet shopping and out-of-town supermarkets.

[2]

I still believe that how retail commerce develops is centred on two quite different <u>creeds</u> – one that is built on greed and gain and another on experience and ethics – and that the latter will be the future. How we buy has changed irreversibly. It has changed not just as a consequence of the internet and the recession, but of wider social issues and changes.

[3]

In addition to this choice and flexibility, the legacy of the internet has meant we tap into trends faster, demand more choice, but also gain access to how goods are made so we demand higher ethical behaviour and standards. We know that online shopping and commerce won't replace the High Street either. People <u>crave</u> social interaction. We are neurologically wired to connect. That's why farmers' markets are more popular than ever. Nevertheless, we cannot ignore the internet.

[4]

Therefore the <u>visionary</u> and creative retailers and entrepreneurs of tomorrow are delivering just that. Where the more traditional retailers have left the High Street, a new breed is moving in. One who puts their values at the heart of what they do. And then wrap it up in a Positive Experience – what I call The PX factor.

[5]

The ethos of these retailers is built on reducing your need to buy more. These are brands catering to shoppers who want things to feed their souls as well as make them feel good. Also great retailers know that today we don't want to be bored when we shop – we want to be thrilled. We want a social experience that we can't get online.

[6]

This could mean a hairdresser sharing a space with a fashion label. Next door would be the cheesemonger sharing space (and rents/rates) with a niche wine shop, and perhaps an organic butcher. All of which requires a creative vision that is also backed up with help from central and local government. Local councils along with the townspeople could decide what shops or social spaces their high street needs and then offer businesses incentives to take the long-term view.

Ultimately, all of this comes down to vision. It requires the people in positions of influence and power to understand how we all want to live today and to do something about it. We still want our High Street. We still want to shop. And we still want to do it in places we trust.

Speaking
Collaborative task and discussion (Parts 3 and 4) ▶ CB page 76

1 Which of these statements are true about the exam?

1 You need to talk about all the points.

2 You should take it in turns to give your detailed opinion as you go through the points.

3 You should ask your partner for their opinion.

4 You do not need to reach the same decision.

5 The examiner will let you continue speaking until you finish.

6 You should give examples to support your opinion.

> Here are some issues that some people think are affected by advertising, and a question for you to discuss.
>
>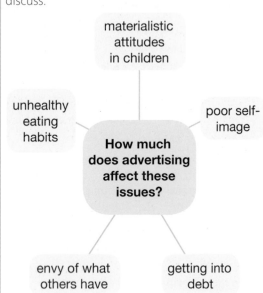
>
> materialistic attitudes in children
>
> unhealthy eating habits
>
> poor self-image
>
> **How much does advertising affect these issues?**
>
> envy of what others have
>
> getting into debt
>
> Talk to each other about how much advertising affects these issues.
>
> Now you have about a minute to decide which issue is the most worrying.

2 Look at the exam task and the extracts from some candidates' discussions. Complete the phrases for agreeing and disagreeing. Then say which points the candidates are talking about.

1 **A:** Yes, I can see that advertising can make people feel bad about the way they look. You feel a bit inferior when you see all the models in size-zero clothes.

 B: *I couldn't agree* .... It can be depressing when you're older, so it must be very hard on teenagers, who always seem to compare themselves to their peers.

2 **A:** Advertisers have got a lot to answer for when it comes to unhealthy eating. They promote fast food and things full of salt and fat.

 B: *I can't* .... *with that* but don't you think upbringing and families have to take some responsibility for that, too?

3 **A:** I think they should cut out all advertising during kids' programmes. It's the only way.

 B: *I'm* .... *I just don't think* it's that simple. Cut down on it, maybe, and avoid advertising chocolate and expensive toys.

 A: No, I really don't think that would work. *We'll just have to* .... *to differ!*

4 **B:** Someone I know got addicted to shopping because of advertising and just bought and bought – you know, on one of these shopping channels. She had to sell her house to pay her debts!

 A: .... *not!* That must have been awful for her.

 B: .... *it was.* She never really got over it.

Grammar
conditionals: advanced features ▶ CB page 77

1 Choose the correct alternatives to complete the sentences.

1 *Provided/Unless* you buy a new phone, you won't be up-to-date with the latest apps.

2 *Had I known/If I knew* how much it would cost to run, I would never have bought that particular car.

3 You should work harder, *otherwise/unless* you won't earn enough to go on holiday.

4 I don't mind telemarketing on the whole, *provided that/supposing* they don't call late at night.

5 *Should/What if* you be unlucky enough to buy something that doesn't work, you have rights as a consumer.

6 *Were I to/Only if* buy something faulty, I'm quite prepared to return it to the shop.

7 I'll keep shopping there *even if/providing that* the prices go up.

8 *Supposing/Unless* inflation increases, will prices also go up?

Writing
Report (Part 2) ▶ CB page 78

1 Look at the exam task and the sample answer. Match the headings (1–7) with the report sections (A–F). There is one heading you do not need to use.

1 Recommendations
2 Conclusion
3 Environment and facilities
4 Value for money
5 Refreshments
6 Shops
7 Introduction

> A new shopping centre has recently opened in your town. The developers have conducted a survey, and have asked you to write a report summarising the responses. You should comment on the popularity of the centre and make recommendations for any improvements that need to be implemented.
>
> Write your **report** in **220–260 words** in an appropriate style.

2 Choose the correct alternatives to complete the comments about the survey.

1 *While/However* a little more than a quarter were in favour of extending the centre, the rest had no strong opinions on the idea.

2 A minority of those questioned *made/expressed* concerns about the restroom facilities.

3 Strange as it may *feel/seem*, there were no unfavourable comments at all about the design of the centre.

4 The *clear/apparent* contradiction between the two sets of comments can be explained.

5 *Notwithstanding/Nevertheless* the limited time available for doing the survey, we managed to interview several hundred shoppers.

6 The satisfaction with the range of shops in the centre is *described/reflected* in the responses to questions 3 and 4.

3 Choose a shopping centre that you are familiar with and do the exam task in Activity 1.

Eastside Shopping Centre

A

The aim of this report is to summarise survey responses regarding the popularity of the Eastside Shopping Centre and to outline recommendations for improvements to the services offered to shoppers.

B

While the majority of those surveyed were happy with the range of shops provided in the centre, it was generally felt that the number of clothes shops was excessive and that there was a lack of outlets selling household goods or fresh food. Shoppers expressed their concern that at least ten stores remained empty, feeling that this was depressing.

C

At present there is only one café open with tables inside. Most of those questioned would rather have seating outside the café as this would accommodate more people and would be less claustrophobic.

D

Most people were satisfied with the current decoration and design of the open areas of the centre, and the water features were singled out for particular praise. However, concerns were raised about the unreliability of the lifts, which often forces elderly people to shop only on the ground floor or to have to negotiate steep stairs to the upper level.

E

The existing empty stores could be leased to household goods and food businesses. In addition to this, outdoor tables for the café would contribute to a livelier atmosphere. The problem of accessing the upper level must be dealt with, either by improving the reliability of the lifts or by installing escalators.

F

If the above recommendations are implemented, I am sure that the popularity of the centre will increase and result in a subsequent rise in profits.

8 Passing through

Listening
Sentence completion (Part 2) ▶ CB page 80

1 Match the definitions (1–10) with the words and phrases (A–J).

1 remove something you do not want or need
2 disadvantage
3 new to the profession of journalism
4 release your feelings of annoyance
5 do something difficult you are unprepared for
6 finance yourself before getting paid
7 recognise the unusual
8 addicted to
9 submit work that has not been requested
10 something to encourage you to do something

A hooked on
B incentive
C dive in at the deep end
D downside
E filter something out

F have an eye for the quirky
G send something on spec
H rookie writer
I pay for expenses up front
J vent your frustration

2 ▶ 14 You will hear a man called Peter Harris giving a presentation to students about his work as a travel writer. For questions 1–8, complete the sentences.

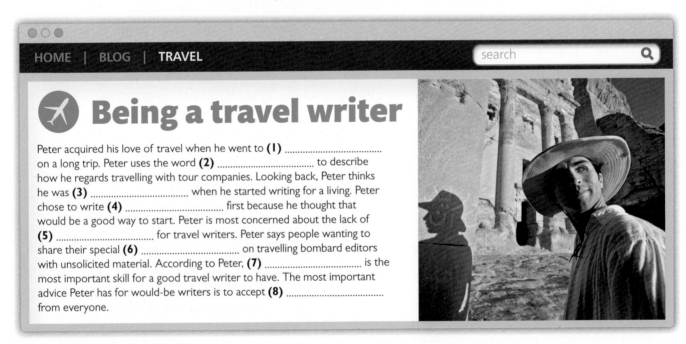

HOME | BLOG | TRAVEL

search 🔍

✈ Being a travel writer

Peter acquired his love of travel when he went to **(1)** .... on a long trip. Peter uses the word **(2)** .... to describe how he regards travelling with tour companies. Looking back, Peter thinks he was **(3)** .... when he started writing for a living. Peter chose to write **(4)** .... first because he thought that would be a good way to start. Peter is most concerned about the lack of **(5)** .... for travel writers. Peter says people wanting to share their special **(6)** .... on travelling bombard editors with unsolicited material. According to Peter, **(7)** .... is the most important skill for a good travel writer to have. The most important advice Peter has for would-be writers is to accept **(8)** .... from everyone.

Grammar
reported speech ▶ CB page 81

1 Find and correct the mistakes with reported speech in six of the sentences.

1 She asked me if I need a lift to the airport on Saturday.

2 He asked whether he can get a flight before he booked the holiday.

3 Jack said he didn't consider flying if he were able to avoid it.

4 It's reported that there had been an avalanche in the mountains.

5 John said he would see me on Saturday, all things being equal.

6 My sister is always saying that you couldn't change what people think about a place.

7 He asked me unless I could help him with his homework.

8 The police officer asked why had I not parked in the car park instead of the road.

2 Rewrite the sentences from a travel blog in direct speech.

1 Sarah said we shouldn't forget to book tickets in advance for the theme park, otherwise we'd have to wait.
'Please .... to wait.'

2 Jack was sure that if we stayed in that hotel, we wouldn't regret it.
'If .... it.'

3 Carlo said that he had never stayed in a worse hotel and that we should avoid it at all costs.
'I .... avoid it at all costs!'

4 Lee said we should try taking the boat along the coast because the views were beautiful.
'Try .... beautiful.'

5 Sue asked whether anyone had stayed at a campsite in the area they could recommend.
'Can I ask .... recommend?'

6 The guide asked if any of us knew anything about the area already.
'Do .... anything about the area already?'

7 We had to ask the coach driver if it would be possible to stop for refreshments.
'Would .... to stop for refreshments?'

8 The customs official insisted that we went through the red channel.
'You .... through the red channel.'

Use of English
Word formation (Part 3)
▶ CB page 82

1 Read the article. For questions 1–8, use the word given in capitals at the end of some of the lines to form a word that fits in the gap in the same line.

Are travel blogs a good thing?

Planning a holiday used to be rather daunting as (0) ...prospective... travellers had to visit travel agents, pore over brochures or plough through guidebooks. There were numerous pitfalls. Travel agents had a financial interest in selling holidays, brochures made locations look (1) .... and guidebooks were often outdated. But now people's (2) .... of other sources of information is greater, and they are more likely to turn to blogs written by travellers and online reviews of hotels and destinations. These provide an endless stream of apparently accurate facts, creating the (3) .... of knowledge. But are they reliable? Bloggers ask for (4) .... to their posts in the form of comments, but this often results in the (5) .... of conflicting accounts. Clearly, blogs are (6) .... personal and bloggers may also have an axe to grind. This could cause them to write negative things, which could be (7) .... for readers who should always check the (8) .... of both the writer and the information. The bottom line is, blogs can be useful but take them with a pinch of salt!

PROSPECT
RESIST
AWARE
IMPRESS
REACT
ESTABLISH
INTENSE
LEAD
AUTHENTIC

2 Read the article again and decide if the statements are true (T) or false (F).

1 In the past, people often read travel brochures before booking a holiday.

2 Blogs perform a useful function in disseminating accurate information.

3 Blogs should be read with some degree of cynicism.

Speaking
Long turn (Part 2)
▶ CB page 83

1 Look at the exam task. Then read a candidate's answer, ignoring the gaps. Which part of the task has the candidate not answered?

> Look at the pictures. They show people experiencing different problems while travelling. Compare two of the pictures and say what the reasons for the problems might be and how the people might be feeling.

> It's quite clear that the people are waiting at an airport and in all **(1)** ...., they've been waiting for quite a while. I'd be **(2)** .... if they got away any time soon. Looking at the **(3)** .... of the queue, they must be feeling a bit fed up! However, what I can't be **(4)** .... of is the reason behind the delay. It could be that their flights have been cancelled because of bad weather or there **(5)** .... even be a strike at the airport. Of course, they could just be waiting to check in and they all arrived at the same time. They're probably feeling pretty angry about the wait but maybe they've become resigned to it – the children seem to be happy playing on the floor.
>
> In the second picture, I **(6)** .... that the bad weather came as a surprise because the driver of the car wouldn't have gone out into a blizzard if he had known it was coming. He's got to push his car **(7)** .... it's stuck in the snow. That **(8)** .... it's impossible for the tyres to grip the road properly. Another problem for him must be the cold, **(9)** .... as he doesn't seem to be wearing winter clothes. He must be feeling worried about **(10)** .... he will be able to complete his journey at all.

2 Read the candidate's answer again and complete it using the words in the box.

because   imagine   length   means   might   particularly
probability   sure   surprised   whether

3 Read the follow-up question and choose the best answer.

> Whose journey do you think will be most affected by the problem?

A The man pushing the car. He's cold and miserable.

B Probably the people at the airport because they might miss connections as a result of the delay.

Reading
Cross-text multiple matching (Part 6)
▶ CB page 84

1 Read four commentaries on the subject of doing voluntary work abroad. For questions 1–4, choose from the commentaries (A–D). The commentaries may be chosen more than once.

Which commentator

1 expresses a different view from the others about the real value of volunteering?   **1** ☐

2 has a similar opinion to Commentator A about the benefits of the experience to the volunteer?   **2** ☐

3 shares Commentator D's concerns about what volunteers feel they are able to do?   **3** ☐

4 holds a similar opinion to Commentator D about changes in modern attitudes to volunteering?   **4** ☐

HOME | FEATURES | **TOURISM**

search

Can YOU *really* help?

Four commentators write about the increase in the number of people doing volunteer work abroad.

A

Over the years, many students have chosen to do voluntary work overseas but now this has become far more complicated. The reason may be the growth of 'voluntourism' agencies which are driven by an underlying commercial agenda. This is not the only complication, however. The relationship between different countries is complex and many emerging market countries, those with growing international economies, are booming. Some are arguably better run than so-called developed countries and, consequently, the view that help is a one-way gift is old-fashioned. In this case, agencies do have a part to play. Voluntourism should be seen as a two-way exchange which is as good for the giver as the receiver. The volunteers themselves probably remain convinced of their ability to change the world but what is actually more valuable for them is the way the experience of listening to and learning from other cultures can bring about wider changes in the way they view things.

B

There are many so-called 'voluntourism' agencies that specialise in arranging trips for well-meaning students and other people who want to do voluntary work abroad. These agencies charge the volunteers for the service but the volunteers themselves are unpaid. In general these volunteers have the interests of the communities at heart and want to help. But how much good they actually do may depend on the extent to which the trips are organised with the needs of the target communities in mind, rather than those of the volunteers. For example, on average, volunteers only stay a fortnight, which is not enough time for them to make their mark on the community they work with. Voluntourism agencies have been attacked for promoting something which on the surface maintains to be humanitarian but is in fact a source of profit for them. Ultimately, however, voluntourism establishes important access routes to money and aid for communities in desperate need. These connections could be impossible to make without the presence of volunteers.

C

The impact of volunteering on those who choose to do it can be very different. Volunteers may arrive with preconceptions, unprepared to try and understand the local culture. This may be because their underlying assumption is that it is inferior to their own and that their aim is to change it, an ambition that is quite impossible. As a result of this, volunteering may not always be a positive experience. Volunteers need to approach the challenge in the right way. Many who react negatively have not grasped the fact that their expectations were unrealistic. They have not understood that in the end, volunteering is as much about what they can learn and share, (which may or may not lead to policy change), as what they can change on the ground. Surely that is where the true importance of volunteering lies. Of course, this should not dissuade the more idealistic students from joining the schemes but they should be encouraged to see it as more of an educational experience and focus on what they can learn from it.

D

It is said that volunteering enables people to become more concerned and aware global citizens and then potentially push for international policy change. Ultimately, this may be the biggest benefit of doing voluntary work, rather than what any idealistic volunteer dreams they can achieve during their trip, which is usually far beyond what is possible. What volunteers often underestimate, however, is the fact that new ideas put into practice in the developing world can also have relevance back home. The spread of such ideas can be an important outcome of the growth of volunteering in general. Of course, this type of 'reverse innovation' is not what was imagined years ago but it is a sign of shifting times and changing attitudes.

Vocabulary
describing trends ▶ CB page 86

1 Match 1–8 with A–H to make collocations.

1	reach	A	steeply
2	remain	B	a level
3	fall	C	a peak
4	a brief	D	a trend
5	grow	E	stable
6	maintain	F	dip
7	moderate	G	substantially
8	reverse	H	growth

2 Complete the second sentence so that it has a similar meaning to the first sentence, using the word given. Do not change the word given. Use collocations from Activity 1. You may need to change the form of some collocations.

1 The number of people travelling through the airport was highest in August.

REACHED

The number of people travelling through the airport .... in August.

2 There has been a huge increase in tourism this year.

GROWN

Tourism .... this year.

3 The number of visitors to the island has fallen dramatically.

STEEP

There .... the number of visitors to the island.

4 We have maintained the level of visitors to the museum this year.

STABLE

The number of visitors to the museum .... this year.

5 The shares index fell slightly before recovering to its previous level.

BRIEF

There .... the shares index before it recovered to its previous level.

6 Although many travel companies had financial difficulties last year, they seem to have recovered now.

TREND

Although many travel companies had financial difficulties last year, it seems as though .... now.

Grammar
verb patterns with reporting verbs ▶ CB page 87

1 Complete the sentences with the correct form of the verb in brackets. Add any other words necessary.

0 The travel agent advised *me to visit* (me/visit) Rio.

1 My sister really regrets .... (not go) Buenos Aires when she was in Argentina.

2 The traveller explained .... (he/want) to get a visa for Russia.

3 The person who wrote the brochure claimed .... (it/be) a beautiful place.

4 I suggested .... (buy) good sun cream for anyone going to the desert!

5 The politician announced .... (he/give) special concessions to the tourist industry.

6 I really object .... (people/smoke) in public places.

7 We agreed .... (meet) at an Italian restaurant on Saturday evening.

8 I was invited .... (attend) the launch of the new cruise ship.

2 Rewrite the sentences in reported speech using the verbs in the box. There are two verbs you do not need to use.

accused admitted claimed encouraged objected persuaded reassured warned

1 'I think it would be a good idea to travel to Australia,' said Charlie's father.

2 'It was you who took my pen!' John said to Sue.

3 'Be careful you don't forget to take your passport,' said Jan's mother.

4 'You must take that trip – you won't regret it,' she said to me – so I did!

5 'I don't accept your insinuation, Mr Johnson', said the politician.

6 'Norway is the most beautiful country in the world!' she said.

Writing
Proposal (Part 2) ▶ CB page 88

1 Look at the exam task and tick (✓) the one thing candidates should do in their proposal.

1 explain why coming to England to study is a good thing

2 indicate which countries the college should advertise in

3 consider how to make the relevant information interesting for the students

4 point out the benefits to the college of having foreign students

> Your college wants to give foreign students thinking about coming to study in your country better information about the college and surrounding area. Students have been asked to submit proposals for different ways of providing this information and outline how best to proceed. A decision will then be made on which proposal to implement.
>
> Write your **proposal** in **220–260** words in an appropriate style.

2 Complete the proposal with the words in the box.

addition   aim   also   confident   outline   overall   well   while

> ### Providing information about the college to foreign students
>
> **Introduction**
> The (1) .... of this proposal is to explain why I believe that making a DVD would be a good way to give foreign students additional information about our college and the surrounding area. I shall also (2) .... aspects that could be focused on in the DVD.
>
> **The benefits of making a DVD**
> (3) .... sending more printed information would be a comprehensive way of giving foreign students additional information, a purpose-made DVD would be more attractive and entertaining. It would present the college and facilities in a lively manner and highlight several different aspects of student life.
>
> **What to include in the DVD**
> To give a(n) (4) .... impression of college life, the DVD should show scenes of students in class and also in places such as the cafeteria and library, as (5) .... as relaxing outside in the summer weather and at a social event. In (6) .... to this, current students could be interviewed to say what they enjoy about being here. We could (7) .... include shots of the town centre and beach to show the attractions of staying in our area.
>
> **Recommendations**
> Assemble a project group to coordinate the filming.
> Engage the photographic studio in town to carry it out.
> Ask students to create and record the audio script for the film.
> Find a local band to supply the backing track for the finished DVD.
>
> **Conclusion**
> I feel (8) .... that a DVD as outlined above would be a popular and successful way of giving foreign students a good impression of our college, as well as valuable information.

3 Read the proposal again and find formal equivalents of the words and phrases below.

1 extra

2 full and complete

3 show

4 who are there now

5 put together

6 employ

7 give us

8 described

Multiple-choice cloze (Part 1)

For questions 1–8, read the text below and decide which answer (A, B, C or D) best fits each gap. There is an example at the beginning (0).

Travellers or tourists?

People's attitude to tourists tends to be somewhat unfair – they say tourists arrive in large numbers, **(0)** *A disrupt* the everyday life of residents and leave without having **(1)** .... with the local culture.

So people often prefer to describe themselves as travellers, **(2)** .... that this is a superior way of seeing the world. But is this simply the last stronghold of snobbery? Is it just the **(3)** .... of people involved in mass tourism that turns travellers into tourists and creates negativity? After all, tourists **(4)** .... prosperity to an isolated area that might otherwise be neglected. And while some residents in tourist hot spots moan about the endless ebb and **(5)** .... of camera-carrying visitors, others embrace the accompanying financial benefits.

(6) ...., many who like to think of themselves as travellers are actually secret tourists – they hanker **(7)** .... popular destinations and resent the hassle of organising their own trips.

Finally, tourists enjoy sharing their experiences, whereas travellers may **(8)** .... the company of others. Which is really preferable?

0	A disrupt	B destroy	C damage	D distress
1	A occupied	B involved	C absorbed	D engaged
2	A implying	B inferring	C appealing	D persuading
3	A dimension	B size	C volume	D capacity
4	A carry	B bring	C distribute	D convey
5	A flow	B movement	C stream	D tide
6	A Alternatively	B Conversely	C Ironically	D Correspondingly
7	A to	B after	C on	D with
8	A repel	B object	C deny	D shun

Open cloze (Part 2)

For questions 9–16, read the text below and think of the word which best fits each gap. Use only one word in each gap. There is an example at the beginning (0).

Mr or Mrs Right?

What are the key requirements for the ideal partner? People come up **(0)** *with* different formulae and priorities. Some say it's empathy, **(9)** .... may be a good starting point, though I wonder whether that's enough to sustain a long-term relationship. Others claim a keen **(10)** .... of humour is vital and that couples who laugh together establish a happy basis to build on. Physical attraction is also high on the list – luckily, we all have our own concept of **(11)** .... makes someone good-looking, **(12)** .... we'd all fall for the same person! So they might not be handsome **(13)** .... everyone's eyes but if they don't appeal to you, things quickly fall apart.

(14) .... it may be true that opposites attract, I wonder whether this creates a short-term connection based **(15)** .... curiosity – surely the longest relationships require shared interests.

As **(16)** .... me, I'm looking for a meeting of minds – personality is top of my list. Mind you, I haven't found my ideal partner yet!

Word formation (Part 3)

For questions 17–24, read the text below. Use the word given in capitals at the end of some of the lines to form a word that fits in the gap in the same line. There is an example at the beginning (0).

To become an expat or not?

If you harbour **(0)** ....*aspirations*.... of leading a perfect life abroad, you're not alone. **(17)** ...., most people feel like this immediately after returning from a particularly enjoyable holiday overseas. But before rushing into anything, take a moment to consider your motivation.

Are you unhappy with your current situation? Even if you are, moving abroad is **(18)** .... to change that – relocating will probably only add to your problems. If you yearn for an easy life, forget it. What on holiday appeared a **(19)** .... lifestyle may turn out to be incredibly boring once you're stuck with it, and adapting to a new way of life can be **(20)** .... challenging.

Remember too that you often need official **(21)** .... to work in another country, which may involve providing proof of financial **(22)** .... or employment.

So the dream of just **(23)** .... and going wherever you like is impractical. However, for every expat who regrets their move, there are others who say it was **(24)** .... In the end, the dream is yours.

ASPIRE	
SURPRISE	
LIKE	
LEISURE	
EXPECT	
APPROVE	
STABLE	
ROOT	
WORTH	

Key word transformation (Part 4)

For questions 25–30, complete the second sentence so that it has a similar meaning to the first sentence, using the word given. Do not change the word given. You must use between three and six words, including the word given. Here is an example (0).

Example

0 Some people have been saying what a good move emigrating would be.

ARGUED

It *has been argued that* emigrating would be a good move.

25 The size of the population is unlikely to change much in the near future.

STABLE

The size of the population .... in the near future.

26 'I think Joe should seriously reconsider his plans,' said the careers advisor.

RECOMMENDED

The careers advisor .... his plans.

27 It doesn't matter if you think you know the subject well, you must revise for the exam.

HOWEVER

You must revise for the exam, ... you know the subject.

28 It was only after telling everyone that it was his birthday that John got lots of cards.

HAVING

John only got lots of cards .... it was his birthday.

29 However hard she tries, she still manages to offend people.

MATTER

It .... she tries, she still manages to offend people.

30 Whatever film you want to see will be good for us.

MIND

We .... film you want.

9 Reading the mind

Use of English
Open cloze (Part 2) ▶ CB page 90

1 Read the article. For questions 1–8, think of the word which best fits each gap. Use only one word for each gap.

Why can't we tickle ourselves?

The answer to the question is assumed to **(0)** ....*be*.... that it comes down to the element of surprise. If you tickle yourself, you're expecting the feeling, so you don't or can't react to it. But brain scans have indicated that brain activity is the same **(1)** .... a person is expecting to be tickled or not. So what's really **(2)** .... on?

Our brains are constantly processing information which is retrieved from all our senses, and this enables us to **(3)** .... sense of our surroundings. An important aspect of the process **(4)** .... differentiating between events caused by external factors and those we choose to initiate ourselves. **(5)** .... seems to be some evidence that activity in the brain changes when responding to stimuli from these two different sources, so **(6)** .... appears that we're able to differentiate **(7)** .... the two, and this affects our reaction.

This finding for me takes **(8)** .... the magic – I prefer the idea that if a baby laughs when being tickled, it's simply having fun! ●

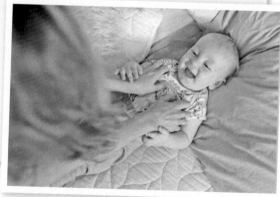

2 Read the article again. How does the writer feel about the research?

1 interested in the discoveries already made
2 keen to find out more about how the brain works
3 sad that some enjoyable things have a scientific explanation

Vocabulary
expressions with *brain* and *mind* ▶ CB page 91

1 Complete the expressions with *brain* or *mind*.

1 ....-boggling
2 .... damage
3 .... teaser
4 .... reader
5 .... storm
6 .... scan

2 Match the statements and questions (1–6) with the responses (A–F).

1 I'm not sure what I should take into account when planning the psychology project.

2 Would you like to come to the theatre this evening?

3 I'm planning to give up my job to go and live in the country and grow vegetables.

4 I think you should talk to your tutor – he'll be able to help you.

5 Have you ever considered studying psychology?

6 Would you like to be rich?

A No, it's never crossed my mind – it's not a particularly interesting subject.

B That's a real brainwave – he could probably sort me out.

C You're out of your mind – that's a crazy idea!

D That's a no-brainer – who wouldn't?

E Not really, thanks – I wouldn't mind having a quiet night in. I'm pretty tired right now.

F You have to bear in mind that your decision affects other work already going on.

Grammar

future in the past ▶ CB page 92

1 Complete the conversations with the correct form of the verb in brackets.

1 **A:** Are you coming out tonight?
   B: I _____ (finish) my assignment but, actually, I think I can leave it until Saturday.
   A: Great – let's go!

2 **A:** What's the matter?
   B: I thought my friend _____ (be) angry with me for turning up late but she was late herself.
   A: You must have been pretty annoyed with her!

3 **A:** The psychology lecture today was awful – the lecturer wasn't well.
   B: I think she _____ (cancel) the lecture had we not all turned up.
   A: I agree – maybe she should have done that.

4 **A:** You look very cold.
   B: When I left the house, I had no idea it _____ (snow) this afternoon.
   A: I was prepared – I saw the weather forecast last night!

5 **A:** You've done really well to get the job.
   B: Thanks – I never thought I _____ (get) it!
   A: It's a no-brainer – you deserve it.

Speaking

Long turn (Part 2) ▶ CB page 93

1 Look at the exam task and the pictures. Which two pictures would you choose?

Look at the pictures. They show situations where creating an illusion is important. Compare two of the pictures and say how the people are benefitting from the illusions and how difficult it might be to create them.

2 ▶ 15 Listen and answer the questions.

1 Did the candidate choose the same pictures as you?

2 Did the candidate answer the task fully?

3 Do you know the final word the candidate has difficulty remembering?

3 Listen again and tick (✓) the phrases the candidate uses when he is unsure of a word.

What's it called?   Sorry, it's gone.
I can't remember the exact word.
It's on the tip of my tongue.   What's the word?
No, that's not the word I'm looking for.
I'll kick myself later.

Reading
Gapped text (Part 7)
▶ CB page 94

1 Read the article and missing paragraphs and answer the questions.

1 What is *The Shallows*?
2 Who is Nicholas Carr?
3 Who is Dr Small?
4 Why is the internet thought to be bad for us?
5 Why is the internet thought to be good for us?

2 Read the article again. Six paragraphs have been removed from the article. Choose from the paragraphs A–G the one which fits each gap (1–6). There is one extra paragraph which you do not need to use.

3 Match the underlined words in the article and paragraphs with their meanings (1–7).

1 harmful
2 related
3 impressionable
4 answer
5 persistent
6 short-lived
7 superficial

4 Complete the sentences with words from Activity 3.

1 The barrage of advertising online is .... and inescapable.
2 A(n) .... expression of anxiety crossed his face but it disappeared almost immediately.
3 If taken in regular doses, the drug can have a(n) .... effect on the liver.
4 A shopping trip can definitely be a(n) .... to depression!
5 The manager had to answer a large number of questions .... to the way he had been running the department.
6 The teacher gave the student's essay a(n) .... look and then handed it back without a mark.

A
We have moved a long way since then. But here is the really important thing. Carr writes: 'If, knowing what we know today about the brain's plasticity, you were to set out to invent a medium that would rewire our mental circuits as quickly and thoroughly as possible, you would probably end up designing something that looks and works a lot like the internet.'

B
The Shallows is a book by Nicholas Carr. It is an elegantly written cry of anguish about what one admirer calls 'the uneducating of Homo sapiens' and a rewiring of neural pathways and networks that may yet deprive the human race of the talents that, ironically enough, drove our journey from caves to PC terminals.

C
'The point is, to play successfully, you have to pay an incredible amount of attention to what your team-mates are doing, to the mechanics of the game. You can set up a thesis for *The Depths*, just as much as *The Shallows*. And it seems to me that to say that some neural pathways are good and some are bad – well, how can you possibly say that?'

D
'This is because the brain is very sensitive to any kind of stimulation. If you have repeated stimuli, your neural circuits will be excited. But if you neglect other stimuli, other neural circuits will be weakened.' Carr argues that the online world so taxes the parts of the brain that deal with <u>fleeting</u> and temporary stuff that deep thinking becomes increasingly impossible. As he sees it: 'Our ability to learn suffers and our understanding remains shallow.'

E
Among the people with walk-on roles in *The Shallows* is Scott Karp, the editor of a renowned American digital media blog called Publish2, whose reading habits are held up as proof of the fact that plenty of people's brains have long since been rewired by their enthusiastic use of the internet.

F
I get a more convincing <u>antidote</u> to the Carr thesis from Professor Andrew Burn of the University of London's Institute of Education. Equating the internet with distraction and shallowness, he tells me, is a fundamental mistake, possibly bound up with Carr's age (he is over fifty). 'Is there anything in his book about online roleplaying games?'

G
But then there is the downside. The tool I use to write can also double as many other things. Thus, while writing this, I was entertained by no end of distractions. I watched YouTube videos, bought something on Amazon, updated my status on my social media and at downright stupid hours of the day – 6 a.m. or almost midnight – I once again checked my messages on various devices.

HOW THE INTERNET IS ALTERING YOUR MIND

Like most newspapers' content, what you are about to read was written using a computer connected to the internet. Obviously, this had no end of benefits, mostly <u>pertaining</u> to the relative ease of my research and the simplicity of contacting the people whose thoughts and opinions you are about to read.

1 ☐ It often feels as if all this frantic activity creates a constant state of twitchy anxiety. Moreover, having read a hotly controversial book about the effect of digital media on the human mind, I may have very good reason to feel scared. Its thesis is simple enough: not only that the modern world's <u>relentless</u> informational overload is killing our capacity for reflection, contemplation and patience but that our online habits are also altering the very structure of our brains.

2 ☐ The writer then argues that the internet's 'cacophony of stimuli' and 'crazy quilt' of information have given rise to '<u>cursory</u> reading, hurried and distracted thinking, and superficial learning' – in contrast to the age of the book, when intelligent humans were encouraged to be contemplative and imaginative.

3 ☐ Dr Small, the director of the Memory and Ageing Research Centre at the University of California, Los Angeles, is a specialist in the effects on the brain of the ageing process. 'Even an old brain can be quite <u>malleable</u> and responsive to what's going on with technology,' he tells me.

4 ☐ When I ask him how I might stop the internet's more <u>malign</u> effects on my own brain, he sounds slightly more optimistic than Carr: 'Try to balance online time with offline time,' he tells me. 'What's happening is we're losing the circadian rhythms we're used to; you go to work, you come home, you spend time talking with your kids.'

5 ☐ 'His argument privileges activities of the skimming and browsing kind. But if you look at research on kids doing this, or exploring virtual worlds such as *Second Life* and its successor, *Sansar*, the argument there is about immersion and engagement.'

6 ☐ This all sounds both comforting and convincing, until I return to *The Shallows* and read a particularly sobering sentence: 'We are welcoming the frenziedness into our souls.' There's something chilling about those words and even twenty stupid minutes on YouTube and an impulse buy from Amazon cannot quite remove them from my brain.

Listening
Multiple matching (Part 4) ▶ CB page 96

1 ▶ 16 You will hear five short extracts in which people are talking about a psychology book they have all read. While you listen, you must complete both tasks.

Task 1

For questions 1–5, choose from the list (A–H) the reason each speaker gives for reading the book.

A It was a present from a friend.

B It provided an extra resource for work.

C It was the result of a chance discovery.

D It formed a compulsory part of their studies.

E It was part of a special deal from a shop.

F It was recommended by someone else.

G It appeared to be a way to improve a relationship.

H It seemed to be relevant to their current course.

Speaker 1 [1]
Speaker 2 [2]
Speaker 3 [3]
Speaker 4 [4]
Speaker 5 [5]

Task 2

For questions 6–10, choose from the list (A–H) the main reason why each speaker would recommend the book to others.

A It gives an easy overview of psychology for students.

B It is a good starting point for new students of psychology.

C It is written in an engaging way.

D It introduces interesting ideas for non-specialists to follow.

E It describes experiments used in psychological research.

F It could inspire people to start learning about psychology.

G It is useful for people to update their knowledge.

H It uses accessible clear non-scientific language.

Speaker 1 [6]
Speaker 2 [7]
Speaker 3 [8]
Speaker 4 [9]
Speaker 5 [10]

Grammar
future in the past: advanced features ▶ CB page 97

1 There is a mistake in four of the sentences. Identify and correct them.

1 My research paper was to have been published this Tuesday but it's been put back until Friday.

2 I was thinking of writing to my tutor to ask for some help but I don't think I would.

3 I had forgotten to complete the form, so I had to do it there and then.

4 He were going to mention his memory problem but he didn't want to worry her.

5 I'm disappointed that she remembered I was coming to visit – it was supposed to a surprise!

6 He was going to leave the institute but is given an unexpected research opportunity instead.

2 Rewrite the sentences using the words in brackets.

1 I intended to write to you but I didn't have time. (*going*)

2 I might have done more work tonight if you hadn't called round. (*thinking*)

3 The government intended to fund more research into brain injuries. (*planning*)

4 At the time it was not going to be possible to tell her the truth about her condition. (*would*)

Writing
Email (Part 2) ▶ CB page 98

About the exam:
In Writing Part 2, you may have the choice of writing an informal letter or email. This will be a response to part of a letter or email you have received.

Strategy:
- Read the task carefully and note the points you need to include.
- Identify the function(s) you should use (e.g. advising, reminding, requesting).
- Plan your email/letter by grouping points into paragraphs.
- Write in an informal style throughout.
- Include interesting opening and closing sentences.

1 **Look at the exam task below and the sample answer in Activity 2. Tick (✓) the things the candidate has done.**

1 answered all the points in the task
2 written under the limit
3 used an appropriate tone
4 given interesting opening and closing remarks
5 not sequenced the paragraphing clearly

> You have received an email from an English friend.
>
> > The exams start next week and I'm getting really stressed out about them. I try to get in some revision whenever I can but nothing seems to stay in my head. You're really good at remembering stuff, so I wondered if you could give me any tips?
> >
> > Cheers,
> >
> > Ted
>
> Write your **email** in reply. Write **220–260** words in an appropriate style.

2 **Complete the email with the words in the box.**

don't   need   suggest   tempted   work   worth

> Hi Ted,
>
> Thanks for your email – I got it this morning. It sounds as if you're really having problems, so I'll do my best – although I'm not the world expert, you know!
>
> The most important thing is to try to relax. The more stressed out you get, the less information will stay in your head. And stress usually comes when you feel that you're out of control, so what you have to do is organise yourself. Why **(1)** .... you make a timetable of when you're going to revise and stick to it? Don't be **(2)** .... to only focus on the topics you like! Then you'll have some direction. That's much better than trying to fit revision in at random moments.
>
> Secondly, you **(3)** .... to make sure you don't do too much at once, and take lots of breaks. It gives your brain a chance to remember things better. Everyone has their own memory techniques. What seems to **(4)** .... for me is to read a whole section on a topic once to get the general picture. Then I go back and note down all the things I want to remember. For me, writing things down in note form helps me remember them. Some people like to read through their notes again just before going to sleep. They say it helps the memory. It's **(5)** .... a try!
>
> And finally, I'd **(6)** .... you get an early night before the exam. It's better to have a fresh brain in the morning than a tired one.
>
> I'll be thinking of you. Do let me know how you get on.
>
> Take care,
>
> Kitty

3 **Read the exam task, make notes and write your email.**

> You have received an email from an English friend.
>
> > You know this college quiz that I was talking about? Well, I'm on the team and we've got our first game next Saturday! I'm scared stiff and regretting saying I'd do it. I'm sure my mind will go blank. You've done this before – any tips?
>
> Write your **email** in reply. Write **220–260** words in an appropriate style.

Reading
Multiple choice (Part 5)
▶ CB page 104

1 Read the article and decide if the statements are true (T) or false (F).

1 Spriggs is a fully trained guide dog.
2 Puppy walkers keep the dogs for less than two years.
3 Gareth started working for the charity when he was a teenager.
4 The writer used to have a dog himself.

2 Read the article again. For questions 1–6, choose the answer (A, B, C or D) which you think fits best according to the text.

1 Why does the writer start to feel more relaxed in the first paragraph?
   A He knows he will shortly regain his sight.
   B He has survived a difficult experience.
   C He begins to have faith in his guide.
   D He is approaching the end of the journey.

2 Gareth believes that a successful guide dog is ultimately the result of
   A the breeding and quality of the dog.
   B the level of training the dog is given.
   C the early stages of care when the dog is young.
   D the interaction between owner and dog.

3 When working in rehabilitation, Gareth was
   A encouraged by the degree of independence the blind people had.
   B surprised by the value of his own contributions.
   C confident that he could learn from the experience.
   D undeterred by his physical problems.

4 The writer mentions the 'fish and chip shop' to
   A illustrate the talents of a good guide dog.
   B correct a common illusion.
   C explain a difficult procedure.
   D emphasise the importance of training done by owners.

5 When taking part in the experiment, the writer believes that
   A being in control of the dog is a very powerful feeling.
   B knowing how to direct the dog takes time.
   C relying on the dog takes considerable courage.
   D reacting to the dog's affection is important.

6 What is the writer's reaction to the experience?
   A He would like to do the same work.
   B He can identify with the satisfaction Gareth gets from his job.
   C He values the experience of being dependent on a guide dog.
   D He wishes that he could have another dog of his own.

A working life: the guide dog trainer

As mobility instructor for **Guide Dogs for the Blind**, Gareth Evans has the rewarding job of matching dogs to their owners.

I'm blindfolded and frightened. Cars are roaring past as I <u>stumble</u> along busy Leamington Spa pavements, terrified I'll unwittingly stray into the path of a vehicle. But Spriggs, the black Labrador whose brown training harness I'm desperately <u>clinging</u> to, soon has me at ease, calmly steering me around hidden obstacles, pedestrians, workmen and parked cars with every wag of his tail. Spriggs is close to finishing his training with Guide Dogs for the Blind and will soon be partnered with a visually impaired person.

At some point Spriggs will have been tutored by Gareth Evans, a local man who has worked with the charity for close to sixteen years. 'It has to be a partnership when you take on a guide dog,' he explains. 'We can only get the dogs to a certain level and then the owners have to take over and they will get out of that partnership what they put in.' Evans grew up in nearby Warwick surrounded by puppies – his family were regular 'puppy walkers' for the charity, the name given to families that look after a puppy for its first 12–14 months before handing it back for training, as well as breeders. 'Guide dogs have always been in my life and I'd always wanted to work for the charity.' He achieved that ambition when he was nineteen, spending five years working in the kennels before a broken wrist led him to <u>shadow</u> the organisation's rehab workers, who provide training and guidance to help people live independently. 'What impressed me most was how you could give someone the smallest piece of advice, some of it not even related to dogs, that would make a huge difference to their lives, such as how to make the text on their television screen bigger,' he remembers. 'So I retrained as a rehab worker and did that for eight years.' Four years ago he became a mobility instructor for the charity, which means that as well as finishing off the dogs' tuition with advanced training, he helps match dogs to owners, provides support while they get to know each other and makes annual aftercare visits.

Evans thinks there are many myths about the role of guide dogs. 'A lot of people think they take their owners for a walk, that the owner says, "Right, off to the fish and chip shop, please," and the dog takes them there,' he says. 'The owners are the ones in control and who need to know where they are going. The dog is only helping them look out for roads and obstacles, it's not actually taking them anywhere – although if it learns a route, it might <u>pop into</u> a shop if the owner visits frequently.' He talks of the occasional embarrassment suffered by owners whose guide dogs betray their love of takeaways by padding into the kebab shop even if the owner wishes to walk past.

When I am <u>blindfolded</u> and partnered with Spriggs for my walk, I immediately realise how big a jump it is from trusting your own eyesight to trusting that a dog will guide you safely around town. For the first five minutes I am genuinely scared that my life is held in the paws of a canine I've never met but I slowly become attuned to Spriggs' subtle movements when he pulls me to the left or right to avoid obstacles or as he prepares to stop at a kerb. I marvel as he obeys my command to turn right at one pavement edge. All the while Evans is telling me what to do, how to give the dog feedback, to pat him affectionately when he has done well, along with numerous other instructions.

By the time I take the blindfold off, I have genuinely bonded with Spriggs, to the extent that Evans jokes: 'I'd better check your bag to see you haven't stolen him,' and I get an inkling of the incredible bond that dogs and owners must share. On the train back to London I spot one of Spriggs' black hairs on my leg and it reminds me of my childhood pet Sid, a Jack Russell terrier I still miss to this day. It then strikes me why Evans has been with Guide Dogs for the Blind for so many years: when you play a key part in <u>forging</u> so many beautiful relationships, partnerships that lead to vastly improved lives, why would you want to work anywhere else?

Vocabulary
expressions for describing compatibility ▶ CB page 102

1 Choose the correct alternatives to complete the conversations.

1 **A:** I love your new dress – the colour really *fits/suits* you.

   B: The assistant said it *matched/fitted* my eyes and skin tone.

   A: I need something new for going out – my old dress doesn't *fit/suit* me anymore since I lost weight.

   B: Well, that new shop in town has loads of good things – they ought to *match/suit* your style.

2 **A:** There are so many cultural possibilities in London – there aren't many cities that can *fit/match* it for theatre and museums.

   B: Agreed, though there are others that can *suit/match* its history.

   A: The cosmopolitan lifestyle in London *suits/fits* me, though.

3 **A:** Have you found a course that *matches/suits* your needs?

   B: Kind of – though I've had to compromise. There's nothing that's a perfect *fit/suit*.

   A: That's a shame – though often things turn out better than you expect – it might end up *suiting/fitting* you quite well.

Grammar
whoever, whatever, etc.
▶ CB page 103

1 Replace the underlined words in the sentences with the words in the box. Add any other words necessary.

---
however   whatever   whenever   whichever (×2)
whoever
---

1 I'll play tennis with <u>anyone who</u> turns up!

2 This is the restaurant I eat in <u>every time</u> I come to visit London.

3 You are being so difficult – <u>everything</u> I suggest seems to be wrong!

4 <u>It doesn't matter which</u> holiday you choose, it will still cost a lot.

5 <u>It doesn't matter how</u> long you practise, you'll never be as good as Sue.

6 I can't decide what meal to have. I'll probably prefer <u>the one</u> you choose anyway – I usually do!

2 Choose the correct answers to complete the sentences. In some sentences more than one answer may be possible.

1 You can say .... you want about it. I think it's a great idea.
   A what   **B** whatever
   C whichever   **D** that

2 That's all .... I can say on the matter – I've made up my mind.
   A whatever   **B** that
   C which   **D** what

3 You can come and stay with me .... you like!
   A however   **B** whenever
   C wherever   **D** whatever

4 It's a difficult decision for her to make by herself, ... you might think about it.
   A however   **B** whatever
   C whichever   **D** whoever

5 .... well you think you know a person, don't lend them any money!
   A Whenever   **B** However
   C Whichever   **D** Whatever

Use of English
Open cloze (Part 2) ▶ CB page 106

1 Read the article. For questions 1–8, think of the word which best fits each gap. Use only one word in each gap.

Does your *personality* really fit?

When you decide to change your job, a prospective employer could ask you to take a personality test to see **(0)** *how* well you would fit into the organisation. Every company wants to employ **(1)** .... right person; in these days of financial constraints, they can't risk **(2)** .... a mistake by selecting someone who isn't up to the job or compatible **(3)** .... the culture of the company. The question **(4)** ...., are these tests any good?

One of their attractions lies in their apparent practicality – applicants complete the test, findings are analysed and the perfect candidate for the job is revealed. But that's also **(5)** .... leads some people to regard the tests with scepticism. It appears efficient to put people into neat pigeonholes but in reality, it can **(6)** .... counter-productive. One downside of the testing is that it stereotypes people, possibly holding them **(7)** .... from fulfilling their potential.

It may be that such tests do have a part to **(8)** .... in a selection process, but their results should be treated with caution.

Listening
Multiple matching (Part 4) ▶ CB page 107

1 ▶ 17 You will hear five short extracts in which parents talk about choosing the most appropriate pet for their children. While you listen, you must complete both tasks.

Task 1

For questions 1–5, choose from the list (A–H) the reason each speaker gives for choosing the particular pet for their children.

A a life-long love of the animal

B a desire to preserve a lifestyle

C a hope that the children would get fitter

D a wish to help the children with schoolwork

E a dislike of the noise some pets can make

F a fear of the cost of keeping some pets

G a passion for nature

H a family decision

Speaker 1	1
Speaker 2	2
Speaker 3	3
Speaker 4	4
Speaker 5	5

Task 2

For questions 6–10, choose from the list (A–H) how each speaker feels about their decision to buy each pet.

A concerned how the children feel about having a pet

B disappointed about the result of getting the pet

C resentful about the work they have to do

D surprised about how successful it's been

E relieved they don't have to exercise the pet

F afraid of the reaction of other people to the pet

G guilty about their initial reaction to the idea

H worried about the long-term effect of the pet on the children's lives

Speaker 1	6
Speaker 2	7
Speaker 3	8
Speaker 4	9
Speaker 5	10

2 Listen again and complete the sentences from the recording with a word or expression that means the same as the word(s) in brackets.

Speaker 1

1 We contacted pet owners to identify the .... (*potential problems*)

2 I'd hate my travelling to be .... (*cut down*)

Speaker 2

3 I was .... of anything that might run up bills. (*concerned*)

Speaker 3

4 Exercise is my greatest .... (*dislike*)

5 We .... together that we'd find an animal that would be pretty easy-care. (*decided*)

Speaker 4

6 I didn't want the .... some pets would cause. (*general stress*)

7 My fears were .... (*not real*)

Speaker 5

8 It gives me an excuse to get out without having to .... it. (*give a reason for something*)

Grammar

participle clauses ▶ CB page 108

1 Match the uses of participle clauses (1–3) with the sentences (A–C).

1 to express a reason or condition

2 to talk about something that took place just before the action in the main clause

3 to replace a relative pronoun or verb

A Having realised I had missed the bus, I decided to walk.

B Courses specialising in teaching communication skills can be very useful.

C Worrying about arguing with my boss meant I didn't actually raise the issue at the meeting.

2 Rewrite the sentences in Activity 1 without using participle clauses.

3 Rewrite the sentences using participle clauses.

1 I applied early, so I was disappointed not to get tickets.

2 The politician continued his speech once he had got the hecklers to be quiet.

3 Anyone who wants to improve their image often goes to a stylist.

4 She answered the door after she put the phone down.

5 I understood the question, so I was able to give an answer.

6 I work with talented people, which makes for an exciting workplace.

Speaking

Collaborative task and discussion (Parts 3 and 4) ▶ CB page 109

About the exam:

After the collaborative task in Part 3, you will be asked some questions related to the same topic. These questions can be directed to one candidate or to both to discuss.

Strategy:

• Give as full an answer as you can with reasons and examples to support your opinion.

• You can comment on your partner's question after he/she has given an answer; this may develop into a discussion.

• Remember that, as in Part 3, any discussion should be balanced and show interaction.

1 ▶ 18 Look at the exam task. Then listen to different candidates doing the task and complete the phrases they use to agree, disagree and cooperate.

Here are some types of partnerships and a question for you to discuss.

business partnership

marriage

speaking test partnership

What do you think is important for these partnerships to succeed?

comedy double act

government coalition

Talk to each other about what is important for these partnerships to succeed.

Now you have about a minute to decide which type of partnership is the most difficult to make succeed.

1 I agree up to a(n) _____, but I think having different hobbies can be refreshing in a way.

2 That may _____ be so, but don't you think they also need to have the same outlook and ambitions?

3 I'm not _____ convinced. Suppose you get two very strong personalities together …

4 Isn't it sometimes the _____ that the serious one is really the brains behind the partnership?

5 I _____ say you're right but then that would risk the coalition …

2 ▶ 19 Listen to two candidates discussing the decision question and tick (✓) the phrases they use.

1 What an interesting question!

2 As we said, …

3 Which would you say … ?

4 It's not an easy choice …

5 If we're thinking long term, …

6 I would definitely opt for …

7 I'm with you there.

8 Let's go for …

3 Read the Part 4 questions and two responses to each. Which is the weaker response in each case?

1 Some people make prenuptial agreements before they get married. Do you think this is a good thing? Why/Why not?

> **A** I would never make a prenuptial agreement. I think they're terrible things.
>
> **B** In some cases it can be a good thing – it really depends on the couple involved. I suppose it gives a sort of security but, on the other hand, surely, you only marry someone you trust.

2 Do you think it's necessary to like someone to be able to work with them well? Why/Why not?

> **A** That's an interesting one! I don't think it's really necessary because a working relationship is different to a personal one. Two people could complement each other with their skills and abilities and produce good work together but they don't have to get on very well.
>
> **B** Best friends don't always make the best work colleagues. Just because you like someone doesn't mean that you'll work well together. In fact, it could hurt your friendship, couldn't it? There could be competition and rivalry. No, not a good thing, in my opinion.

Writing
Formal letter (Part 2)
▶ CB page 110

1 Look at the exam task and the sample answer. Six sentences have been removed from the letter. Choose from the sentences (A–F) the one which fits each gap (1–6).

> You work for a new website that helps match people and careers.
>
> You have been asked to write to the careers advisors at secondary schools and colleges to inform them about how your website can help their students. You should explain
>
> • why the website was set up.
> • what the website does.
> • how successful it has been.
>
> Write your **letter** in **220–260** words in an appropriate style.

Dear Sir or Madam,

(1) ....

(2) .... Students often find the range of professions very confusing and many stumble into a career by chance rather than find one that really suits them. That is where we at *Students' Choice* come in. We have done a great deal of research into the different career opportunities available to students today and also consulted expert educational psychologists. As a result, our website provides valuable assistance for students who are about to make those all-important choices.

(3) .... There is information about the range of careers open to students, interviews with prospective employers on the type of applicants they are looking for and tests that students can take to show them the type of work that suits their personalities and requirements.

(4) .... There is a blog section on the website where you can read about many of these students' experiences.

(5) ....

(6) ....

Yours faithfully,

Paul Abbeyfield

pabbey@studentschoiceab.com

A I sincerely hope that *Students' Choice* can supplement the careers advice that you give your students and help them to make the right choices.

B We have been operating the website for over eight months now and in that time have helped hundreds of students to select suitable careers.

C Should you need further information, please contact me at the email address below.

D As you know, the choice of a future career is both an important and challenging one.

E I am writing to you to give you some information about our new website, *Students' Choice*, which has been set up to help match students and future careers.

F The website offers help in several ways.

2 Do the exam task.

> You are a university student and you are looking for a summer job doing voluntary work. You have found a website that offers a service to find voluntary work for students. Write an email to the website to ask them to find appropriate work for you. You should explain
>
> • the type of work you are looking for.
> • how the experience could benefit your studies.
> • your availability and any expenses you might have.
>
> Write your **email** in **220–260** words in an appropriate style.

Multiple-choice cloze (Part 1)

For questions 1–8, read the text below and decide which answer (A, B, C or D) best fits each gap. There is an example at the beginning (0).

Does what we see match the reality?

I suppose it's human **(0)** ...*A, nature*... to try to judge someone by their appearance. The downside is that it's then hard to alter that original judgement, which was only created by the first impression they **(1)** .... on us.

At any initial encounter, we **(2)** .... note of the person's clothes, how they talk and whatever their body **(3)** .... indicates to us. But can this information be trusted? Does it actually reveal the truth? A talkative person may appear friendly and warm **(4)** .... they are actually self-centred, while an introvert may **(5)** .... as arrogant when they are the sweetest person in the world once you see beneath their quiet exterior.

Why do we assume we can understand someone simply **(6)** .... on what we suppose is proof taken from a very short acquaintance, or that their appearance accurately **(7)** .... their personality? If we rely on our initial judgements too heavily or are too ready to **(8)** .... to conclusions, we may be making a big mistake.

0	**A** nature	**B** feeling	**C** disposition	**D** temperament
1	**A** got	**B** put	**C** gave	**D** made
2	**A** place	**B** take	**C** write	**D** keep
3	**A** manner	**B** movements	**C** language	**D** signs
4	**A** alternatively	**B** in spite of	**C** even if	**D** as well as
5	**A** come through	**B** come down	**C** come out	**D** come across
6	**A** hung	**B** grounded	**C** fixed	**D** based
7	**A** reflects	**B** acts	**C** gives	**D** paints
8	**A** arrive	**B** spring	**C** reach	**D** jump

Open cloze (Part 2)

For questions 9–16, read the text below and think of the word which best fits each gap. Use only one word in each gap. There is an example at the beginning (0).

Are dancers different?

It's been suggested that dancers are different from the rest of us – **(0)** ....*but*.... how, and why?

The answer appears to lie **(9)** .... the fact that they have a greater understanding of their own bodies and a heightened ability to perceive and react to things as they happen. For example, dancers seem to be able to identify their own pulse rate instinctively, **(10)** .... actually checking places on the body where it's normally measured, **(11)** .... as on the wrist. This was established through a test in **(12)** .... pulse rates in different people were monitored electronically. When asked **(13)** .... they thought their rate was, it was dancers who gave the most accurate assessments.

What does this prove? Is **(14)** .... simply that dancers think about their bodies more than anyone else? If **(15)** ...., that would hardly be a surprise given the constant rehearsing they do and the physical strain they are under. Dancers are multi-taskers, striving to combine movement, acting, and partnering this **(16)** .... musicality. There are many complex demands made on their brains, so it's no wonder that maintaining their bodies is a priority.

Word formation (Part 3)

For questions 17–24, read the text below. Use the word given in capitals at the end of some of the lines to form a word that fits in the gap in the same line. There is an example at the beginning (0).

How important is our mindset?

Although we may do it **(0)** subconsciously,
we continually assess the **(17)** ....
of things that happen to us in order to decide
what actions we should take and how we feel
about them. However, we're all different and
our **(18)** .... mindset will affect our
response – that's what steers us and suggests
possible courses of action. But it can also trip
us up.

If our mindset is too **(19)** ...., our
reactions to an event are led by our need
to evaluate it; we require a **(20)** ....
outcome such as 'I'm always wrong!' However,
we may over-react to the experience, expressing
our feelings **(21)** ...., thereby causing
misunderstandings or unhappiness.

Analysing something with this kind of dark
mindset can mean our interpretation of it
becomes **(22)** .... and, obviously, this
kind of **(23)** .... is unhealthy.

Luckily, people with more open mindsets seek
to learn from every experience. They have a
(24) .... rather than downbeat approach
to life. It's clear which mindset is desirable!

CONSCIOUS
SIGNIFY

PERSON

JUDGE

COMPREHEND

APPROPRIATE

BALANCE
NEGATIVE

CONSTRUCT

Key word transformation (Part 4)

For questions 25–30, complete the second sentence so that it has a similar meaning to the first sentence, using the word given. Do not change the word given. You must use between three and six words, including the word given. Here is an example (0).

Example

0 Staying another night would have meant paying more.

IF

I would have had to pay more if I had stayed another night.

25 People will always want entertainment, providing that they have the time to enjoy it.

LONG

There will always be a need for entertainment, ... the time to enjoy it.

26 Scientists did not expect to make a discovery in the treatment of cancer.

BREAKTHROUGH

There .... in the treatment of cancer.

27 I thought very hard but couldn't remember the answer.

RACKED

I .... to remember the answer, but failed.

28 The building is unusable in its present state.

PURPOSE

The building .... in its present state.

29 However hard I look, up to now I haven't been able to find a job.

ALTHOUGH

I haven't been able to find a job .... really hard.

30 I don't think my future job prospects are very good, which is worrying.

ABOUT

I .... my future job prospects.

11 Face value

Vocabulary
words to describe emotions ▶ CB page 112

1 Complete the conversations with words formed from the verbs in the box. Use one verb for each conversation. There is one verb you do not need to use.

---
amuse   astonish   blame   celebrate   embarrass   exhilarate   frustrate
---

1 **A:** Well, that was ....! I could feel myself going red.

   B: Yes, the whole thing was a complete .... for everyone.

2 **A:** I find skiing .... The speed is thrilling.

   B: I don't get that sense of .... at all – it just scares me!

3 **A:** Did you find that stand-up comedian ....?

   B: Not really. I prefer different types of ...., like reading.

4 **A:** What's the best .... you've ever been to?

   B: I'd say my graduation. We had a big .... party afterwards.

5 **A:** His resignation was .... It was so unexpected.

   B: Yes, I had no idea – there was such a mood of .... around the office.

6 **A:** Apparently, ... is the commonest cause of unhappiness at work.

   B: Yes, it's so .... when people don't listen to your ideas!

Use of English
Open cloze (Part 2) ▶ CB page 113

1 Read the article. For questions 1–8, think of the word which best fits each gap. Use only one word in each gap.

Looking past *the obvious*

Do scientists bother **(0)** ....*to*.... to read science fiction? We like to imagine them **(1)** .... hard-headed people who would find such fiction frivolous, totally lacking in value, but, apparently, many do enjoy **(2)** ....

So what's the attraction? Maybe they find it exhilarating to discover things science fiction presents as possibilities, **(3)** .... the existence of new life forms or living robots. But that's probably too simple **(4)** .... explanation. Creating a society peopled with alien beings enables a writer to address issues of morality and values in a meaningful **(5)** .... creative way. Readers can question **(6)** .... own values and ideals **(7)** .... feeling uncomfortable or embarrassed.

Finally, the fascination may simply be whether the science in fiction is really so far-fetched. How many things once dismissed as fantasy are now part of everyday life? Looking beyond the obvious is good for us, taking us **(8)** .... of our comfort zones, challenging us and encouraging us to think outside the box.

Listening
Multiple choice (Part 3)
▶ CB page 114

1 ▶ 20 **You will hear an interview with Karen Simpson and Jason Todd, two fashion designers. For questions 1–6, choose the answer (A, B, C or D) which fits best according to what you hear.**

1 What is Karen's attitude towards consumers of fashion?

  A They are often uninterested in ethics.

  B They are only concerned with having fun.

  C They are very influenced by the media.

  D They are uninformed about many issues.

2 What does Jason think about combining ethical approaches with fashion design?

  A It's too complicated for many people to try.

  B It's more difficult than he'd expected.

  C It's often misunderstood by consumers.

  D It's ignored by the industry in general.

3 What do Karen and Jason both say about their design styles?

  A They try to produce something recognisably their own.

  B They are motivated by their own experiences.

  C They want to do things that other designers don't.

  D They understand the need to adapt to a changing market.

4 Karen says her priority in her clothes is that they

  A are chosen for sensible reasons.

  B are comfortable to wear.

  C have a reasonable price tag.

  D have a practical use.

5 Jason regards the production process as

  A challenging owing to the pressures of time.

  B satisfying because of the teamwork involved.

  C demanding due to changes in marketing requirements .

  D rewarding because he can see his designs come to life.

6 What do Karen and Jason both think about the future of ethical fashion?

  A Finances could become a bigger problem.

  B Fashion could influence the wider business world.

  C It will be difficult to maintain their ideals.

  D They will have to sell their clothes to a wider market.

Grammar
passive forms ▶ CB page 115

1 **Rewrite the sentences in the passive.**

1 They thought the antique chair was worth thousands of pounds but it wasn't.

2 Experts have to authenticate works of art before they go on sale.

3 I'm not keen on people I don't know selling things to me!

4 The museum will display the new exhibits in a specially designed area.

5 He'll have finished the sales catalogue by the end of the day.

6 They have reduced the price of the entrance tickets for families.

2 **Complete the second sentence so that it has a similar meaning to the first sentence, using the word given. Do not change the word given. You must use between three and six words, including the word given.**

1 She wants people to take her seriously as an artist.

  BE

  She .... as an artist.

2 If people think a painting was done by a famous artist, it will be worth a lot.

  HAVE

  If a painting .... by a famous artist, it will be worth a lot.

3 The high valuation really took the art collector by surprise.

  ABACK

  The art collector .... the high valuation.

4 People think the artist made a fortune through his abstract work.

  THOUGHT

  The artist .... a fortune through his abstract work.

5 The manager of the gallery believed he was showing a genuine masterpiece.

  SHOWN

  The manager of the gallery believed that .... was a genuine masterpiece.

6 Young artists often copy famous paintings for practice.

  ARE

  Famous paintings .... young artists for practice.

Reading
Cross-text multiple matching (Part 6)
▶ CB page 116

1 Read four extracts from drama school blogs about the acting process. For questions 1–4, choose from the blogs (A–D). The blogs may be chosen more than once.

Which blogger

1 expresses a different view from the others about what's important when preparing for a role? `[ 1 ]`

2 has a similar view to A about an actor's assessment of his or her own performance? `[ 2 ]`

3 has a different opinion to C about what makes a good performance? `[ 3 ]`

4 shares B's opinion about what is most satisfying about acting? `[ 4 ]`

2 **Complete the sentences with the correct form of the underlined words in the blogs.**

1 Household chores can be .... but, unfortunately, they have to be done!

2 My cousin is a(n) .... lawyer and I think he'll do very well. However, he still faces years of studying and taking exams.

3 A colleague interrupted me today with an extremely simple question and I think my expression .... what I thought about it.

4 When I sit down to take an exam, I have a(n) .... – I put my pen and pencils in a row along the top of the desk.

5 When I started studying English, our teacher made us learn new vocabulary .... It was pretty boring but I still remember the words.

6 I'm not a very .... person. I much prefer to plan well ahead rather than make last-minute decisions.

HOME | BLOG | **COMMENT**

Playing a part

Four aspiring actors comment on how drama school training helps them prepare for a new role.

A

Some actors have little <u>rituals</u> that they have to carry out every time they start a new part, which may be based on superstition. For them, acting involves a deep personal investment. However, there are also practical considerations when taking on any new part. Is it better to learn all the words <u>by rote</u>, or through some kind of emotional memory? The script itself is fixed, but there are a million ways in which an actor can imagine saying the lines. Wherever this imagination comes from, the actor must first draw on things that they have experienced and know to be true. Because of this, actors are not necessarily the best judge of their own performance since they are too close to it, but if they use the practical techniques learnt in drama school, they will be better equipped to take on demanding roles and face their critics knowing they have performed well.

B

It's a strange thing that the world of the theatre is often connected with deceit and lying – after all, that's the stuff of good drama, and actors are simply playing a part. But really it's the opposite, as acting is essentially connected with bringing out some kind of truth. The fact is that truth is everything to do with humanity. And the best part of an actor's job is to convey that and change the way people think about it. However, if an audience doesn't believe in a character on stage, it's not worth doing. For an actor, finding a way inside a character requires different skills but to be honest, acting is not as spontaneous as we imagine it to be – it's really all about thinking, evaluating and planning every move beforehand so that an illusion is created that will hold an audience. That's when acting is at its most demanding, and practicalities like learning the lines are actually quite <u>mundane</u>. When a performance is a revelation, opening people's eyes to something new, and completely truthful in what it says about life, it lifts both audience and the actors on to a different level. So much of what is done in drama schools is based on achieving that.

C

Most acting workshops teach actors to be flexible and loose in their approach to a role, to use their imagination and be as open as possible, responding intuitively to any given situation. This is key to the success of actors when establishing a new character. When it comes to fixing the emotions of a character, there is no point in trying to create unrealistic emotions because what people in real life do is react to other people around them; they don't walk around summoning up states of anger or fear at a moment's notice. Actors have to do the same thing night after night, and may lose the ability to see how well it is being done or even engage emotionally. The irony is that actors must appear to be <u>spontaneous</u>, yet they know what the other characters on stage are going to say. The audience must believe in their characters and their motivations, and for as long as they remain convinced, the actors have succeeded.

D

Drama schools teach <u>aspiring</u> young actors that there is no one right way to do things – there are different approaches to developing a character, although the practical techniques of voice projection and so on are clearly the same. Some actors totally immerse themselves in the character they're playing, even staying in character when off-stage. Others consider this self-indulgent, and rely on imagination and spontaneity to carry them through. After all, imagination is not something concrete that can be manipulated and the aim of the actor is to <u>convey</u> his or her version of the truth of the play to the audience. It's every actor's dream to reach an audience and help them look at something in a new way.

Grammar
linking adverbials ▶ CB page 119

1 **Choose the correct alternative in each sentence.**

1 *In contrast/In view of* his appearance, I don't think we can offer him the job.
2 *In spite of/Given* her poor fashion sense, I'd love to employ her.
3 *Despite/As well as* his lack of qualifications, he dresses really badly.
4 I think she interviewed well. *Alternatively/Even so*, we can't give her the job.
5 He doesn't fit our company image. *Consequently/On the contrary*, we won't be taking him on.
6 She's worked really hard at college. *Furthermore/In contrast*, she's got great qualifications.
7 *In addition to/Apart from* his poor dress sense, he seems to fit the bill as far as the job itself is concerned.
8 She looks very smart. *In contrast/Alternatively*, he looks rather scruffy.

2 **Complete the text with the words in the box.**

apart from   as a result   clearly   consequently
despite   given   nor   whereas

(1) .... what many people do almost instinctively, it seems wrong to judge someone purely on the clothes they wear. (2) .... , these might not reflect the real person. (3) .... possibly sending mixed messages, clothes can't show a person's abilities (4) .... the skills they have, and (5) .... , no one should judge a person by their appearance!

People change their facial expressions according to their mood, but if an expression is used often, it can change a person physically. (6) .... of facial movements, someone who smiles a lot may have lines around the eyes, (7) .... someone who frowns a lot could develop wrinkles on their forehead or above the eyes. (8) .... these physical signs, why shouldn't we judge someone's personality by their appearance?

Speaking
Long turn (Part 2)
▶ CB page 118

1 **Look at the exam task and the pictures. Then complete the sentences with the words in the box.**

confidence convinced denying doubt doubtful
hard question suppose

1 There's no .... the fact that the woman is pretty surprised!

2 It's .... whether the footballer's going to calm down any time soon.

3 I'm .... that the parents have very strong feelings about their child.

4 I think I can say with .... that the woman had absolutely no idea about the presents.

5 There's no .... about it. Those parents are having an extra special moment.

6 There's no .... in my mind that they're feeling angry.

7 It's .... to say who has the strongest feelings but it's probably the parents.

8 I .... the parents' feelings will last the longest.

> Look at the pictures. They show people showing different emotions. Compare two of the pictures and say how the people are feeling and what might have made them feel this way.
>
> Follow-up question: Which people do you think have the strongest feelings?

2 ▶ 21 **Listen to a candidate doing the task and complete his answer.**

> Right, I'd like to discuss these pictures – the one with the woman getting the presents and the footballers.
> **(1)** .... , in both the pictures the people are feeling **(2)** .... about something but they're in very different situations and have very different feelings.
>
> The people in the first picture are enjoying a **(3)** .... moment, and they all seem to be very happy because they're laughing, **(4)** .... there's no doubt that the footballers have very negative feelings. They're **(5)** .... not laughing!
>
> The people in the first picture are very excited to see the woman happy. I think they're her family and maybe it's her birthday and they've been planning to give her a surprise for a long time. They're glad that it's **(6)** .... out to be a success, and she's feeling happy that her family have been so thoughtful.
>
> **(7)** .... , the footballers are showing completely different emotions. They both look **(8)** .... , even aggressive, and the referee is trying to stop them having a fight. Maybe the one in green and yellow kicked the other one, or perhaps tried to push him out of the way and he didn't like it. I'm **(9)** .... that it'll be difficult to calm them down, but in a competitive game like football emotions are often very intense but quite short-lived.
> I **(10)** .... the referee will sort everything out.

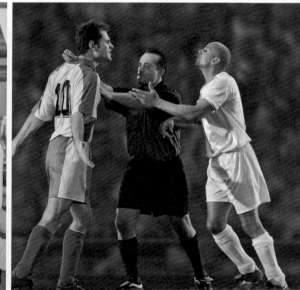

Writing
Essay (Part 1) ▶ CB page 120

1 **Look at the exam task. Do you agree with the opinions expressed?**

> Your class has watched an online discussion programme about the importance of honesty today. You have made the notes below.
>
> **The importance of honesty today**
> - to our friends and family
> - to ourselves
> - to those in authority
>
> **Some opinions expressed in the discussion**
>
> 'It's impossible to be honest with our friends all the time. It can be hurtful!'
>
> 'It's quite normal to pretend things to ourselves. But sometimes we need to be straight.'
>
> 'I'm pretty sure most people have lied at some time or another to authorities about minor matters but for important things you should tell the truth.'
>
> Write an essay for your tutor discussing **two** of the points in your notes. You should **discuss why you think honesty is or isn't important, giving reasons** to support your opinion.
>
> You may, if you wish, make use of the opinions expressed in the discussion but you should use your own words as far as possible.
>
> Write your **essay** in **220–260** words in an appropriate style.

2 **Read two introductory paragraphs for the essay. Find examples of the following:**

1 a phrase giving the writer's opinion
2 a contraction
3 impersonal language
4 a general factual statement
5 an indication of what is going to follow
6 a reflective rhetorical question

A

I think it's important to be completely honest. I learnt when I was a child that it's always best to tell the truth. If we aren't honest, I think this can give us a bad conscience and make us feel guilty. So, to show you why I think this is very important, I'd like to give you some examples.

B

From an early age, most children are taught that honesty is the best policy and it can sometimes be quite refreshing to hear the honest, direct opinions of a child. However, as we grow older, our decisions about how honest we should be are influenced by many other things such as the desire to avoid hurting others unnecessarily or when considering the possible consequences of being totally honest. So, how honest should we be?

3 **Which of the two introductory paragraphs in Activity 2 is more appropriate to begin the essay? Tick (✓) three of the reasons below for your choice.**

1 It introduces the points for discussion clearly.
2 It is written objectively.
3 It writes about 'I' all the time.
4 It summarises the writer's opinion.
5 It engages the reader.

4 **Which items from Activity 2 (1–6) should be avoided in an introduction to an essay?**

5 **Choose the two points from the essay prompts that you would like to focus on and make notes for the rest of the essay. Then write your essay.**

81

12 Brilliant ideas

Listening
Sentence completion (Part 2)
▶ CB page 122

1 ▶ 22 You will hear a man called Tony Hopkins giving a presentation to students about his work as a toy designer. For questions 1–8, complete the sentences.

Tony's toys

Tony thinks that writing **(1)** .... when he was at school was the strangest thing he did.

Tony thinks of designing toys as a(n) **(2)** .... that he really enjoys.

To play Tony's first game people used a(n) **(3)** .... to move a shuttlecock.

Tony's game didn't fit in with the **(4)** .... of the company he applied to first.

Tony doesn't understand why an initial **(5)** .... stops people designing toys.

Tony is convinced that aspiring toy designers need **(6)** .... from people who really want to help them.

According to Tony, asking for **(7)** .... from companies is important.

Tony feels that **(8)** .... is a vital quality for new designers to have.

Vocabulary
multi-part verbs: science and research
▶ CB page 123

1 Rewrite the sentences, replacing the multi-part verbs with the correct form of the verbs in the box. There is one verb you do not need to use.

clarify conduct consider contest intend propose

1 A study into different ways of learning was carried out.
2 It's rather hard to make the difference between some words clear.
3 A new project has been put forward to develop space travel further.
4 I have always taken issue with the conclusions drawn by the head of department.
5 The project set out to prove the statistics were flawed but it was unsuccessful.

2 Find and correct mistakes with word order in four of the sentences.

1 The students looked the possibility into of developing the project.
2 The results took account into any demographic differences.
3 Scientists carried intensive checks out on all the equipment.
4 They put several useful suggestions forward but were ignored.
5 The findings were noted in detail down, for further analysis.

Grammar

cohesion ▶ CB page 124

1 Choose the correct alternative in each sentence.

1 The scientists conducted various experiments *so/in order to* confirm the data.

2 The lecturers, *like/as* the students, were unhappy with the proposed changes to the syllabus.

3 They worked on the design *until/while* they felt it was perfect.

4 The project went ahead as planned *but/despite* not for long – it was scrapped after two months.

5 In all the projects I was involved with I had no problems *except/apart* with one man who was very difficult to work with.

6 *Even/Although* I agree in principle with the findings, I have some issues with the details.

emphasis with inversion ▶ CB page 126

2 Complete the sentences with the correct form of the verb in brackets. Add any other words necessary.

1 At no time .... (*tell*) us what her idea for a new invention was.

2 Not only .... (*move into*) a new flat last month, he changed his job as well.

3 Seldom .... (*know*) a better person to work on creative ideas with.

4 Under no circumstances .... (*change*) your job without consulting me!

5 Scarcely .... (*choose*) her design course than she changed her mind.

6 Hardly .... (*finish*) painting the flat when my friend spilled coffee over the wall.

3 Rewrite the sentences using inversion. Start with the words in brackets.

1 She had only just woken up when the builders arrived. (*hardly*)

2 This is the most beautifully designed house I have ever seen. (*never before*)

3 He has never told anyone why he decided to move to a different company. (*at no time*)

4 It's not often that I see people working together so creatively. (*rarely*)

5 He closed the front door and immediately realised he'd left his key inside the flat. (*no sooner*)

6 You must never open the door to strangers at night! (*under no circumstances*)

Use of English

Key word transformation (Part 4) ▶ CB page 127

1 Choose the correct alternative to complete the second sentence so that it has a similar meaning to the first sentence. Ensure the second sentence uses the word given and that the answer is between three and six words long, including the word given.

1 Allegedly, students remember things with less difficulty when they see them than when they hear them.

EASIER

Allegedly, *it is supposed to be easier for students to/ students find it easier to* remember things when they see them than when they hear them.

2 Children find it more interesting to visit museums than read about history.

PREFER

Children *prefer visiting museums to reading/prefer to be able to visit museums than read* about history.

3 The museum guidebook didn't give enough information for tourists.

WAS

The museum guidebook *was not as informative enough as/was less informative than* tourists wanted.

4 I never return things I've bought to a shop – it's too much hassle!

BACK

I *never take back anything/never take something back* I've bought to a shop – it's too much hassle!

5 It's rare that I speak to my friend nowadays.

HARDLY

I *hardly ever speak to my friend/hardly do I speak to my friend* nowadays.

6 There is a rumour of a change in the management structure next year.

BE

The management structure *is rumoured to be changing/is going to be changing* next year.

Reading
Gapped text (Part 7) ▶ CB page 128

1 **Read the article quickly and decide if the statements are true (T) or false (F).**

1 Some famous people refuse to accept the truth of certain scientific facts.

2 Brian Cox used to be a pop star.

3 He doesn't use social media.

4 He is depressed about future scientific investigations.

5 He believes that colonising another planet will be good for our species.

2 **Read the article again. Six paragraphs have been removed from the article. Choose from the paragraphs A–G the one which fits each gap (1–6). There is one extra paragraph which you do not need to use.**

3 **Match the adjectives from the article (1–6) with their meanings (A–E).**

1	telegenic	A	unable to talk, express oneself
2	inured to	B	appealing, good on television
3	tongue-tied	C	generally, in all aspects
4	combative	D	typical of a person's attitude
5	trademark	E	accustomed
6	all-round	F	eager to fight or argue

4 **Complete the sentences with the correct form of the underlined words/phrases in the text and paragraphs.**

1 There has been a .... of burglaries in our area in recent weeks.

2 The plans to change school start times have come .... recently. Parents and teachers have protested.

3 It takes some parents ages to .... the fact that their children often play computer games late into the night.

4 When the science prize was announced you could have .... in the hall.

5 My elder brother always used to .... for me when I got bullied at school.

6 I have my own opinions and I'm not going to .... to anyone else's!

A
It is, he adds 'a very pure way of communicating. There's a wonderful thing that happens when thousands of people in a room all think about something difficult and start to understand it. Sometimes you can <u>hear a pin drop</u> when you are talking about general relativity.'

B
'I am a bit less combative [now],' he admits. 'Outwardly. I have realised that confrontation is not the way forward,' he demurs today. 'I think that people like me – in all different fields – have a responsibility to try and civilise the debates.'

C
Cox quite fancies a trip into space himself, but he has professional and personal commitments on Earth that prevent him traversing the planets. As well as the TV and radio shows and the tours, he still lectures. He is married to TV presenter Gia Milinovich, and they have a nine-year-old son, George.

D
Does Cox feel that all this is bringing us closer to understanding the universe? 'I think the mysteries are increasing, actually, certainly in cosmology,' he says. The universe is not behaving as the data from the Hubble telescope, and the discovery of the Higgs Boson particle by the LHC, suggest it should.

E
Talking about family and fame is the only time Cox becomes tongue-tied. He says he has become inured to unsought public recognition but still likes to go to places where he is unknown, like France (he is big in Estonia, apparently, as well as here and in Australia).

F
This time he'll be broadcasting from an observatory outside Sydney which means he can look straight at 'the centre of the galaxy: there's a black hole there, four million times the mass of the sun, a very exotic object'.

G
'Well,' comes Cox's trademark, straight-to-the-point reply to the latter, 'we can see it.' Cox was, famously, in a rock band while studying physics at university. He re-entered the public sphere years later as an academic to combat a government spending review that was 'accidentally bad for physics'. He was an immediate hit with the viewing public.

PROFESSOR BRIAN COX:
CAN SCIENCE SURVIVE IN OUR POST-TRUTH WORLD?

In our post-truth universe, where facts <u>kowtow</u> to personal belief, where does that leave science? Prof Brian Cox thinks carefully before saying: 'It is important for people in my position – by which I mean scientists that have some sort of public voice – to say that not all opinions are equal.' The popular physicist, TV presenter and all-round cheerleader for rational thought has seen long-held facts <u>under fire</u> of late. Among them is the belief of one public figure that the Earth is flat and of another that the Big Bang didn't happen.

1 [ ] Broadcasters quickly <u>cottoned on to</u> the fact that he was telegenic and a born communicator on one hand, and quite feisty on the other. When I interviewed him several years ago after the TV series *Wonders of the Solar System* made him a star, he was regularly getting into fights on Twitter with anyone whose views he considered ridiculous.

2 [ ] And there have been plenty of those of late, following a <u>spate</u> of discoveries breathing new excitement into our discussions of the universe. Nasa announced the discovery of a new solar system of seven Earth-sized planets that may have 'potential for life' and revealed plans for a new telescope that could study 'dark matter', the mysterious and currently unidentified substance which it is thought might unlock astronomical mysteries.

3 [ ] In spite of these disappointments Cox seems upbeat. His undying sense of awe and wish to share it is essentially optimistic. He regularly gives lecture tours about the universe in eight- or nine-thousand-seat arenas. In his days with the band he was always at the back hiding behind the keyboards. Does he get stage fright now, alone in front of all those people? 'No, I really enjoy it,' he says. 'There is complete freedom because it's my show, so I can do what I want.'

4 [ ] His own sense of awe is undimmed. He thinks that life, in the form of microbes, will be discovered in his lifetime on Mars or on Jupiter's moon, Europa. And he is excited by the possibilities of mining asteroids for iron and plans for galactic travel and eventual Mars-colonisation. 'There's everything you need on Mars to go and live there.' Plus, it's harder for a species to destroy itself if it is spread over two or more planets.

5 [ ] How does travelling affect his family life? 'I do less of it now,' he says. Is George into science? 'Yes and no. You know what seven-year-olds are like.' How does he feel about you being famous? 'It's not a thing I want him to be conscious of particularly. We don't talk about it.' He laughs awkwardly. 'We stay out of everybody's way.'

6 [ ] His early ambition, 'to keep science in the public eye', has spiralled into a wider spokesman's role on behalf of public service broadcasting, investment in research and education. And he's one of the few people <u>sticking up</u> for knowledge in a world where, as the classicist Mary Beard put it, 'ignorance is something to be proud of'.

Vocabulary
expressions with *matter*
▶ CB page 128

1 Choose one word from each pair of words in the box to complete the sentences. There is one pair you do not need to use.

black/dark data/fact honour/pride
ideas/opinion interest/question pressure/time
principal/principle

1 I know nothing about it – as a matter of ...., I've never even seen that report before.

2 Whether he was right or not is a matter of .... – people take very different positions on it.

3 I'm not really involved but just as a matter of ...., what did he say?

4 Surely, they'll find out the truth soon – it can only be a matter of ....

5 I can't change my stance on the situation now – it's become a matter of ....

6 I'm going to do well this time – it's a matter of ...., as I don't want to fail again.

85

Speaking
all parts ▶ CB page 125

1 **Look at the Part 2 task, answer and pictures. What mistake(s) has the candidate made?**

1 not addressing both parts of the question
2 not comparing the pictures
3 giving too much description
4 not speculating

> Compare two of the pictures and say what the people might be discussing and how they might be feeling.

In the first picture there are two men standing in the middle of the countryside looking at some papers – they're probably plans of some kind because I think they're building a bridge or road. I can see it in the background. Maybe they're checking the work that other people have done or maybe they're making sure that everything is all right. They look like engineers because they're wearing special jackets that make them easy to see, and white helmets for protection. In the second picture there's a group of young people sitting in a circle and discussing something. They may be doing a college project, and they're possibly having some kind of seminar because they have laptops and notepads with them. One girl is sitting in the middle and is obviously taking charge of the discussion. They're all wearing casual clothes, and three of them are wearing red tops. The girls are all wearing jeans. They're all obviously engaged with the discussion and enjoying it because they're smiling.

2 **Look at the Part 3 task and the two extracts from candidates' discussions. Answer the questions.**

1 Which comments relate to Extract 1 and which to Extract 2?

   A The candidates interact with each other.
   B The candidates develop one idea before moving on.
   C The candidates take turns to give their ideas on different topics.
   D The candidates address the task.
   E The candidates concentrate on personal responses.

2 Which extract is a better response to the task?

> Here are some aspects of our lives that have been affected by recent developments in technology and a question for you to discuss.
>
>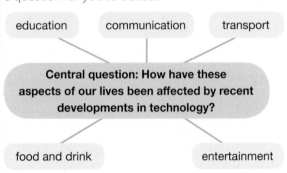
>
> education   communication   transport
>
> **Central question: How have these aspects of our lives been affected by recent developments in technology?**
>
> food and drink   entertainment
>
> Talk to each other about how these aspects of our lives have been affected by recent developments in technology.
>
> Now you have about a minute to decide which of these aspects of our lives has benefited most from developments in technology.

Extract 1

A: Communication is very different today from the past. People don't have much time, so they talk to friends on the phone or by email rather than meeting up. It isn't a good thing. It's really important for people to meet face-to-face.

B: I don't use public transport much. I like to walk everywhere or cycle. It's better for your health. I really believe that travelling by bus or underground is also unhealthy. You can pick up all sorts of colds and things.

A: I enjoy watching soap operas on TV. They're great. I also go to gigs quite a lot. I like it when they use lots of special lighting and effects. I also like the atmosphere when there is a big crowd.

Extract 2

A: Education is changing a lot, I think. It's down to the equipment teachers have got in the classrooms.

B: I completely agree with you. They can use these wonderful electronic whiteboards and the students have tablets and laptops. They don't have to spend a lot of time looking things up in books – they can browse online.

A: True! Also, students don't have to write everything down in notebooks. They can type their notes or work on screens.

B: I think technology has allowed teachers to develop new teaching methods to help their students. It makes learning much more interesting and fun, too.

A: You're right. OK, so what do you think about food and drink?

Writing
Essay (Part 1)
▶ CB page 130

1 **Look at the exam task and tick (√) the things you should include in your answer.**

1 a reference to how science is taught at university

2 a discussion of why adults dislike science subjects

3 an outline of why science at school can be boring

4 the importance of students developing a competitive streak

5 detailed examples of experiments

6 reasons why we need students to follow scientific careers

7 the pros and cons of two of the ideas

8 your own opinion

> Your class has attended a panel discussion on how to make science more interesting for young people at school. You have made the notes below.
>
> **Ideas for making science more interesting for young people at school**
> - organising visits to science shows and exhibitions
> - providing better training for science teachers
> - setting up local and national science competitions

> **Some opinions expressed in the discussion**
>
> 'Some science exhibitions have fun experiments that the kids can get involved in.'
>
> 'It's not really the training that's important – it's the type of people who become science teachers.'
>
> 'I think competitions might make science too serious, particularly if the students feel pressurised by the school.'

Write an essay for your tutor discussing **two** of the points in your notes. You should **explain which idea you think would be most successful, giving reasons** to support your opinion.

You may, if you wish, make use of the opinions expressed in the discussion but you should use your own words as far as possible.

Write your **essay** in **220–260** words in an appropriate style.

2 **Complete these extracts from a candidate's answer with the words in the box.**

> also   apart   hear   nevertheless   one   only   other
> see   such   while

1 .... watching a teacher doing an experiment in class can be relatively unexciting, participating in fun experiments at a science show is far more likely to interest young people.

2 Not .... can competition give a focus to what the kids are doing in class but it can .... promote teamwork and healthy rivalry.

3 .... from bringing science to life, visits to shows can be really informative, too.

4 On the .... hand, we need to invest in better training for teachers but on the .... hand, we need suitable people to apply for the training!

5 We often .... that the country needs more scientists and engineers.

6 As I .... it, in the end it is down to the quality of the teacher and the teaching methods he or she uses in the classroom.

7 Making science lessons interesting for young children is a difficult challenge. ...., it is something we definitely need to address.

8 Some TV science shows .... as *The Big Bang Theory* have become very popular with children and teenagers.

3 **Do the exam task in Activity 1.**

Multiple-choice cloze (Part 1)

For questions 1–8, read the text below and decide which answer (A, B, C or D) best fits each gap. There is an example at the beginning (0).

It's the same, isn't it?

It's **(0)** ..A, common.. knowledge that the correct answer to 'Which weighs more, a pound of lead or a pound of feathers?' is 'They're the same.' Anyone who says 'lead' is going **(1)** .... the facts. But is this actually the **(2)** ....?

Psychologists suggest it's possible for two objects with identical mass to feel unequally heavy and this is to **(3)** .... the distribution of the weight. One experiment **(4)** .... some way to supporting this theory. Scientists placed a lump of lead in a cardboard box, then filled an identical box with a bag containing the same weight of feathers. Volunteers were blindfolded, given each box **(5)** .... and asked which was heavier.

So what happened? The majority **(6)** .... the box with lead in it. The apparent explanation for their choice is the lead sitting in the bottom of the box **(7)** .... it difficult to control and it therefore felt heavier. **(8)** ...., the feathers were equally distributed, making the box easier to manage.

Whatever the answer, it's a fun quiz question!

Open cloze (Part 2)

For questions 9–16, read the text below and think of the word which best fits each gap. Use only one word in each gap. There is an example at the beginning (0).

The perfect partner

It's impossible to look into relationships and understand what people see in each other, and psychologists come up **(0)** ....with.... different suggestions to explain this.

Facial attraction is high on the list – luckily, we all have our own concept of **(9)** .... makes someone good-looking, **(10)** .... there could be competition! A person might not be attractive **(11)** .... everyone's eyes but for the right person, the face fits.

Some say the secret is empathy, **(12)** .... may be a good starting point, though I wonder whether it's enough to sustain a long-term relationship. Others think a shared **(13)** .... of humour is vital and that those who laugh together stay together.

(14) .... it may be true that opposites attract, this could just be a temporary feeling based more **(15)** .... idle curiosity than genuine affection.

Whatever the secret, it clearly lies deeper than surface attraction. As **(16)** .... me, I'm still looking for the face that fits!

0	**A** common	**B** usual	**C** normal	**D** everyday
1	**A** opposed	**B** opposite	**C** against	**D** counter
2	**A** way	**B** case	**C** idea	**D** proof
3	**A** bring up	**B** come to	**C** keep on	**D** do with
4	**A** goes	**B** moves	**C** gets	**D** takes
5	**A** by row	**B** by rote	**C** in time	**D** in turn
6	**A** took up	**B** went for	**C** got on	**D** kept with
7	**A** made	**B** caused	**C** created	**D** formed
8	**A** At least	**B** Consequently	**C** In contrast	**D** Comparatively

Word formation (Part 3)

For questions 17–24, read the text below. Use the word given in capitals at the end of some of the lines to form a word that fits in the gap in the same line. There is an example at the beginning (0).

Great – or popular?

Some actors are described as great while others are not, but what is it that creates this **(0)** ...distinction... ? — **DISTINCT**

Actors who make regular **(17)** .... — **APPEAR**
in blockbuster films are popular, but often remain **(18)** .... themselves at all — **RECOGNISE**
times, and are therefore not considered 'great'. Conversely, so-called 'great' actors seem to be able to disappear completely into every role they take on – you forget who the actor actually is. It's not just a question of their **(19)** .... or technical skill – it's — **VERSATILE**
that each new character they play is totally **(20)** .... — **BELIEVE**

It is therefore somewhat **(21)** .... that — **IRONY**
'great 'actors may not **(22)** .... be — **NECESSARY**
popular off-screen and their films may not make money. Could it be that audiences don't warm to them because, unlike their extrovert celebrity counterparts, they appear to be **(23)** .... and lacking in charisma? — **INTEREST**

Maybe truly great actors need to be **(24)** .... in real life but still able to — **LIKE**
disappear into someone else once the camera starts rolling.

Key word transformation (Part 4)

For questions 25–30, complete the second sentence so that it has a similar meaning to the first sentence, using the word given. Do not change the word given. You must use between three and six words, including the word given. Here is an example (0).

Example

0 It's true that the company might go into liquidation if it's not careful.
   DANGER
   It's true that the company _is in danger of going_ into liquidation if it's not careful.

25 The moment I shouted he ran away.
    SOONER
    No .... he ran away.

26 I'm sure that it was the sound of the rain that disturbed me.
    MUST
    It .... of the rain that disturbed me.

27 I managed to finish all the homework before the deadline!
    SUCCEEDED
    I .... the homework before the deadline!

28 I took the only course open to me and changed my job.
    DID
    What I ...., which was the only course open to me.

29 They don't allow people who arrive late at the opera house in until the interval.
    ARE
    People who arrive late at the opera house .... until the interval.

30 My application for the job was turned down because I didn't have the right qualifications.
    GROUNDS
    My application for the job was turned down .... I didn't have the right qualifications.

Common language errors at C1 Advanced: Writing and Speaking

Grammar

Agreement: nouns and pronouns

My father loves to cook. ~~She~~ He often makes meals for ~~her~~ his friends and they ask ~~her~~ him for recipes.

Agreement: subject and verb

Information on the new system ~~are~~ is hard to find.

The company's two directors, who had originally set up the firm, ~~was~~ were caught embezzling funds.

Articles

To me, ~~the~~ music is the purest art form there is.

The bold painting at the very end of the exhibition is a perfect example of modernism.

Verb tense

First she ~~had~~ researched the market and then she planned the product.

The course ~~is~~ has been running for three years now.

Verb formation

The course would have interested me if it ~~would have~~ had included more practical work.

I have ~~being~~ been thinking about this idea for some time now.

~~To help~~ Helping my local community is really important to me.

I recommend you ~~seeing~~ see the new play at the National Theatre.

Irregular verbs

The group's new album has ~~catched~~ caught the public's imagination.

Word order

We have rarely had ~~rarely~~ a student drop out.

Questions

I wonder what ~~will~~ such companies will produce in the next five years.

What do you think ~~did happen~~ happened next?

Linking words and phrases

She thinks it's a good idea. ~~Similarly,~~ Conversely, he hates it.

Clothes made of natural materials ~~namely~~ such as cotton are popular in hot weather.

It was a tough project but we got there ~~at the end~~ in the end.

~~Contrary~~ Compared with my first job, the second one was simple.

The company was great, and ~~at any rate~~ what's more even the food was good.

Punctuation

Commas

What I like best, is the sense of atmosphere. (✗)

What I like best is the sense of atmosphere. (✓)

The man in the corner who is from France is very nice. (✗)

The man in the corner, who is from France, is very nice. (✓)

There are many things I'd love to do such as, climb a mountain. (✗)

There are many things I'd love to do, such as climb a mountain. (✓)

Question marks

How many exams per term should pupils have. Research suggests that three is too many. (✗)

How many exams per term should pupils have? Research suggests that three is too many. (✓)

I wanted to ask how you came to that view? (✗)

I wanted to ask how you came to that view. (✓)

Apostrophes

The schools headmaster has resigned. (✗)

The school's headmaster has resigned. (✓)

It is expected that student's results will improve. (✗)

It is expected that students' results will improve. (✓)

I love eating fish and chip's. (✗)

I love eating fish and chips. (✓)

Quotation marks

The future is in wind power, said the director. (✗)

'The future is in wind power,' said the director. (✓)

Hyphens

His eighty year old widow spoke movingly of his life. (✗)

His eighty-year-old widow spoke movingly of his life. (✓)

They had a five minute wait for the train. (✗)

They had a five-minute wait for the train. (✓)

Spelling

Omission of silent letters

lam (✗)

lamb (✓)

sychiatry (✗)

psychiatry (✓)

Suffixes and prefixes

comprehensable (✗)

comprehensible (✓)

inpossible (✗)

impossible (✓)

Homophones

right/write/rite

whole/hole

accept/except

there/their/they're

weak/week

too/two/to

Letter doubling

appologise (✗)

apologise (✓)

reccommend (✗)

recommend (✓)

Letter order

peice (✗)

piece (✓)

calander (✗)

calendar (✓)

Some interactive spoken language

I am agree with you. (✗)

I agree with you. (✓)

That's my feeling. (✓)

Let's consider this idea. (✓)

Why don't we discuss about this? (✗)

Why don't we discuss this? (✓)

You make a good point. (✓)

You give a good point. (✗)

What's your view? (✓)

What're your view? (✗)

I can't go along with that. (✓)

I can't take that. (✗)

I hadn't thought of that. (✓)

I hadn't thinking about that. (✗)

Activities

1 Find and correct the grammatical mistakes in the sentences. What grammatical area is each mistake in? Use the notes on common errors to help you.

1 Hardly he had finished the work than the boss arrived.

2 She lent him the book she had borrowed from library the previous week.

3 I wonder what might Sue be doing on Saturday evening.

4 The boss proposed we working overtime, but we refused.

5 People often finds it difficult to accept criticism.

6 She finished the work he starts the previous day.

7 He's never been teached to behave politely!

8 It was a difficult task but at the end we completed it.

2 Find and correct the mistakes with spelling and punctuation in the sentences. Use the notes on common errors to help you.

1 I wanted to ask you where you buy your clothes?

2 The local schools' results were excellent – it's the best school in the area.

3 Our three week holiday turned out to be very expensive.

4 I think it's a shame that more girls' don't play football.

5 Young people should take a more responsable attitude towards their studies.

6 Although it was an unfortunate occurence, the punishment was necessary.

7 I received an email yesterday asking me a purely rethorical question – pointless!

8 The man who's car is parked outside is my boss.

9 It's a pretty difficult situation said my sister.

10 Can you tell me how often you get the chance to go to the cinema.

3 Find and correct the mistakes in the conversations. Use the notes on common errors to help you.

1 A: The weather is strange for this time of year – what are your view?
  B: Yes, I am agree with you. It seems to be raining all the time.
  A: Let's hope it improves soon!

2 A: I think that we should accept the new contract after all.
  B: No, sorry, I can't take that. I think it's a terrible idea.
  A: Well, we may not have much choice.

3 A: We could always change the appointment – it probably wouldn't be too difficult to rearrange my diary.
  B: I hadn't thought to that. You're good at thinking outside the box!
  A: It's called lateral thinking!

4 A: We need to talk about these ideas on the task sheet – what do we start with?
  B: Let's consider about this idea first. I think it's an important issue.
  A: Sorry, I'd rather discuss about this one first.

5 A: It's important to study hard before an exam.
  B: You give a good point. I'll do my best!
  A: Me too!

Exam strategies: Writing and Speaking

Writing

General advice

- Read the question carefully and make sure you do everything that you are asked.
- Keep as close to the word limit as you can, otherwise you risk missing information out or going off the point.
- Make sure you plan carefully and divide your points into paragraphs.
- Use a range of linking words and discourse markers to create interesting sentences and guide the reader through your answer.
- Use an appropriate style, depending on the question type and the reader.
- Use a range of vocabulary and structures throughout.
- Check your work for grammar, spelling and punctuation mistakes.

Part 1: Compulsory question

1 Match the advice (1–3) with the reasons (A–C).

1 Do not copy words and phrases directly from the opinions given in the essay task.

2 Do not address all three points given in the task.

3 Use an appropriate semi-formal and impersonal style.

A You will not have time or space to do this.

B You need to show your own range of vocabulary and structures.

C An essay needs to be balanced and objective.

2 Look at a short extract from a candidate's answer to an essay question. Which piece of advice from Activity 1 above has the candidate forgotten?

> I think there is far too much advertising on television. When I'm watching a film, I get fed up when there are adverts every fifteen minutes or so. I never watch them anyway, so they don't encourage me to go out and buy things. What's the point? I particularly dislike adverts that are aimed at children. Get rid of them all!

Part 2

3 Match the advice (1–3) with the reasons (A–C).

1 Choose the question which you are most interested in and have some ideas about.

2 Remember to write in an appropriate style.

3 Make sure you organise your answer well, according to the task type.

A If your style is too formal or informal, you could offend the envisaged audience.

B Your answer is more likely to interest the reader and show your best language.

C This makes it clearer for the reader to follow your arguments or main points.

4 Look at a short extract from a candidate's answer to the exam task on page 17. Which piece of advice from Activity 3 above has the candidate forgotten?

> This is a proposal to show why we need up-to-date technology here at the college and what sort of equipment the college should invest in. Firstly, I think it would be a good idea to have interactive whiteboards in every classroom as it makes it possible for teachers to communicate more easily. In addition to this, I believe that the college should provide tablets and laptops for all the students who can't afford them themselves. These days it is essential for students to have access to the internet. I would recommend that the college also looks into the possibility of ...

Speaking

General advice

- Listen carefully to the instructions given by the Interlocutor throughout the test.
- In Parts 2 and 3, you can refer to written questions on the paper you are given with the pictures or discussion task.
- Ask the Interlocutor to repeat any instructions you are not sure about.
- Speak clearly so that both the assessor and Interlocutor can hear you.
- Remember that there are no right or wrong answers to the questions you are asked.

Part 1: Interview

1 Match the advice (1–3) with the reasons (A–C).

1 Don't give an answer that is too long and detailed.

2 Don't answer a question with one word.

3 Don't ask your partner for a reaction.

A These questions are directed at individual candidates.

B This doesn't allow you to show your English ability.

C This could take up too much time. It may also indicate that a candidate has prepared or rehearsed an answer. Your answers should be spontaneous.

2 Look at the question and a candidate's answer. Which piece of advice from Activity 1 above has the candidate forgotten?

> **Q:** What's your favourite way of spending your free time?
>
> **A:** I'm really keen on reading – detective fiction in particular. So every spare moment I have, you'll see me with my nose in a book. I've never been especially sporty – the most exercise I get is the occasional walk in the countryside – but even there I take a book to sit and read! How about you, Kim?

Part 2: Long turn

3 Match the advice (1–3) with the reasons (A–C).

1 Remember to talk about only two of the pictures.

2 Listen carefully, refer to the question above the pictures and answer all parts of the task.

3 Don't describe the pictures in detail.

A By doing this you show a range of language for different functions.

B You won't have time to do the task well if you don't do this.

C This is not part of the task and only shows a limited use of structure.

4 Look at the extract from a candidate's answer. Which piece of advice from Activity 3 above has the candidate forgotten?

> These two pictures show people competing in different kinds of sports outside – two guys are playing golf and in this one a group of kids are playing some sort of ball game in teams. The third picture is a bit different in that it's an indoor sporting event – two teams are playing ice hockey and they're being cheered on by a big crowd.

Part 3: Collaborative task

5 Match the advice (1–3) with the reasons (A–C).

1 Make sure you interact with your partner and ask for and comment on opinions.

2 Do not rush through all the points.

3 Refer to the question in the centre of the mind map.

A This helps to focus you on the task and make sure you stay on the point.

B This encourages a good discussion and shows your communication skills in English.

C This may not give you time for a good discussion. It's better to deal with a few points well.

6 Look at the extract from a Part 3 discussion between two candidates. Which piece of advice from Activity 5 above have the candidates forgotten?

> **A:** OK, we need to talk about why people choose to go into these different careers. The first one: teaching. Well, that's because they want to help others, isn't it?
>
> **B:** Yes, I agree. The next one: a police officer. They probably want to make people's lives safer. What about a politician?
>
> **A:** I think people do that because they want to help society. The next one is …

Part 4: Discussion

7 Match the advice (1–3) with the reasons (A–C).

1 Develop your answer by giving reasons and examples.

2 Listen to your partner's answer and think about whether you agree or not.

3 Remember you can ask the Interlocutor to repeat the question.

A You may not hear or understand the question well the first time. It's better to check rather than misinterpret the question.

B The Interlocutor may ask for your opinion or you may want to add your ideas when your partner has finished.

C This gives you the chance to give a full answer and show a range of language.

8 Look at the question and a candidate's answer. Which piece of advice from Activity 7 above has the candidate forgotten?

> **Q:** How far do you think people's opinions are influenced by their parents' beliefs?
>
> **A:** Quite a lot. Parents' views are important.

Practice test

Reading and Use of English

For questions **1–8**, read the text below and decide which answer (**A**, **B**, **C** or **D**) best fits each gap.
There is an example at the beginning (**0**).

Example:

0   **A** in other words   **B** in addition   **C** in fact   **D** in truth

```
   A   B   C   D
0 ▬▬  ☐   ☐   ☐
```

Exceptionally talented or just over-confident?

According to a study on what lies at the heart of success, it seems that the key is not what might be expected, **(0)** _A, in other words_ talent, hard work or a good education, but instead it's total, unadulterated confidence. Why is this?

Confident people tend not to be **(1)** .... by their own shortcomings and often have **(2)** ....-than-life personalities. This means they are more visible in the workplace, pushing themselves forward at every opportunity and so **(3)** .... promotion over those who may be more competent but appear on the **(4)** .... to be less talented. Confident people are often admired and their opinions valued; **(5)** ...., they are able to influence attitudes in the workplace.

These findings could have implications for recruitment procedures generally, as a typical job interview often involves a group task which unfairly **(6)** .... the over-confident. Displays of confidence may carry too much **(7)** .... with interviewers, meaning that better but quieter candidates are **(8)** .... down.

What's the result? A less efficient workforce.

1	**A** put back	**B** put off	**C** put under	**D** put across
2	**A** bigger	**B** wider	**C** greater	**D** larger
3	**A** being	**B** making	**C** reaching	**D** getting
4	**A** top	**B** head	**C** surface	**D** front
5	**A** consequently	**B** because	**C** while	**D** as
6	**A** supports	**B** favours	**C** shows	**D** demonstrates
7	**A** consideration	**B** power	**C** force	**D** weight
8	**A** moved	**B** sent	**C** turned	**D** passed

Part 2

For questions **9–16**, read the text below and think of the word which best fits each gap. Use only one word in each gap. There is an example at the beginning (**0**).

Write your answers **IN CAPITAL LETTERS**.

Example: 0 B E T W E E N

Dancers or athletes?

Are dancers really just athletes? There are certainly similarities **(0)** ....between.... them and it has long been acknowledged that their level of fitness is similar. In fact, experiments where footballers took **(9)** .... in training sessions with dancers showed that **(10)** .... was the players who got tired first!

Many people already view dancers as elite athletes. Unfortunately, **(11)** .... is also apparent is that while dancers possess an enviable range of flexibility, **(12)** .... to mention amazing muscular strength, they are also highly susceptible to injury. And **(13)** .... from those lucky enough to perform at the highest level, they may have little specialist support when something serious occurs, so potential careers can be cut short.

To return to the original question, many would argue that dancers are more than athletes. **(14)** .... training equally hard, they have the added pressure of needing to look graceful and **(15)** .... everything appear effortless.

So it is not only the physical capabilities of dancers that is admirable but the artistry with **(16)** .... they perform.

Part 3

For questions **17–24**, read the text below. Use the word given in capitals at the end of some of the lines to form a word that fits in the gap **in the same line**. There is an example at the beginning **(0)**.

Write your answers **IN CAPITAL LETTERS**.

Example: | 0 | P E R S O N A L I T Y

Sleeping: more than meets the eye

It seems that one of the many things that has an effect on our **(0)** ....personality.... is   **PERSON**
the position we sleep in! How can this be?

Apparently our sleeping position partly determines how we feel when we wake
up. To **(17)** ...., people who sleep on their backs with their arms   **CLEAR**
stretched out typically awake feeling **(18)** .... and eager for the day   **VITAL**
ahead. Conversely, those who sleep face down with their arms outstretched
awake feeling fatigued, as this position seems to generate a sense of losing
control. **(19)** ...., those who sleep lying straight tend to show signs   **AMUSE**
of **(20)** ...., although whether this is simply because they feel stiff in   **STUBBORN**
the morning is **(21)** ....!   **DEBATE**

Most people appear to sleep on their side with their knees drawn up, described
as 'the foetal position'. Actually, this is **(22)** .... because although the   **SURPRISE**
position is often said to denote stress, people who sleep like this awake feeling
(23) ...., having somehow worked through their problems overnight.   **FRESH**

It's unclear what it means if you are a **(24)** .... sleeper and change   **REST**
your position frequently!

Part 4

For questions **25–30**, complete the second sentence so that it has a similar meaning to the first sentence, using the word given. **Do not change the word given.** You must use between **three** and **six** words, including the word given. Here is an example **(0)**.

Example

0 The irate customer refused to speak to anyone other than the store manager.

ON

The irate customer .... to the store manager and no one else.

The gap can be filled with the words 'insisted on speaking', so you write:

Example: **0** | INSISTED ON SPEAKING |

---

25 I was just about to call you to tell you about the rearranged meeting.
POINT
I was .... you to tell you about the rearranged meeting.

26 My sister was totally shocked when she won the lottery.
CAME
Winning the lottery .... my sister.

27 Joe originally intended to drive but the bad weather caused him to change his mind.
WAS
Joe's .... drive but the bad weather caused him to change his mind.

28 It was heavy snow on the line that delayed the train.
HELD
The train would have arrived on time if it .... heavy snow on the line.

29 She realised she'd lost her keys the moment she arrived home.
SOONER
No .... she realised she'd lost her keys.

30 He clearly felt very strongly about the situation, which took me by surprise.
STRENGTH
It .... about the situation that took me by surprise.

Part 5

You are going to read a magazine article. For questions **31–36**, choose the answer (**A**, **B**, **C** or **D**) which you think fits best according to the text.

The man who wants to teach the world

Helena de Bertodano meets Salman Khan.

What Salman Khan, the founder of the non-profit online school Khan Academy has to say to the parent of an eleven-year-old in the USA is frankly terrifying: 'If your child is not placed in the fast track for math in sixth grade, his chances of becoming a doctor or an engineer are probably zero. And it's decided when he's eleven years old.'

This is exactly what happened to his cousin, Nadia. Usually a straight-A student, she had done poorly in a maths streaming test in sixth grade because she had failed to understand one concept. This one test result, Khan says, might have harmed her academic destiny. Nadia's distraught mother turned to Khan for help. Khan tutored her remotely over the phone and Nadia passed her retake with flying colours. Soon, many more relations and friends wanted Khan's help. Unable to handle the volume of requests, at the suggestion of a friend, he started to record his lessons on video and post them on YouTube. 'At first I was dismissive,' Khan says. 'I thought YouTube was for dogs on skateboards.'

Now Khan has more than 6,500 videos to his name, which have been watched on YouTube and his own website over 1.2 billion times. His friendly, avuncular style, coupled with his knack for making difficult concepts seem simple, has helped children – and adults – all over the world move into the fast track. He says his aim is to create 'the world's first free, world-class, virtual school where anyone can learn anything'. Some teachers are wary of him, thinking that he is trying to supplant them, but many more embrace his approach and have started 'flipping' the classroom, encouraging students to watch Khan's videos at home and then tackling maths problems together in class.

You might expect a man with such influence to have state-of-the-art headquarters but Khan's premises are unprepossessing. Arriving at an unmarked red door, sandwiched between a clothes shop and a Chinese restaurant, I decide I have the wrong address – especially after ringing the bell for ten minutes with no response. Eventually, I rouse someone on the telephone and the door is opened. When his assistant shows me in, Khan appears at first to be slightly annoyed at this interruption. Sitting on a leather swivel chair behind a heavy oak desk surrounded by pictures of his wife – a doctor – and their two children, he continues to work for a few minutes. But once he warms up, it becomes clear that the initial awkwardness is down to shyness, not rudeness. 'I'm not very good when people want to meet me,' he says. 'I want to hide a little bit.'

Khan believes that the rigidity of the school system is outdated and deadens a child's natural curiosity. 'Aged one to four, kids are excited by anything new, they want to figure it out, then all of a sudden, when they turn five, you start seeing fewer curious kids, by nine or ten you see very few with any curiosity, and by eighteen it's very much the exception. Curiosity is just stamped out of them. I'm convinced it's indoctrination, not a genetic thing. Kids are herded together, the bell rings, you're rewarded for passivity, you're rewarded for compliance, that's what keeps you moving through the system.'

Private school education makes little difference, he says. Nor does he believe that student–teacher ratio is an issue. 'The idea that smaller classes will magically solve the problem of students being left behind is a fallacy.' As he points out, if a teacher's main job is lecturing to the students, it doesn't really matter how many students are in the classroom. What matters is the 'student-to-valuable-human-time-with-teacher' ratio. What his videos do, Khan says, is free teachers up for more personal interaction.

He thinks bigger classes with more teachers would provide a more creative learning ground. In his ideal classroom there would be 75–100 students of widely varying ages, with three or four teachers. Some students would be working at computers; others would be learning economics through board games; others would be building robots or designing mobile apps; others would be working on art or creative writing. His dream is nothing short of revolutionary. 'In 500 years I hope people look back and say, "Imagine, kids had to learn in classrooms that were like factories and it was unheard of for an eight-year-old to truly, deeply understand quantum physics. Isn't that strange?".'

31 Why did Khan initially start to record videos?

   A It was easier to explain concepts in a video than on the phone.

   B It enabled him to advertise his services worldwide.

   C It was impossible for him to respond personally to each request for assistance.

   D It was a more popular medium for young people to use.

32 One value of the videos is that they can

   A be used as an additional tool for teachers in class.

   B be shown to students as a reward for hard work.

   C act as a substitute for formal learning.

   D help students prepare for a topic they will study.

33 When visiting Khan the writer is

   A annoyed by Khan's lateness.

   B surprised by Khan's choice of location.

   C embarrassed by the way Khan addresses him.

   D impressed by the style of furnishings in Khan's home.

34 The writer mentions different children's ages to illustrate his idea that

   A it is quite natural for children to grow disillusioned with formal education.

   B the older a child is, the less able they are to assimilate new information.

   C a child's growing lack of interest in learning is a result of experience at school.

   D younger children need more motivation to remain interested in education.

35 In Khan's opinion, the suggestion that a lower student–teacher ratio solves the problem of ineffective learning is

   A an illogical assumption.

   B as yet unproven.

   C unworkable in practice.

   D counterproductive to general opinion.

36 When Khan compares classrooms to factories in the final paragraph, he is implying that

   A classrooms produced what industry demanded.

   B children were part of an inflexible system.

   C teaching methodology produced student clones.

   D small numbers of teachers dealt with large numbers of students.

Part 6

You are going to read four reviews of an exhibition of paintings by Lowry, an English artist who was famous for painting scenes of northern industrial cities. For questions **37–40**, choose from the reviews **A–D**. The reviews may be chosen more than once.

An art exhibition by Lowry

Four reviewers comment on an exhibition of paintings by Lowry.

A

There is a painting at the start of this riveting exhibition that stays in mind and it typifies the effect Lowry's work has had on our sense of what he called 'the northern industrial scene'. No other artist has painted factories and chimneys stretching far into the distance like stage sets so insistently and so recognisably. However, what belongs to Lowry's imagination and what belongs to the actual world he observed is a question that runs through this exhibition. What impresses me is that the pictures seem to show an almost purist emotional detachment, on the part of the observing artist, but this is part of their strength, as is the similarity of the scenes. Lowry has patched together elements taken from different cities so they are not narrowly specific, yet they are deeply familiar to people who grew up in these places. Their sameness is their greatest attribute.

B

A good exhibition may enhance or deepen our understanding of an artist, but very few transform our perception of an already well-known name. However, this is the most radical and exciting re-evaluation of a British artist I have ever encountered, and a thrilling display of how paint conveys ideas, time and place; the paintings show a self-contained world at once fascinating and convincing in its relation to the artist's own experiences. The initial impression as you walk into a room of his paintings is sameness; you have to look for difference, which is there. The curators of this exhibition have produced a display that demonstrates both why such repetition was important and how Lowry developed beyond it. The exhibition traces the evolution of Lowry's work, which he described as 'to put the industrial scene on the map, because no one had done it'. This is a modest aim for such an achievement. In these unique paintings there is darkness and light, while fictional scenes and true representation can be found side by side.

C

This is an interesting exhibition, although it has several flaws; it is not easy for the visitor to follow how the artist developed over the course of his lifetime as the exhibition is not designed in order of date. Another, in my opinion, is that too many similar paintings are grouped together. We know that most people consider the greatness of Lowry's work to lie in his particular choice of style, topic and technique but this way of grouping simply means that we are overcome by an impression of sameness which is unfortunately repetitive and boring for the discerning visitor. To avoid this I should like to have seen more of his lesser-known portraits and late seascapes included, which are of at least similar, if not more, interest than those exhibited. The current exhibition, focusing as it does on his industrial and urban scenes, makes it appear that Lowry was the only artist painting such topics in the nineteenth century. This is untrue and the influence of those other artists can be clearly seen in Lowry's work.

D

This noteworthy exhibition is guaranteed to polarise opinions, which is why it is so important to see it for yourself. It is extraordinarily hard to catch the tone of Lowry's paintings in the gallery, however well they are shown. My sense is that this comes directly from the curious absence of feeling at the heart of Lowry's art. He painted his own small world and once he established his style, it never really changed. He repeated himself, shuffling the scenery in picture after picture just as life repeats itself, the crowds he painted going to and fro among the same dark buildings day after day. His people were faceless, with sticks for limbs, small in stature and generally remote. Movement was implied, though never achieved. Strangely, for me it is not these popular scenes but those of individuals, as well as his haunting pictures of the sea and hillsides with houses piercing the sky like broken teeth – that are his best work. However, it is his figures that most ordinary people will recognise instantly and which are a central feature of this exhibition.

Which reviewer

agrees with reviewer D about the involvement of the artist with the figures he depicts?   37 [   ]

has the same view as reviewer C about Lowry's less famous works?   38 [   ]

has a different opinion from the others about the value of going to the exhibition?   39 [   ]

shares the same opinion as reviewer A about the importance of Lowry as an artist?   40 [   ]

Part 7

You are going to read an article about the making of a popular television detective series. Six paragraphs have been removed from the article. Choose from the paragraphs **A–G** the one which fits each gap (**41–46**). There is one extra paragraph which you do not need to use.

Scott and Bailey

On Silver Street in Bury, Manchester, an old Barclays Bank building has been turned into the headquarters of the Major Incident Team of the Manchester Metropolitan Police. They don't actually exist, the Manchester Metropolitan Police, but you would never know that if you looked around the building.

41	

This rigorous authenticity is one of the things that makes *Scott and Bailey* different from other police dramas and extends further than office ephemera. This is largely down to the involvement of Di Taylor, a retired CID detective inspector and co-creator of the series. And it helped it attract an audience of 9.4 million viewers in its first year.

42	

It's clever and it's funny: Wainwright has a remarkable way of creating sprightly dialogue. The plots are convincing and the characters are credible: it's particularly good on the way women relate to each other. There is the friendship between two female detectives and the more complicated friendship between Scott and Murray, who is her contemporary and long-standing friend but also her boss.

43	

The original idea belonged to Suranne Jones and actress friend Sally Lindsay. It was given to Wainwright to write. Wainwright had met Di Taylor through a mutual friend and wanted to take the female heroes out of the regular police and put them onto the major incident team (MIT), 'which is much more interesting than burglaries and car theft'.

44	

'I find them very masculine and there's little that entertains me.' Wainwright is particularly bored with the stereotype of the lone male detective who is brilliant but troubled. 'I like to take people into dark areas but I also like to make them laugh. Di is a born detective but she has a robust personality and she's deeply human as well. And very funny. I wanted to reflect that in the series.'

45	

'When I got talking to her, the penny began to drop,' the actress says. 'The Detective Chief Inspector I play is a brilliantly shifting character, which is really good going on TV. She's imperious, funny, larky, annoying, beady, entertaining – it's very unusual to get so many flavours.'

46	

This is indicative of the feedback *Scott and Bailey* has received. Taylor says, 'I've had people phoning me whom I haven't spoken to for years – people who've been really high up on murder cases, who absolutely love it. The police all talk about it on their shifts the next day, which to me is the biggest compliment anyone could pay.'

A

Why is it so popular? Well, the thing that resonates most strongly with its actors, creators and critics is the script. Written by the acclaimed Sally Wainwright, the series concerns two female detective constables, Janet Scott (Lesley Sharp) and Rachel Bailey (Suranne Jones), their DCI, Gill Murray (Amelia Bullmore), their intriguing personal lives and quite a lot of gruesome murder.

B

The director of this episode is Morag Fullarton. He is aware of striking a balance between what is authentic and interesting and what is authentic and dull. 'Are we going to do what is procedurally correct and will be boring, or are we going to dispense with that and make it more interesting for the viewer?'

C

As well as creating multi-faceted characters like Murray, authenticity is achieved in others ways, too. For one episode they were allowed to shoot in a real prison. 'I've been refused access there before, for another programme,' the locations manager says, 'but the lady from the prison service loves *Scott and Bailey* because it's very true to life.'

D

The women are believable and sympathetic. Rachel Bailey is bright but rather chaotic, an instinctive detective who takes risks, both personally and professionally; Janet Scott is her older colleague, with two daughters, a husband she's bored with and a colleague who's in love with her. There's a lot of chat and some very serious issues discussed in the cafeteria. Alongside that are the crimes. This is television drama at its best: fresh and intriguing and very compelling.

E

Posters urging the report of domestic abuse adorn the walls of the reception area and in the detectives' office there is a scruffy, studenty atmosphere – jars of Coffee-mate on top of the fridge, Pot Noodles and a notice urging 'Brew fund due. You know who you are – pay up!' The desks are strewn with cold and flu medicine; the walls of the DCI's office are hung with framed certificates.

F

So Wainwright did just that when she created Gill Murray. When Amanda Bullmore was cast in the role, she had no idea that her character was based on a real person. She read the script and then went up to Manchester to meet Wainwright, who said, 'We're taking you out to dinner to meet Di who's been very instrumental in all this – just sit next to her and soak it all up.'

G

Talking to the CID inspector made Wainwright realise that she could write a cop show that was exciting and different. Wainwright is not a fan of most police dramas. She doesn't even like *The Wire*.

Part 8

You are going to read about four independent jewellery designers. For questions **47–56**, choose from the designers (**A–D**). The designers may be chosen more than once.

Which designer

is concerned about the sourcing of her materials?	47
is claimed to have the wrong attitude to business?	48
uses the same combination of metals and precious stones in each piece of jewellery?	49
creates designs that feature different versions of the same symbol?	50
intends her jewellery to stand the test of time?	51
designs pieces to reflect her beliefs that everything is linked by patterns?	52
uses inspirations from experiences when she was young?	53
makes jewellery that is easily attributable to her?	54
does not work exclusively on making jewellery?	55
was originally inspired by a social connection?	56

Shining lights

A Emma Franklin

'It has always been about animals,' Emma Franklin says. 'My friend's grandmother had an amazing stag brooch with huge antlers and that's where it started. Everyone has a relationship with an animal in my collection.' Franklin has focused on jewellery design since her teens and graduated from Central Saint Martins, setting up her own business immediately. Based in East London, Franklin hand-makes each necklace, bangle, ring, cufflink and pin, featuring any of fourteen animal heads, from a pig to a triceratops, as well as a shotgun. All her pieces are made in solid silver, plated in twenty-two-carat yellow gold or black rhodium, with black diamonds and freshwater pearls. Bespoke commissions, predominantly engagement rings, not all animal-related, are becoming more frequent. Franklin's robust designs are instantly recognisable, as she has discovered. 'Recently in a pub this girl was wearing one of my rings at the bar, so I introduced myself. She was completely star-struck and fetched over her dad, who had bought it for her. I had to explain that it was really me who was excited.'

B Alexandra Jefford

'My design style constantly evolves,' Alexandra Jefford says. 'But even though I try new things, I can't kick my art background. I'm really inspired by art, architecture, design, furniture design.' Jefford graduated with a degree in fine art, began designing jewellery ten years later and sold her first piece, a gold ring, on its first outing, at dinner with a friend. Her designs, produced on a project-by-project basis rather than as collections, include her signature Alphabet series for which she designed a slim font. Her recent O project interprets that letter in various typefaces. She combines jewellery design with other artistic pursuits such as sculptural welding and life drawing. Fans range from her daughter's friends to her mother's friends, although she doesn't always want to sell. 'I become emotionally involved with all my pieces, so I find it really hard to let go. There are still some pieces that I hide "for the family museum". My husband says that I work as a shopper rather than a seller.'

C Hattie Rickards

Hattie Rickards' first collection of twelve rings, entitled *Revealed*, was an instant success after its November launch. Her second, *Geo*, came out to even greater acclaim. 'The ethos behind *Geo* is connection and relationships, bringing tessellating or geometrical shapes together making one, for example, the *Kindred* ring, where two puzzle pieces fit neatly together.' Hampshire-born Rickards set up on her own last year. 'I wanted to create a high-end, luxury jewellery brand with an ethical backbone, which coincided with a gap in the market.' All Hattie Rickards' jewellery is made using Fairtrade precious stones from Thailand and India and eighteen-carat, Fairtrade, fair-mined gold from Colombia. HRJ is one of the first twenty companies to become a certified user of this type of gold, many of its pieces having the premium 'ecological' label. There are no plans for e-commerce, as Rickards believes this detracts from the meaning behind the piece. 'I am passionate that people understand the symbolism behind my work. I don't want it to just be a ring on a website. The story is so important.'

D Mawi Keivom

Mawi Keivom is known for her architectural statement jewellery: chunky box chains with coloured pearls, spiked gold rings and brightly coloured gems.

Born in the north-east of India, forty miles from the Burmese border, into the Mahr tribe, Keivom draws her influences from a peripatetic childhood with her diplomat parents that took them to Africa, the Middle East, South-east Asia and Europe. Keivom studied fashion design in New Zealand, then, after a stint in New York, moved to London, where she met her husband, Tim Awan, and together they set up Mawi – she as the jewellery designer, he as the business brain. 'My style of jewellery is very individual and not for the faint-hearted. I have a very strong vision that translates into an industrial, graphic aesthetic offset with crystals and pearls that are a little bit feminine. I don't try to do something that is for the moment. My pieces are classics in their own right, not trend-specific.'

Writing

Part 1

You **must** answer this question. Write your answer in **220–260** words in an appropriate style.

1   Your class has had a presentation from several visiting speakers about how people should be encouraged to improve their general health and fitness. You have made the notes below.

Ways of encouraging people's general health and fitness
- government regulation
- media campaigns
- increased sports facilities

Some opinions expressed during the presentation by the speaker
'People should take responsibility for their own health and fitness.'
'People take more notice of what they see on television than what they are told by teachers or politicians.'
'People don't do sport because the facilities are few and far between.'

Write an essay for your tutor discussing **two** of the ideas in your notes. You should **explain which way you think is most effective** for encouraging people in general, **giving reasons** to support your opinion.

You may, if you wish, make use of the opinions expressed during the presentation but you should use your own words as far as possible.

Part 2

Write an answer to **one** of the questions **2–4** in this part. Write your answer in **220–260** words in an appropriate style on the separate answer sheet.

---

2   You read this notice at your local sports and leisure centre.

> The council is planning to close the centre for several months to carry out repairs. It also intends to make improvements to the facilities and services it offers. The director of the centre would like you to send a proposal outlining where you think improvements can be made to the facilities and the services.

Write your **proposal**.

3   Your company has sent you on a-six month exchange to work in a branch in a different country. You have been asked to write a report on the exchange for your manager. You should say what differences there were in the work routine and work place, what you learnt from the experience and whether you would recommend the exchange for other employees.

Write your **report**.

4   You see the announcement below on an international student website.

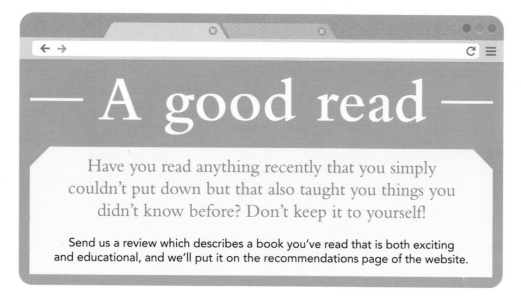

— A good read —

Have you read anything recently that you simply couldn't put down but that also taught you things you didn't know before? Don't keep it to yourself!

Send us a review which describes a book you've read that is both exciting and educational, and we'll put it on the recommendations page of the website.

Write your **review**.

Listening

Part 1

▶ 23 You will hear three different extracts. For questions **1–6**, choose the answer (**A**, **B** or **C**) which fits best according to what you hear. There are two questions for each extract.

Extract One

You hear two university students talking about stories.

1   How does the man feel about stories in today's world?

    A   He is afraid people find them confusing if they can't concentrate.

    B   He is concerned that people don't concentrate enough nowadays to read them.

    C   He is worried about the effect on people's concentration of not reading them.

2   What do they both think about stories?

    A   Longer stories are better for developing characters.

    B   People find longer stories more interesting than shorter ones.

    C   It's a pity that people are not interested in complex stories.

Extract Two

You hear part of a radio programme in which two people are talking about computer games.

3   What is the woman's attitude towards computer games?

    A   She dislikes their lack of social interaction.

    B   She is concerned about their complexity.

    C   She regrets their increasing popularity.

4   What do the speakers agree about?

    A   There is a renewed interest in board games of the past.

    B   Computer games reflect the demands of modern society.

    C   It is important for people to play games they can learn from.

Extract Three

You hear two archaeologists talking about the role of technology in preserving the past.

5   What is the woman doing?

    A   justifying the way technology has developed over time

    B   complaining about the complexities of current technology

    C   correcting a widely held view about technology

6   What do both speakers think about preserving the past?

    A   It is harder to pass on information about the present than it was in the past.

    B   The effect history can have on the future is hard to determine.

    C   Facts about the past are becoming harder to identify.

Part 2

▶ 24 You will hear a woman called Carol Street giving a presentation about how she made a huge lifestyle change. For questions **7–14**, complete the sentences with a word or short phrase.

A NEW LIFE AS A ZOOKEEPER

When Carol chose her first job, it was the feeling of **(7)** .... that she wanted most from it.

Carol's biggest dislike was becoming a **(8)** .... after starting her first job.

Carol thinks that the birthday present that changed her life was given to her as a **(9)** .... by a friend.

Carol uses the word **(10)** .... to describe how she felt about the job of a zookeeper.

Carol thinks that it was her **(11)** .... that got her the job as a zookeeper.

What upsets Carol in her job is being accused of having **(12)** .... animals.

Carol gets a sense of security from understanding the changing **(13)** .... of the animals.

In her job, Carol is careful not to be too kind to the **(14)** ...., even though she'd like to.

Part 3

▶ 25 You will hear an interview with a man called Jim Horton and a woman called Jenny Simmons, who both work as voice actors. For questions **15–20**, choose the answer (**A, B, C** or **D**) which fits best according to what you hear.

15 What does Jim say about working as a voice actor?

    A   He resents the time it takes from his private life.

    B   He gets bored by some of the work.

    C   He finds the range of work too demanding.

    D   He dislikes the commercial side of the work.

16 Jenny says that the hardest thing for her about becoming a voice actor was

    A   dealing with technology.

    B   reading a script clearly.

    C   having a short rehearsal time.

    D   working in a recording studio.

17 When he's working on a new project, Jim finds it

    A   helpful to work with the director.

    B   stressful to find the right tone of voice.

    C   easy when he has performed a similar role before.

    D   exciting when the role is something new for him.

18 What do both Jenny and Jim agree about portraying a character?

    A   It involves a different approach each time.

    B   It should be as real as possible.

    C   It requires a team of people to help.

    D   It can be upsetting sometimes.

19 What does Jim say about working on video games compared with films?

    A   The pay is not as good.

    B   They're harder because of the schedule.

    C   The scripts are more difficult to read.

    D   They're more demanding on the actor's voice.

20 What advice would both Jenny and Jim give to would-be voice actors?

    A   Develop good general acting techniques.

    B   Go to as many auditions as possible.

    C   Employ a good agent.

    D   Keep trying even when it's hard.

Part 4

▶ 26 You will hear five short extracts in which people are talking about an adventure competition they took part in. **While you listen, you must complete both tasks.**

TASK ONE

For questions **21–25**, choose from the list (**A–H**) the reason why each speaker chose to take part in the competition.

A   a long-held ambition

B   a friend's recommendation   Speaker 1 [ ] 21

C   the location of the competition   Speaker 2 [ ] 22

D   the desire to overcome a fear   Speaker 3 [ ] 23

E   the need to get fitter   Speaker 4 [ ] 24

F   the extension of a hobby   Speaker 5 [ ] 25

G   the prize on offer

H   a dissatisfaction with life

TASK TWO

For questions **26–30**, choose from the list (**A–H**) what each speaker enjoyed most about taking part in the competition.

A   establishing new friendships

B   having time away from work   Speaker 1 [ ] 26

C   discovering an aspect of their personality   Speaker 2 [ ] 27

D   developing a new skill   Speaker 3 [ ] 28

E   spending time with old friends   Speaker 4 [ ] 29

F   being able to accept their limitations   Speaker 5 [ ] 30

G   finding an unexpected interest

H   making family feel proud

Speaking

Part 1

The Interlocutor will ask you and the other candidate some questions about yourselves.

▶ 27 Listen to the recording and answer the questions. Pause the recording after each bleep and give your answer.

Part 2

The Interlocutor will give you and the other candidate three different pictures and ask you to talk on your own about two of your pictures for about a minute. You will also have to answer a question about your partner's pictures.

▶ 28 Listen to the recording and answer the questions. When you hear two bleeps, pause the recording for a minute and answer the question. Then start the recording again. When you hear one bleep, pause the recording for thirty seconds and answer the question.

Candidate A

- Why might the people have chosen to study in these places?
- What difficulties might they have?

Candidate B

- Why might the people have chosen to enter these competitions?
- How difficult might it be to prepare for them?

Part 3

The Interlocutor will ask you and the other candidate to discuss something together.

▶ 29 Look at the task and listen to the Interlocutor's instructions. When you hear the bleep, pause the recording for two minutes and discuss the task.

After two minutes, start the recording again and listen to the Interlocutor's instructions. When you hear the bleep, pause the recording for one minute and complete the task.

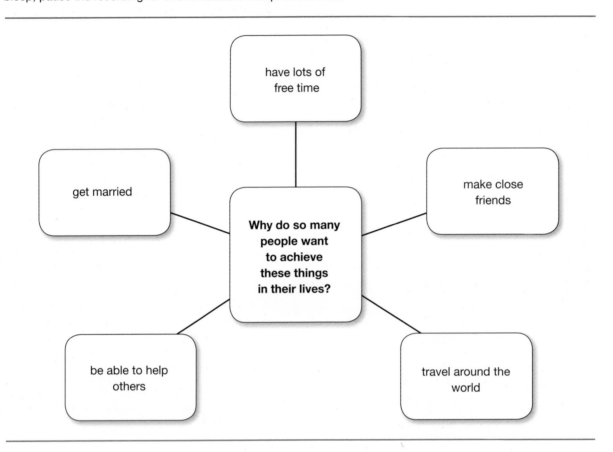

Part 4

The Interlocutor will ask you and the other candidate questions related to the topic of Part 3.

▶ 30 Listen to the recording and answer the Interlocutor's questions. Pause the recording when you hear each bleep and discuss the question with the other candidate.

Answer key

UNIT 1

Speaking

1   **1** D **2** B **3** – **4** E **5** C **6** A

Use of English

1   **1** C **2** E **3** A **4** D **5** F **6** B

2   **1** A 'breakdown' of normal values is a negative idea

2 C 'to aspire to something' means you aim for it and hope to achieve it

3 D 'a foot on the ladder' is a collocation meaning to start

4 B 'to be in a position to do something' means to be ready to do something

5 A If you can 'afford' something, then you have the money to pay for it

6 B 'suits' means it is appropriate for them

7 D 'have the space to do something' means you are given the time and freedom to do it

8 A 'a mark of success' means something that symbolises success

Grammar

1   **1** we're glad it's over **2** I'll have lived **3** it had been raining
4 I still haven't finished **5** I made **6** I've known

2 / **3**

1 Verbs of feeling: care (B), feel (B), like (S), prefer (S), want (S)

2 Verbs of knowing or thinking: believe (S), understand (S)

3 Verbs of possession: belong (S), have (B), own (S)

4 Verbs of communicating: agree (B), deny (B)

5 Verbs of sensing: feel (B), hear (B), smell (B), taste (B)

4   **1** B **2** both **3** both **4** both **5** A **6** A

5   **1** smell **2** prefers **3** am seeing **4** is arriving **5** is thinking
6 tastes

Vocabulary

1   **1** high-rise **2** run-down **3** long-standing **4** cut-price
5 sun-soaked, wind-swept **6** theatre-goer **7** drop-down
8 mass-produced

Reading

1   **2** The writer mentions the difficulties expats face and how she now enjoys and appreciates Madrid as a place to live, focusing on how she has finally come to consider it her home.

2   **1** B Yet when I hit the 'Send' button of my phone, I was caught even more profoundly by surprise. For the first time, I had referred to Madrid as my home.

2 D In the United States, not having a Social Security Number made me an outsider, causing numerous inconveniences

3 B Instead of having to gather wood for the night's fires, as I had done when hiking in the South American mountains, I could settle down and focus on my professional goals as a writer.

4 A For me, feeling at home in Madrid has been a slow progressing relationship.

5 D Unparalleled, too, is the nightlife, which will enthral flamenco lovers and clubbing addicts alike.

6 B As expats, we undergo a period of ambiguity, in which we always feel like those who have just arrived.

3   **1** B **2** D **3** E **4** F **5** A **6** C

4   **1** baggage **2** profoundly **3** enthral **4** for good **5** ambiguity
6 mere fact

Listening

1   **1** B I don't have to apologise for anything I do – that's the best. It's up to me

2 H Now I love the large number of people I count as friends but I see who I like when I choose. It's completely in my hands and that's the best thing

3 A But living alone means I can recharge my batteries, chill out, get myself ready for work – and I do have quite a stressful job

4 C Now I love coming home and being greeted by silence – I can always fill it with music or radio programmes if I need to.

5 F I actually like my own company – it gives me time to sort out my thoughts, get things into perspective. It's easier to do that when you're alone.

6 D I've never bothered because the nearest takeaway is at the end of a phone – though I'm sure that's not good for me physically or financially!

7 B although there are countless options open to me, it can be a bit mundane at times and then I have to do something about it

8 H Of course, there can be downsides – paying all the bills on my own isn't always easy

9 G I guess I do miss having someone to chat over problems with, suggest what to do

10 C There are loads of different forms of technology that enable me to keep in constant contact with others, though it'd be good to have someone to sort it out for me when it goes wrong! I'm no good at that sort of thing!

Vocabulary

1   **2** standing **room** only

3 I love cities with lots of open **space** in them.

6 there was **room** for improvement

Grammar

1   **1** They're looking for a place to live, but as yet they haven't found it.

2 Telling people to recycle everything doesn't work, nor does making laws.

3 People in the city use public transport whereas people in the countryside don't.

4 Planning cities carefully has a positive effect on the future, as does saving energy.

5 As the local council can't solve the parking problem, residents will have to do it.

6 No one will stop using cars as long as public transport is so unreliable.

Writing

1 Plan 2

2 **1** issue **2** otherwise **3** currently
4 relatively **5** obstacle **6** encroach

UNIT 2

Speaking

1 **1** pretty sure **2** my opinion **3** guess **4** think it goes without
5 mean to imply **6** far as I'm concerned

Grammar

1 **1** went, hadn't seen **2** left, didn't speak
3 I've been working on **4** had, changed, left **5** was born
6 had read, sent **7** had already decided
8 arrived, was talking, were saying **9** turned, left
10 had booked, checked out

2 **1** was born, moved **2** had never met, went
3 had planned/was planning, was booking, called
4 (have) found **5** turned up, was thinking
6 had been working, lost **7** took **8** had known, couldn't help

Listening

1 **1** A M: This one was different. I'd not had high expectations – I'd
heard speakers could be anything from top-rate to mediocre but,
in fact, I wasn't disappointed.

2 C M: I thought some of the innovative software being
promoted looked cool. I've collected loads of brochures to look at.
F: … though there were a couple of things that I'll take away
with me to try

3 C I fully realise people want to communicate quickly and
succinctly but it's all pretty shallow and creates a false intimacy.

4 A M: They really appreciated the chance to interact personally.
F: If you can see body language and facial expressions, you can
interpret tone, which avoids misunderstandings and creates
deeper relationships.

5 C Then we can make a real difference and it bothers me that
people don't get that.

6 B M: it's important to enjoy working with colleagues – that's
crucial cos we can't do it alone.
F: It's impossible to do it alone – you must be involved with other
professionals in the whole process so the outcome for the patient
is as good as it can be.

Reading

1 3

2 **1** C *as they passed* refers to the whales swimming by Charlotte
2 A *this research* refers back to *two years discovering the
sophisticated ways*
3 D *a different adjective* refers back to *amazing* (how Charlotte
describes an experience that might not be enjoyed by squeamish
people)
4 G *such 'reading' of their language* – refers back to how
Charlotte understood what the wolves were communicating with
their gestures
5 B *at the other end of the zoological scale* contrasts with
elephants discussed in the previous paragraph

6 E *we see this again* – refers to use of sound signals in water
referred to in the previous paragraph/at the end of the paragraph
E the way they use sound and what it means refers forward to the
description of whale communication in the following paragraph

3 **1** A **2** C **3** E **4** G **5** H **6** D **7** B **8** F

Use of English

1 **1** unresponsive verb to adjective
2 contributions verb to plural noun
3 reputation noun to noun
4 misleading verb to negative adjective
5 unappealing verb to negative adjective
6 desirable verb to adjective
7 illegal adjective to negative adjective
8 effective noun to adjective

Vocabulary

1 **1** F **2** E **3** B **4** A **5** C **6** D

2 **1** A **2** C **3** B **4** C **5** A **6** C

3 **1** soft **2** squeaky **3** deep **4** husky **5** monotonous
6 soothing

Grammar

1 / **2**
1 that/who (D) **2** who (ND) **3** who/that (D) **4** that (D)
5 who's (D) **6** when (D) **7** whose (ND) **8** which (ND)

3 **1** Something **that** I enjoy is watching chat shows on TV.
2 He studies with postgraduate students, among **whom** he
seems to excel.
3 I'm going on an IT course, **which** should be very interesting.
4 Celebrities **who/that** are often used to sell products in
advertising campaigns make a lot of money.
5 The lecturer **whose** talks are always really informative is leaving
the university.
6 The woman, **who** was rather well dressed, was talking too
loudly on her mobile.

4 D = defining   ND = non-defining
In class, (D) children who are often reluctant to discuss things
in groups say it's because the groups have been organised by
the teacher. Because of this, (ND) these lessons, which are often
unsuccessful, may not be repeated. However, (D) teachers who
involve the children in the reason for the grouping find that their
lessons are often more successful. So what is their explanation?
(D) Groups which have been organised by the children themselves
tend to be based on friendships. So what happens is that (ND)
children, who on the whole like to get on with their friends, may
find it hard to disagree with each other. They may also agree with
what their friends have said without actually thinking about it
critically. What's important is to listen to everyone in the class,
(ND) whose opinions are equally valuable. It may also be a good
idea to avoid seating children directly opposite each other, (ND)
which avoids confrontation.

Writing

1 **1** The introduction outlines the purpose of the proposal, 'to help
foreign students at our university to become more proficient in
their oral language skills'; mixing with native speakers is just a way
to do this

2 **1–5** Yes to all

3 A 4 B 2 C 3 D 1 E 5

Model answer

Introduction
In this proposal I will set out the current situation in the college, explain the need for state-of-the-art technology and make recommendations for the kind of technology that would help tutors and learners most.

Current situation
The computers available to students for self-study and research are old, slow and they often crash. Although the software needs updating, the age of the hardware means that this is not possible.

Tutors often give PowerPoint presentations in lectures, but are frequently let down if the software fails. When this happens, students do not receive the high level of teaching they should expect, which leads to frustration on the part of both tutors and students.

How new technology would help
If students were able to access the latest software on the latest computers, they would be able to do their detailed research more quickly and efficiently. This would save time, and would be more motivating. If tutors were able to use state-of-the-art interactive equipment in lectures and seminars, their lessons would be more interesting because they could access a wide range of technological tools, which would make their lectures more effective.

Recommendations
For the reasons given above, installing new computers in the study centre and providing interactive equipment in the lecture rooms would enhance the level of both teaching and learning in the college.

I strongly believe that updating the technology in the college would benefit everyone, and that buying the most up-to-date technology available would save money in the long run as it would not need replacing quickly.

USE OF ENGLISH I

Part I

1 B *subject to* plus noun
2 C you 'achieve' a price when reach the price you want to sell a house
3 C 'potential buyer' is a collocation
4 A 'secure a sale' is a collocation
5 D *Although* introduces a contrast between 'most buyers will …' and 'it is worth'
6 A 'do up' is a phrasal verb meaning *improve* or *decorate*
7 B 'room for someone to do something' means there is still the possibility for them to do something
8 D 'put your stamp' on a place means to give it your own look or make it as you like it

Part 2

9 is 10 what 11 less/other 12 instead 13 pay 14 taken 15 from 16 like

Part 3

17 historic/historical noun to adjective
18 instinctively noun to adverb
19 eruption verb to noun
20 towering noun to adjective
21 strength adjective to noun
22 unexpected verb to negative adjective
23 unpleasant verb to negative adjective
24 inescapable verb to negative adjective

Part 4

25 was John who encouraged me
26 no (more) room for anything else
27 did not miss him until
28 was dismissive of
29 had sold out by the
30 did not know who

UNIT 3
Reading

1
1 D D says: … fear that developmental psychologists like Barnes risk 'reading-in' that is … understand the world intentionally and consciously, as adults do …
(A mentions *an intriguing suggestion, based on well-documented research is that while it's* …)
2 C says: This, however, is hardly revolutionary – as most parents of teenagers are already well aware.
(D mentions *too much time confirming what parents … have long known*)
3 D D says: children are like the research and development department/adults are more like the production and marketing section (B mentions the lantern and the spotlight)
4 C C says: One issue Barnes could have addressed is the potential downside … (the others: A = covers all the theories B = thorough and well-informed D = an in-depth volume)

2 1 B 2 A 3 A 4 A 5 B 6 B 7 B 8 A

Vocabulary

1
1 infant: all the others are old
2 child: all the others refer to teenage years
3 aging: the others are positive
4 childlike: the others are all negative
5 pensioner: the others refer to adults but not the elderly

2 1 innocence 2 maturity 3 infantile 4 senility 5 youthful 6 boyish

Grammar

1
1 By the end of the week I **will have finished** this project.
2 Hurry up – the performance **is going to start/starts** in two minutes!
3 I'm sure he**'ll win** the competition.
4 I can't concentrate, so I**'ll stop** work now.
5 This time next week I**'ll be flying** to the USA.
6 Hopefully, they **will have announced** the results by lunchtime.

2
1 will have taken the comments
2 have left home by the time
3 is only a matter of time
4 are sure the broadcast will
5 won't be long before
6 I am going to do

3
1 F I get pretty angry when you leave **it** all up to me to make up after a fight!
2 B The politician made it clear that **it** was important to look after older people.
3 A Most teenagers think **it** is the older generation that doesn't understand them!
4 E I can't stand **it** when families have big arguments.

5 D I find **it** exciting when I make new friends.

6 C Don't worry if you don't get on at first; **it** will be better later.

4 **1** He made **it** obvious to everyone that he didn't like her.

2 I cannot bear ~~it~~ to see children unhappy.

3 Children owe **it** to their parents to look after them in their old age.

4 **It** was great to meet his sister last week.

5 One day **it** may be you who needs help from other people.

6 I think **it** is important for all generations to get along with each other.

5 **1** It is heartwarming to think how different generations could help each other.

2 It is so important in life to experience good relationships.

3 It can be very difficult to understand another person.

4 It can sometimes be tough to get on with siblings.

5 It is important for teenagers to have a role model.

6 It can be emotional to make up with a friend after a quarrel.

Speaking

1 **1** their studies **2** friendships **3** money

2 **2** Oh yes. When you're …; That is so true. We're under…; I agree but I think …; You mean, like, …; Exactly. For support, …; You've got a point but … ; Yeah, but

3 money and friendships

4 **1** say **2** got **3** that **4** still **5** differ **6** Let's

Use of English

1 **1** C 'leave something aside' is a phrase meaning 'ignore it for the moment'

2 D 'role' collocates with 'play'

3 C 'surround' is followed by 'yourself' when it means 'have people around you'

4 C 'sensible' is the only one that means 'practical'

5 A 'lead' is followed by 'to'

6 B 'sense of well-being' is a collocation

7 A 'achieving' is the only one that means 'gaining'

8 D 'out of reach' means 'unattainable'

Listening

1 **1** B Life coaching works on action in the present in order to facilitate a specific outcome later on. I provide support and encouragement so people can take control themselves.

2 A I've always loved helping people and have been through negative experiences myself – this job is all about both.

3 D Some big companies realise this, though I didn't expect to be working within one, which I actually often do.

4 C The basic principle of building robust and lasting relationships starts with how you feel about yourself. Self-esteem creates success and failure in everything

5 A Jon: I'd say it's more being able to use your unique talents, feel you're making a positive contribution to something larger than yourself while not thinking about what you can't do; that's pretty crucial
Clare: It's true that people are rarely able to stop unhelpful thoughts but a life coach can show them how.

6 D Jon: I feel very fortunate when I help people appreciate themselves and realise their own worth.
Clare: seeing clients build up their own self-assurance is probably the greatest feeling

Writing

1 Plan B

2 2, 3, 5

3 1, 2, 5

Model answer

Assistance for new students

Introduction

The aim of this report is to outline the main problems that new students at the college can face and to offer some recommendations as to how these problems might be addressed.

Problems

After conducting a survey of current students at the college, it became clear that many had experienced difficulties finding their way round the college buildings initially. Maps showing location of classrooms and facilities are not well positioned, and have not been updated since extensions to the college were made two years ago.

The survey results also showed that new students felt quite isolated and lonely for the first few weeks. Many didn't know any other students when they arrived and it sometimes took a long time for them to make new friends.

Another common concern was about the pressure of adapting to new teachers and teaching methods, and dealing with the amount of homework they were given. This caused a lot of stress until they became used to the new system.

Recommendations

I would therefore make the following recommendations:

- Ensure that location maps of the buildings are updated and displayed in prominent positions.
- Organise a programme of social events where new students can mix with both existing and new college students.
- Arrange for each new student to be assigned a 'buddy' – an older student who can give them advice and support during the first few weeks.
- These recommendations should help new students to feel less isolated and stressed as they enter a new learning environment, making the transition from school to college easier.

UNIT 4

Listening

1 **1** insurance policy   I also studied accountancy, not as a long-term career plan but as a kind of insurance policy

2 professional contract   After I graduated I was unprepared for how difficult a professional contract was to come by. There's so much competition within the industry

3 rewarding   What's a ballet dancer's everyday life like? It's often routine, some say mundane, but striving for perfection makes it rewarding.

4 determined   Physiotherapists deal with these issues daily, and encourage us to work hard to overcome them. One described us as 'as hard as nails', another as tough, but I prefer determined.

5 gym   Many people don't realise the hours we spend in a gym being monitored by computers

6 flexibility   I learnt early on that my problem was flexibility but improving that has been a long and painful journey.

7 acting   When I spend so much time focusing on technique it's easy to downplay acting, which is crucial for selling the story.

8 stage presence   Finally, what marks out successful dancers? It's that magical spark that some call musicality, others charisma but I think it's stage presence. I'm so lucky to be able to do it.

2
1 a second string to my bow
2 persevered
3 set them up for life
4 start on the bottom rung of the ladder
5 cut out for
6 on top form

Grammar

1
1 doing 2 to act 3 to put 4 to get over 5 to make
6 fulfilling 7 to become 8 to polish 9 feeling
10 to understand 11 to overcome 12 breaking 13 trying
14 to produce

2
1 ✓
2 It was the idea of getting a high-powered job that made me **go** to university.
3 Many people have tried **to** explain the secret of success but they fail to pin it down.
4 My parents helped me **to overcome** financial difficulties when I was trying to get my foot on the property ladder.
5 I really feel that there is nothing to prevent me from **fulfilling** my potential.
6 I have to force myself **to get** up in the mornings but once I'm up, there's no stopping me!
7 ✓
8 It's people who dare **to try** new things that inspire others to do the same.

Vocabulary

1
1 obtain 2 aim 3 beat 4 grasping 5 get 6 accept
7 bring 8 break
2
1 C 2 B 3 E 4 D 5 F 6 A

Use of English

1
1 of/about his chances of success/succeeding
2 should make you (feel) calmer/calm down
3 have a (really/very) bad memory for
4 on the grounds of
5 regret not helping
6 prevented from going away

Reading

1
2

2
1 B this knowledge does not help many of us understand ... how is it going to leave a lasting and useable legacy
2 A a science of performance, underlying principles that help unlock the question of why ...
3 C they have been given extra tuition at home
4 C it determines our motivation. To see how, consider an employee who ... 'they' in the questions refer to these employees
5 A allied with clearly identifiable pathways from shop floor to top floor
6 A damaging because ... abilities of those ranked the lowest cannot be developed ... and refers back to the first sentence 'businesses that focus on recruiting external talent/neglect the cultivation of existing personnel ...'

3
1 = fixed mindset
2 = growth mindset

4
1 ramifications 2 potential 3 ethos 4 anecdotes 5 insight
6 attainment

Grammar

1
1 should have done, must have been
2 needn't have practised, could have won
3 could have done, might have improved
4 did you have to do
5 could have, must be good
6 might not have been

Speaking

1
relationships, education
2
1 true 2 all about 3 My feeling is 4 What about
5 can mean 6 case in point
3
A 6 B 4 C 3 D 5 E 2 F 1

Writing

1
B
2
2, 8
3
Model answer

People may think that the decisions they make about the important things in life, such as which career to follow, are completely their own. However, this is not in fact true. Throughout our lives we are influenced by the actions, opinions and personalities of other people. Our hopes and dreams and even our behaviour are all influenced by the people we live with, meet or learn about.

Undoubtedly, one of the most important groups of people who influence us are family members. They are the first people we know and our parents are our role models for several years. We don't question what they tell us and we copy what they do. Often children want to have the same jobs as one of their parents or another close family member. Their opinion of us continues to matter as we grow older and we do not want to disappoint them.

Another group of people whose influence is significant is our peers. From an early age, most children want to be included in friendship groups and as a result adapt their behaviour and opinions so that they can fit in. Peer pressure is especially important during the teenage years when adolescents are establishing their own independence from the family. Many teenagers will follow their peers' habits or opinions rather than their parents.

In my opinion different types of people influence us at different stages of our lives and it is impossible to say which is the most important. For some people it will be their family while for others it will be their peers. The only definite thing is that whether we are aware of it or not, our aspirations and character development are certainly influenced by others.

USE OF ENGLISH 2

Part I

1 B 'while' leads into a contrast in the second part of the sentence
2 D 'absolute' is an opposite idea to 'relative'
3 D you 'master a skill', meaning you become good at it
4 A 'After all' follows on from the idea of the previous sentence by giving an example
5 B 'private life' is a fixed phrase

6 C 'personal space' is a collocation

7 D a collocation – 'the length = of time something lasts'

8 C 'although' is a connector leading in to the second part of the sentence

Part 2

9 on **10** although/though/while **11** something **12** not **13** have **14** under **15** making/even **16** too

Part 3

17 indisputable noun to adjective

18 rigorous noun to adjective

19 dedication verb to noun

20 endurance verb to noun

21 musicality noun to noun

22 dissimilar adjective to negative adjective

23 explosive verb to adjective

24 repetitive verb to adjective

Part 4

25 had not/never faced a bigger/such a big

26 regret not trying harder/regret not having tried harder

27 gets on my nerves when

28 to make his mark

29 to make dreams come true

30 would rather not take

UNIT 5

Use of English

1 **1** far **2** are **3** how **4** with **5** who **6** in **7** not **8** around

2 A 7 B 4 C 5 D 2 E 8 F 1

3 2

Speaking

2 **1** if **2** must **3** imagine **4** probably **5** say **6** guess **7** might **8** looks **9** suppose **10** sure

Listening

1 **1** D It seemed a logical extension of being an actor and I got hooked pretty quickly.

2 D they'd just like to see a more clearly defined career structure – and the entertainment sector doesn't give that at all. Even people who make it big aren't necessarily working all the time.

3 B I want to spread joy, take people out of themselves, and it's pretty special when I can see I'm having that kind of effect on others.

4 C The bottom line is you need to be thick-skinned and confident in what you're doing but taking constructive comments on board. Take the rough with the smooth, in other words.

5 A Janet: It's definitely higher-profile than ever but there'll be even more comedians trying to get work which will create extra pressure on us all.

Dave: It's high stakes, and understandably people get stressed. Though there may be more opportunities, it's vital to grab them with both hands because if you don't, someone else will.

6 B I don't make enough as a stand-up, which is something I have to address – I need to be realistic and bring in a regular wage for a while.

Grammar

1 **1** doing that **2** They **3** them **4** one **5** that **6** that **7** it **8** they

2 **1** I can't afford **it** **2** I expect **so** **3** Do you think **so**? **4** So **am** I! **5** Of course I **will**.

Reading

1 B

2 **1** C *took his own brother to court/caused such a rift in the family* A talks about 'willing' money to charity and D mentions 'inherited wealth' but only C discusses the consequences.

2 A *may be partly in a person's genes* D mentions inheritance but this is wealth, not biological.

3 C *use money to bribe family members* B talks about money not making people 'like or love you' and A mentions having excess 'to use on' luxuries, but neither reflect use of money for manipulation

4 D *wrong choice of word* A mentions 'fancy language' but not misinterpretation of a particular term.

5 B *We don't need surveys and scientific projects to tell us that* D mentions experts' comments but not the idea that they tell us nothing new.

6 D *you almost cry/want to punch the air* – which are physical reactions

7 A *willed the whole fortune to an animal charity* (outside the family)

8 A *my uncle/in direct contrast my uncle on my mother's side* – writer gives the example of the two uncles

9 B *maintain good health … at least pay for the treatments and care we need*, an example of how money can make life easier

10 C *Now, however, I can see what she meant* – which refers to a grandmother's saying that the writer couldn't understand when she was a child.

3 **1** hoarded **2** generous to a fault **3** the wherewithal **4** get under my skin **5** equally **6** get my head round **7** a rift **8** relative (to)

Grammar

1 **1** owned **2** gave/would give **3** started **4** had gone **5** hadn't got **6** could improve **7** didn't play **8** left

2 **1** is high time you made **2** wish I hadn't changed **3** only I had spoken more **4** would prefer to get up **5** would rather make all **6** wish I had chosen a

Vocabulary

1 **1** misbehaving **2** misfortune **3** misunderstood **4** mistrust **5** misleads **6** misinterpret **7** misprints **8** misgivings

2 **1** Happily **2** Oddly enough **3** Hopefully **4** Understandably **5** Unfortunately **6** Sadly

Writing

1 **1** C **2** E **3** B **4** A **5** D

2 **1** He starts with an interesting short sentence to make us read further.

2 He mentions 'slapstick' humour, which he doesn't usually like, but implies that in spite of this, it's good – thereby emphasising the quality of the series.

3 the writer, the date, the situation, the actors, the channel and viewing time

4 depressed, fed up, unlikely, slapstick, different, glad, aristocratic, eccentric, wonderful, minor, forgetful, lovable, talented, sharp-voiced, witty, superb, amusing, mild, bygone, best, worst, excellent, refreshing, innocent, funny, gloomy

5 By citing his own example and suggesting it will raise a smile. He also uses strong recommendations
(*I can thoroughly recommend …; You won't regret it.*)

UNIT 6

Use of English

1 **1** accuracy **2** portrayal **3** speculation **4** exhibit **5** injuries **6** identification

2 **1** controversial noun to adjective

2 immortalised adjective to verb

3 debatable noun to adjective

4 indisputable noun to adjective

5 remains verb to plural noun

6 analysis verb to noun

7 descendants verb to plural noun

8 conclusive verb to adjective

Listening

1 **1** B M: they feel they have a responsibility to store it for future generations. And we all go to marvel at it in museums and galleries, so there's a point to it.

2 A M: It may be we feel these things somehow define us, but no-one else does. They mean nothing to other people.

F: I reckon that each generation has its own priorities and they just don't fancy being coerced into keeping things that mean nothing to them.

3 A F: Of course, society would lose something if they weren't available but to be honest, they're a minority interest and therefore a luxury we can ill afford …

People need to be trained to set them up and the payback isn't sufficient. If you think about it, technology's taken over – and it's more cost-effective than maintaining a stuffy old building!

4 C M: Students love them because they get a practical slant on subjects that otherwise they'd only read about. That advantage of museums shouldn't be underestimated or undervalued.

F: Be that as it may, it all comes at a cost and priorities are different nowadays. Museums may be important for those keen on history or anyone with a particular interest in a particular thing – like railways or dolls houses.

5 C that was a bit of a slog! The story was so slow it almost stopped – it seemed to go on forever!

6 B F: I reckon most of it was fabricated; certainly, there were characters invented just to up the tension. That seems a cop-out – and worse than that, it's feeding false information to people who see it without knowing anything about what actually happened.

M: It's a film, not a history lesson – that seems a valid thing to do.

Grammar

1 **1** far more **2** like **3** as **4** By far **5** far, much **6** quite **7** much less **8** most

Speaking

1 1, 2, 4, 5, 6

2 3, 7

Reading

1 3

2 **1** D a harmless eccentricity shared by middle-aged men nesting in garages and sheds across the land.

2 C Watching the moving documentary *My Hoarder Mum and Me* put my father's relatively benign symptoms into context

3 A Any Freudian analysts watching will have been scribbling in their notebooks when Jasmine told us she now presents a TV property series that helps people to find their ideal homes.

4 C In need of professional help, Jasmine consulted a Dr Mataix-Cols, who told her hoarding was considered a form of OCD but did not get the attention and research grants it deserved

5 C But she was touchingly appreciative of what Jasmine had done for her and vowed to continue their house-clearing project.

6 B my father likes to squeeze every drop of value from everything he owns

3 **1** mouldy **2** benign **3** impassable **4** dispiriting **5** unperturbed **6** ephemeral **7** incensed **8** potty

4 **1** mouldy **2** impassable **3** incensed **4** ephemeral **5** unperturbed **6** potty

5 **1** B **2** A **3** A

Vocabulary

1 **1** trip **2** tree **3** sector **4** runaway **5** social **6** roots

2 **1** incredible **2** impractical **3** irresponsible **4** unrealistic

3 **1** are forgivable **2** has been/is (very) productive **3** is (very) imaginative **4** (very) changeable **5** variable **6** very/easily accessible

Grammar

1 **1** F **2** B/E **3** A/C/F **4** B/E **5** D **6** A/D

2 **1** A **2** C **3** B **4** A **5** C **6** B **7** A **8** C **9** B **10** A

Writing

1 3

2 **1** well-known **2** claimed **3** considered **4** believe **5** common **6** undeniably **7** generally

USE OF ENGLISH 3

Part 1

1 B 'turned down' is a phrasal verb meaning 'rejected'

2 D 'a niche market' is a collocation meaning 'a specialised area of the market'

3 B 'come into partnership' is a collocation meaning 'to work together'

4 D 'opt' is followed by 'for'

5 A 'totally' is a quantifier meaning 'completely'

6 C 'coping with' is a phrasal verb meaning 'managing'

7 A 'turn your back on something' is a collocation meaning 'move away from'

8 C 'calling the shots' is an expression meaning 'to be in charge'

Part 2

9 it **10** makes **11** is **12** not **13** what **14** as **15** myself **16** for

Part 3

17 unwilling   noun to adjective

18 imaginary   verb to adjective

19 unfinished   verb to adjective

20 behaviour   verb to noun

21 perfectionists   adjective to plural noun

22 insignificant   verb to negative adjective

23 complications   verb to plural noun

24 inconvenience   adjective to negative noun

Part 4

25 wish they didn't have

26 discovery (that/which) the archaeologists made

27 would/might expect people to be less

28 quite impossible to imagine

29 to turn it into a profitable

30 was bitterly disappointed by

UNIT 7

Grammar

1   **1** wouldn't have bought **2** will help **3** wanted **4** go
5 are **6** would be

2   **1** hadn't bought, wouldn't feel

    2 would have contacted, were

    3 had done, would understand

    4 would be, had had

    5 hadn't bought, would be able

    6 had thought, wouldn't be working

Vocabulary

1   customer feedback   junk mail   marketing manager
online shopping   product placement   retail park

2   **1** retail **2** achieve **3** base **4** loyal **5** targets **6** campaigns

Listening

1   **1** B   when it came to finding a job, I wasn't getting anywhere. A mate said, 'You're good at marketing and selling. Why don't you try that?' So I did!

    2 B   experience in the business world is ultimately what counts. I did several internships for free when I was job hunting, and that type of experience is really helpful – it gears you up for the real world.

    3 C   When you're in a tight corner, you've only got yourself to fall back on and, surprisingly, I found that unpredictability thrilling.

    4 A   people admire your courage while having this stereotypical image of young people, which more often than not works against you. That's difficult, but the more you put yourself out there and people see what you can do …

5 D   The best feeling, though, is when my work has helped a client achieve what they want. When they do well, so do I.

6 D   Emily: You'd probably expect me to say, keep at it, but you have to believe that there's a point to it all and you're making a difference, so focus on that.

James: But your aim shouldn't be just getting rich –believe in what you're doing, make it count for something. Then it will give you more satisfaction than you can ever imagine

Use of English

1   **1** D   'up to' is an expression meaning 'it's the responsibility of …'

    2 B   'make a fortune' is a collocation

    3 A   'marketing campaign' is a collocation

    4 C   'word of mouth' is an expression meaning 'personal recommendation'

    5 D   a new product is 'launched' onto the market

    6 D   'a response' from the market

    7 B   'sales pitch' is a phrase meaning 'the advertising the company puts out'

    8 D   if something 'carries weight with somebody', it has a strong influence on them

Vocabulary

1   **1** sour **2** mouldy **3** bald **4** viral **5** bankrupt **6** downhill
7 mad **8** deaf

Reading

1   3

2   **1** G   *it* in *it could have been saved* refers back to the business that closed

    2 C   *That was the year I was* refers back to 2011

    3 A   *these changing attitudes* refers to 'social issues and changes'

    4 E   *digital plays an everyday important and continuing part* refers back to 'we cannot ignore the Internet'

    5 D   *a new breed is moving in. One who puts their values at the heart of what they do. And then wrap it up in a Positive Experience* links with the examples of Uniqlo and the garment repair service

    6 B   *These are brands catering to shoppers who want things to feed their souls as well as make them feel good* links with 'we should be building the same model for smaller businesses'

3   **1** king **2** tap **3** comes **4** incentives **5** knock-on
6 beneficial

4   **1** garment **2** creed **3** overload **4** crave **5** eyesore
6 reinvigorating **7** visionary

Speaking

1   3, 4, 6

2   **1** more (poor self-image)

    2 argue (unhealthy eating habits)

    3 afraid, agree (increased materialistic attitudes in children)

    4 Surely, Yes/Indeed (people getting into debt)

Grammar

1   **1** Unless **2** Had I known **3** otherwise **4** provided that
5 Should **6** Were I to **7** even if **8** Supposing

Writing

1 A 7 B 6 C 5 D 3 E 1 F 2

2 1 While **2** expressed **3** seem **4** apparent
5 Notwithstanding **6** reflected

UNIT 8

Listening

1 1 E 2 D 3 H 4 J 5 C 6 I 7 F 8 A 9 G 10 B

2 1 Australia It started by chance. I'd been on several short family holidays to Europe, America, Africa; then after college I took any job I could to save money for a few days in Singapore, followed by a six-month trek around Australia on my own – just for fun, but it got me hooked.

2 narrow-minded – I hated being what tour companies describe as 'protected' or 'sheltered' but I feel is 'narrow-minded'

3 immature It sounded ideal and at the time I was excited by the concept, but I was probably immature.

4 articles Rather than diving in at the deep end by writing books, I decided articles would be the simplest way in

5 salary The biggest downside is there's no salary, plus you often have to pay for expenses up front and it can be months before a book's published and you get any royalties.

6 observations Editors are swamped with stuff sent on spec by those hoping to pass on their own unique observations

7 (successful) communication That's where your skill comes in – ultimately, successful communication far outweighs your enthusiasm for travel or anything else.

8 feedback Develop your own style and, primarily, never ignore feedback wherever it comes from.

Grammar

1 1 ✓

2 He asked whether he **could** get a flight before he booked the holiday.

3 Jack said he **wouldn't** consider flying if he were able to avoid it.

4 It's reported that there **has** been an avalanche in the mountains.

5 ✓

6 My sister is always saying that you **can't** change what people think about a place.

7 He asked me **if/whether** I could help him with his homework.

8 The police officer asked why **I had** not parked in the car park instead of the road.

2 1 don't forget to book tickets in advance for the theme park, otherwise you'll have

2 you stay in this hotel, you won't regret

3 have never stayed in a worse hotel; you should

4 taking the boat along the coast because the views are

5 if/whether anyone has stayed at a campsite in the area they can

6 any of you know

7 it be possible

8 must go

Use of English

1 1 irresistible — verb to adjective
2 awareness — adjective to noun
3 impression — verb to noun
4 reactions — verb to plural noun
5 establishment — verb to noun
6 intensely — adjective to adverb
7 misleading — verb to negative adjective
8 authenticity — adjective to noun

2 1 T 2 F 3 T

Speaking

1 The candidate does not compare the two pictures by using linkers. He describes them both separately.

2 1 probability **2** surprised **3** length **4** sure **5** might
6 imagine **7** because **8** means **9** particularly **10** whether

3 B – the candidate gives reasons for their opinion

Reading

1 1 B Ultimately, however, voluntourism establishes important access routes to money and aid for communities in desperate need. These connections could be impossible to make without the presence of volunteers. (others point out that volontourism benefits the people doing it rather than the community/country itself)

2 C they should be encouraged to see it as more of an educational experience and focus on what they can learn from it (A: but what is actually more valuable for them is the way the experience of listening to and learning from other cultures can bring about wider changes in the way they view things)

3 C Many who react negatively have not grasped the fact that their expectations were unrealistic. They have not understood that in the end, volunteering is as much about what they can learn and share as what they can change. (D: what any idealistic volunteer dreams they can achieve during their trip, which is usually far beyond what is possible)

4 A Some are arguably better run than so-called developed countries and, consequently, the view that help is a one-way gift is old-fashioned. (D: Of course, this type of 'reverse innovation' is not what was imagined years ago but it is a sign of shifting times and changing attitudes)

Vocabulary

1 1 C 2 E 3 A 4 F 5 G 6 B 7 H 8 D

2 1 reached a peak
2 has grown substantially
3 has been a steep fall in
4 has remained stable
5 was a brief dip in
6 this/the trend has been reversed

Grammar

1 1 not going to/not having gone to
2 (that) he wanted
3 (that) it was
4 buying
5 (that) he was giving

6 to people smoking
7 to meet
8 to attend

2 **1** Charlie's father encouraged him to travel to Australia.
2 John accused Sue of taking his pen.
3 Jan's mother warned her not to forget (to take) her passport.
4 She persuaded me to take the trip – so I did.
5 The politician objected to Mr Johnson's insinuation.
6 She claimed (that) Norway was the most beautiful country in the world.

Writing

1 3

2 **1** aim **2** outline **3** While **4** overall **5** well **6** addition **7** also **8** confident

3 **1** additional **2** comprehensive **3** present **4** current **5** assemble **6** engage **7** supply **8** outlined

USE OF ENGLISH 4

Part 1

1 D 'engage' is followed by the dependent preposition 'with'. The others don't have the same meaning.

2 A 'implying' means suggesting something without actually saying it. The others have the wrong meaning.

3 C 'volume' means the number of tourists. The others have the wrong meaning.

4 B a collocation meaning to make a place financially better

5 A 'ebb and flow' is a fixed phrase meaning 'constant movement'

6 C All the words are linkers, but only 'Ironically' has the right meaning here.

7 B 'hanker after' is a phrasal verb meaning 'want'

8 D 'shun' means 'avoid' in this context. The others have a different meaning.

Part 2

9 which **10** sense **11** what **12** otherwise/or **13** in
14 While/Although/Though **15** on **16** for

Part 3

17 Unsurprisingly   verb to negative adverb
18 unlikely   verb to negative adverb
19 leisurely   noun to adjective
20 unexpectedly   verb to negative adverb
21 approval   verb to noun
22 stability   adjective to noun
23 uprooting   noun to verb
24 worthwhile   noun to adjective

Part 4

25 is likely/expected to remain stable
26 recommended (that) Joe should seriously reconsider
27 however well you think
28 after having told everyone (that)
29 doesn't matter how hard
30 don't mind seeing whatever

UNIT 9

Use of English

1 **1** whether completes the phrases 'whether or not'
2 going part of a phrasal verb
3 make a collocation – make sense of …
4 is verb
5 There introducing the topic
6 it phrase – 'it appears that'
7 between dependent preposition
8 away phrasal verb

2 3

Vocabulary

1 **1** mind **2** brain **3** brain **4** mind **5** brain **6** brain

2 **1** F **2** E **3** C **4** B **5** A **6** D

Grammar

1 **1** was going to finish
2 would be/was going to be
3 would have cancelled
4 was going to snow/would snow
5 would get

Speaking

2 **2** yes **3** simulator

3 What's it called? Sorry, it's gone. I can't remember the exact word. What's the word? No, that's not the word I'm looking for.

Reading

1 **1** a book about the internet and the mind
2 the author of *The Shallows*
3 a doctor who specialises in ageing and the brain
4 It retrains our neural pathways – we don't think so deeply/we don't communicate face to face well now.
5 It can teach us to pay greater attention to things/online roleplaying.

2 **1** G *But then there is the downside.* This contrasts with 'the benefits' in the previous paragraph.

2 B *'The Shallows' is a book by* – refers back to 'a hotly controversial book' in the previous paragraph and 'rewiring of neural pathways' refers back to 'altering the very structure of our brain'

3 A 'since then' In *We have moved a long way since then* refers back to the 'age of the book' and the sentence *But here is the really important thing. Carr writes*: Implies that this Is one of the last references to what he has written.

4 D *This is because* in the phrase 'This is because the brain is very sensitive to any kind of stimulation' refers back to *even an old brain being malleable* in the previous paragraph.

5 F *a more convincing antidote to Carr's thesis* in 'I get a more convincing antidote to the Carr thesis from Professor Andrew Burn' refers back to the 'stopping the malign effect' mentioned in the previous paragraph.

6 C *team mates/mechanics of the game* refer back to 'immersion and engagement' and 'second life' in the previous paragraph.

3 **1** malign **2** pertaining **3** malleable **4** antidote **5** relentless **6** fleeting **7** cursory

4 **1** relentless **2** fleeting **3** malign **4** antidote **5** pertaining **6** cursory

Listening

1 **1** B I'm involved in management training and I had a feeling that this would supplement my reading in that area and enhance my professional life

2 D I probably wouldn't bother if it weren't part of my psychology module, though

3 C It wasn't on my university reading list nor had my tutor mentioned it but I came across a second-hand copy when I was browsing with a friend in a shop – it was cheap and on the flip test it looked worth reading, so I thought I'd give it a go.

4 F I studied psychology many years ago and when I saw a positive review about this book saying it was worth reading, I decided to buy it.

5 G I actually bought this for my student girlfriend but we'd been going through a bad patch and I wanted to share some of her interests to build bridges

6 D It opens your eyes to different ways of looking at things, which can't be bad for people like me.

7 C I hadn't expected it but it's actually pretty accessible. There's a balance of technical information and fascinating details, and it's fairly readable. That kind of thing's unusual in a science book but it brings it all to life.

8 F It gave me the impetus to track down other psychology books, which is why I reckon other people should try it.

9 G I was surprised to discover just how far the field has changed and progressed in recent years and this should guarantee its appeal to ex-students like me, perhaps less to the uninformed reader with only a superficial interest.

10 H Its main selling point is there's not too much jargon, which can be mind-bending and put people off. It's also related to everyday life.

Grammar

1 **1** correct

2 I was thinking of writing to my tutor to ask for some help but I don't think I **will**.

3 correct

4 He **was** going to mention his memory problem but he didn't want to worry her.

5 I'm disappointed that she remembered I was coming to visit – it was supposed to **be** a surprise!

6 He was going to leave the institute but **was** given an unexpected research opportunity instead.

2 **1** I was going to write to you but I didn't have time.

2 I was thinking of doing some more work tonight if you hadn't called round.

3 The government was planning to fund more research into brain injuries.

4 At that time it would not have been possible to tell her the truth about her condition.

Writing

1 1, 3, 4

2 **1** don't **2** tempted **3** need **4** work **5** worth **6** suggest

3 **Model answer**

Hi!

Great to hear from you. Yes, I remember you mentioning the quiz. Well done on getting on the team, and don't worry, you'll be fine! As you say, I've done a fair number of quizzes and to be honest, it's a lot easier once you're doing it than it is thinking about it. It's beforehand when you get the nerves. Try to make sure you get a good night's sleep and relax.

I think you said it's a general knowledge quiz, which will be perfect for you because you know such a lot about so many different topics. The only thing I'd suggest would be to keep up to date with current events and check out recent news reports.

Another important point is not to panic! Unless it's a speed competition, where you have to beat your opponent to answer the question more quickly, you should take your time to think. Sometimes I hear the question and immediately think that I've got no idea. However, if you give your brain some time, you'd be surprised what comes to mind!

Also, don't look at your opponents while you're trying to think – they can really put you off. Just look over their shoulder or the wall! Don't make eye contact with anyone or you might freeze. And another thought – if you get an answer wrong, don't worry about it, move on to the next question. If you're thinking about the last question, you'll miss the next!

These quizzes are supposed to be fun, so enjoy it! Good luck! I'll be thinking of you and keeping my fingers crossed. And please let me know how it goes.

Love,

Beth

UNIT 10

Reading

1 **1** F **2** T **3** T **4** T

2 **1** C But Spriggs, the black Labrador whose brown training harness I'm desperately clinging to, soon has me at ease

2 D 'It has to be a partnership when you take on a guide dog,' he explains. 'We can only get the dogs to a certain level and then the owners have to take over and they will get out of that partnership what they put in'

3 B What impressed me most was how you could give someone the smallest piece of advice, some of it not even related to dogs, that would make a huge difference to their lives

4 B 'A lot of people think they take their owners for a walk, that the owner says, "Right .../The owners are the ones in control"'

5 C trusting that a dog will guide you safely around town. For the first five minutes I am genuinely scared that my life is held in the paws of a canine

6 B when you play a key part in forging so many beautiful relationships, partnerships that lead to vastly improved lives, why would you want to work anywhere else?

Vocabulary

1 **1** suits, matched, fit, suit

2 match, match, suits

3 suits, fit, suiting

Grammar

1 **1** whoever **2** whenever **3** whatever **4** Whichever **5** However **6** whichever

2 **1** A/B **2** B **3** B **4** B **5** B

Use of English

1
1 the — definite article
2 making — collocation – 'make a mistake'
3 with — dependent preposition
4 is — verb completing the phrase – 'the question is'
5 what — relative pronoun
6 be — verb
7 back — phrasal verb
8 play — collocation – 'play a part in'

Listening

1
1 B It was a concern about taking care of the animal when we were away – we're inveterate travellers and I'd hate that to be curtailed – so it had to be something small.

2 F We're not that well-off, so I was wary of anything that might run up bills by ruining furniture or needing the vet, so tropical fish were just the thing.

3 H We came to the conclusion together that we'd find an animal that would be pretty easy-care.

4 D But the final push stemmed from some classwork they had on birds and I felt I should support them.

5 G The great outdoors has always been my big thing. I've tried to instil it in the kids – not easy! ... I thought it would encourage them to get out into the countryside – a dog needs that – but it was me that ended up doing it

6 C Predictably, though, it's me who's ended up cleaning out the hamster's cage and making sure it's fed – it's really backfired on me. Now I'm stuck with it.

7 D though it's hard to believe, up to now I haven't had any problems with the kids forgetting to clean out the tank – they seem to love it.

8 E And at least it walks itself, though the neighbours don't always like it!

9 G I feel bad about what I said because it's worked out for us

10 B It was a failure as far as my initial plan was concerned, though.

2 **1** pitfalls **2** curtailed **3** wary **4** bugbear **5** came to the conclusion **6** hassle **7** unfounded **8** justify

Grammar

1 **A** 2 **B** 3 **C** 1

2 **A** When I realised I had missed the bus, I decided to walk.

B Courses which/that specialise in teaching communication skills can be very useful.

C I was worried about arguing with my boss, which meant I didn't actually raise the issue at the meeting.

3 **1** Having applied early, I was disappointed not to get tickets.

2 Having got the hecklers to be quiet, the politician continued his speech.

3 Anyone wanting to improve their image often goes to a stylist.

4 She answered the door having put the phone down.

5 Having understood the question, I was able to give an answer.

6 Working with talented people makes for an exciting workplace.

Speaking

1 **1** point **2** well **3** entirely **4** case **5** dare
2 2, 3, 4, 5, 7, 8
3 **1** A (too short/abrupt)
2 B (misunderstanding of question)

Writing

1 **1** E **2** D **3** F **4** B **5** A **6** C

2 **Model answer**

Dear Sir or Madam,

I am writing to you to enquire about possible voluntary work for this coming summer. I understand that you find placements for students and I would like to know whether you could help me.

I am currently at university and would like to work as an English Language teacher in one of the African countries you have links with. I would not mind whether the teaching were in a village or larger town, as long as it involved helping children who otherwise might not get the chance to learn.

My first degree was in modern languages and linguistics, and I am now studying to be a teacher. As well as benefiting the children, I believe that doing some voluntary teaching would give me important experience in dealing with a range of challenges that teaching involves. As you know, the type of teaching situation I am likely to encounter here in the UK is very different to that I would experience in Africa and the wider the experience I can gain, the better.

My holidays run from the end of June to mid-September, so that would give me ten weeks' availability.

Should you be able to offer me a placement this summer, please contact me at the email address below, with details of dates and information about whether or not you contribute to travel expenses. Of course, I can supply any further information you might need, and if you need me to attend an interview, I am free most weekends.

I sincerely hope you can help me.

Yours faithfully,

Abby Mansfield

Abb1@ .....

USE OF ENGLISH 5

Part I

1 D 'make an impression on someone' is a collocation

2 B 'take note of something' is a collocation

3 C 'body language' is a phrase meaning what we learn from a person's facial expressions or movements

4 C 'even if' is a linker meaning 'although'

5 D 'come across as' is a phrasal verb meaning 'appear to be'

6 D 'based on' is a collocation

7 A if a person's appearance 'reflects' their personality it gives an accurate impression of it

8 D 'jump to conclusions' is a collocation meaning 'to make assumptions too quickly'

Part 2

9 in — preposition after 'lie'
10 without — preposition
11 such — 'such as' is used to give an example

12	which	relative pronoun
13	what	relative pronoun
14	it	used as the subject
15	so	phrase 'If so' meaning 'if this is the case'
16	with	preposition – 'partner with'

Part 3

17	significance	verb to noun
18	personal	noun to adjective
19	judgemental/judgmental	verb to adjective
20	comprehensible	verb to adjective
21	inappropriately	adjective to adverb
22	unbalanced	noun to negative adjective
23	negativity	adjective to noun
24	constructive	verb to adjective

Part 4

25 as long as people have

26 has been an unexpected breakthrough/was no expectation of a breakthrough

27 racked my brains

28 is not fit for purpose

29 although I have been looking

30 am worried about

UNIT 11

Vocabulary

1 1 embarrassing, embarrassment **2** exhilarating, exhilaration
3 amusing, amusement **4** celebration, celebratory
5 astonishing, astonishment **6** frustration, frustrating

Use of English

1 1 as/being — collocation
2 it — referent back to science fiction
3 like — introducing an example
4 an — indefinite article
5 but/yet/and — conjunction
6 their — possessive pronoun
7 without — preposition
8 out — phrasal verb

Listening

1 1 D my family drummed environmental responsibility into me but I realised that wasn't the case for many people. After I went into fashion design, I wanted to promote those values

2 B I want to make people look good but didn't realise how much of an uphill struggle it would be to achieve this while making them environmentally aware at the same time.

3 A Jason: My designs embody where I'm at in terms of the look I want and the materials I use, and they stand out. I'm always true to what I believe.
Karen: But I do have an identifiable look underlying all my designs so people know what they're getting with me.

4 A I hate waste, so I use recycled materials – it's plain common sense, not just ecologically responsible.

5 D I get a real kick from seeing my abstract concepts take shape.

6 C Karen: It's not plain sailing, and I know it'll be challenging– but this is not just happening in fashion, it's happening in other areas too.
Jason: I'd love to sell huge numbers of clothes but not at the expense of what I believe in, and that'll be tough

Grammar

1 1 The antique chair was thought to be worth thousands of pounds but it wasn't.
2 Works of art have to be authenticated by experts before they go on sale.
3 I'm not keen on being sold things by people I don't know!/I'm not keen on things being sold to me by people I don't know!
4 The new exhibits will be displayed in the museum in a specially designed area.
5 The sales catalogue will be finished/will have been finished by the end of the day.
6 The price of the entrance tickets has been reduced for families./ The price of the entrance tickets for families has been reduced.

2 1 wants to be taken seriously
2 is thought to have been done/painted
3 was (really) taken aback by
4 is thought to have made
5 what was being shown
6 are often copied by

Reading

1 1 B acting is not as spontaneous as we imagine it to be – it's really all about thinking, evaluating and planning every move beforehand/practicalities like learning the lines are actually quite mundane
Other blogs mention imagination/spontaneity/importance of practicalities/line learning, etc.

2 C Actors have to do the same thing night after night, and may lose the ability to see how well it is being done or even engage emotionally (A: actors are not necessarily the best judge of their own performance since they are too close to it)

3 B When a performance is a revelation, opening people's eyes to something new, and completely truthful in what it says about life, it lifts both audience and the actors on to a different level. (C: The audience must believe in their characters and their motivations, and for as long as they remain convinced, the actors have succeeded.)

4 D It's every actor's dream to reach an audience and help them look at something in a new way. (B: And the best part of an actor's job is to convey that and change the way people think about it)

2 1 mundane **2** aspiring **3** conveyed **4** ritual
5 by rote **6** spontaneous

Grammar

1 1 In view of **2** In spite of **3** As well as **4** Even so
5 Consequently **6** Furthermore **7** Apart from
8 In contrast

2 1 Despite **2** Clearly **3** Apart from **4** nor **5** consequently
6 As a result **7** whereas **8** Given

Speaking

1 1 denying **2** doubtful **3** convinced **4** confidence
5 question/doubt **6** doubt/question **7** hard **8** suppose

2 1 Obviously 2 strongly 3 special 4 whereas 5 certainly
6 turned 7 Conversely 8 angry 9 convinced 10 suppose

Writing

2 1 I think (used several times in A)
2 it's, aren't, I'd
3 children are taught
4 From an early age
5 I'd like to give you some examples.
6 So, how honest should we be?

3 B is better – reasons 1, 2 and 5

4 1 the introduction should just introduce the topic, not give the writer's opinion
2 although contractions can be used, it looks rather informal

Model answer

B

From an early age, most children are taught that honesty is the best policy and it can sometimes be quite refreshing to hear the honest, direct opinions of a child. However, as we grow older, our decisions about how honest we should be are influenced by many other things such as the desire to avoid hurting others unnecessarily or when considering the possible consequences of being totally honest. So, how honest should we be?

Firstly, let's consider how open we should be with our friends and family. In my opinion, it is all a question of who we are talking to and what we are talking about. Friends and family are the people I go to for advice, so I would need to be honest with them about any problems or difficulties I have. However, there are certain topics that I would probably not be open with them about, either because they would not understand or because it might hurt them unnecessarily. We have to balance the value of telling people the truth against the consequences.

Secondly, we should think about being open and honest with figures of authority. Clearly it's important to tell the truth to the police as to do otherwise could cause problems for ourselves and others. However, should we be honest to car park attendants, train guards, etc.? An interesting question!

To summarise I think each person needs to develop his own moral standards regarding honesty. Personally, I would like to think I am honest in so far as I do not cause unnecessary hurt to others but everyone is different!

UNIT 12

Listening

1 1 jokes (for radio) Like, while I was at school, I wrote stories for comics, cartoon captions and, most bizarrely, jokes for radio.
2 puzzle I get a buzz from trying to work something out – other people call it problem-solving or lateral thinking but I regard it as a puzzle.
3 glove Then I thought of this table-top game where you punch it forward not with a racquet but with a glove.
4 brand image The people at the first company were friendly and made positive comments but were worried about finance and my idea didn't really suit their brand image.
5 rejection I know some incredibly creative people who throw in the towel at the first rejection – I don't get that at all.
6 honesty I realise you need to bounce ideas off people who should provide some support and back-up, but more crucially, honesty – I'm certain that's vital if they're to be any practical use. Telling white lies isn't helpful.

7 feedback They won't necessarily give advice or make suggestions but should provide feedback on why they've turned you down; if not, request it
8 patience You must be determined but there's a difference between persistence and making a nuisance of yourself. First and foremost you need patience. If you get annoyed, they'll think it's easier to work with someone else.

Vocabulary

1 1 A study into different ways of learning was conducted.
2 It's rather hard to clarify the difference between some words.
3 A new project has been proposed to develop space travel further.
4 I have always contested the conclusions drawn by the head of department.
5 The project intended to prove the statistics were flawed but it was unsuccessful.

2 1 The students looked **into** the possibility of developing the project.
2 The results took **into** account any demographic differences.
3 Scientists carried **out** intensive checks on all the equipment.
4 ✓
5 The findings were **noted down in detail**, for further analysis.

Grammar

1 1 in order to 2 like 3 until 4 but 5 except 6 Although

2 1 did she tell
2 did he move into
3 have I known
4 must/should you change
5 had she chosen
6 had I/we finished

3 1 Hardly had she woken up when the builders arrived.
2 Never before have I seen such a beautifully designed house.
3 At no time has he told anyone why he decided to move to a different company.
4 Rarely do I see people working together so creatively.
5 No sooner had he closed the front door than he realised he'd left his key inside the flat.
6 Under no circumstances must you open the door to strangers at night!

Use of English

1 1 students find it easier to
2 prefer visiting museums to reading
3 was less informative than
4 never take back anything
5 hardly ever speak to my friend
6 is rumoured to be changing

Reading

1 1 T 2 T 3 F 4 F 5 T

2 1 G 'reply to the latter' refers back to the statement that 'the Big Bang didn't happen'
2 B 'less combative' refers back to 'getting into fights'
3 D 'all this' refers back to 'discoveries/new solar system/plans for a new telescope', etc.

4 A 'pure way of communicating' and 'wonderful thing that happens' refers back to the huge 'arenas' he gives talks in

5 C 'a trip into space himself' refers back to 'galactic travel'

6 E 'talking about family and fame' refers back to comments about his family, and 'tongue-tied' refers back to 'awkwardly'

3 1 B 2 E 3 A 4 F 5 D 6 C

4 1 spate 2 under fire 3 cotton on to 4 heard a pin drop 5 stick up 6 kowtow

Vocabulary

1 1 fact 2 opinion 3 interest 4 time 5 principle 6 pride

Speaking

1 1, 2, 3

2 1 Extract 1: C, E; Extract 2: A, B, D
2 Extract 2

Writing

1 3, 6, 7, 8

2 1 While 2 only, also 3 Apart 4 one, other 5 hear 6 see 7 Nevertheless 8 such

Model answer

Science subjects can divide opinion among students at school. Some love them and others loathe them. Those who love science obviously find doing experiments and finding out how things work fascinating whereas others find it boring and dry. However, the world needs good scientists and schools must try to motivate more students to become interested in science subjects.

One way of doing this, I believe, is to take students out of the classroom. Laboratories are useful and important places to work, but students are more likely to be interested if they see how science works in the real world. There are, for example, a lot of science shows and exhibitions these days where students can see amazing experiments and even encourage young children to take part.

Another way of interesting students in science is encouraging them to take part in the increasing number of science competitions now available. These can challenge students to work together to invent or design things with the possibility of a prize as motivation. Some people feel that competitions can create too much pressure, but as long as it's the students who choose whether to enter or not, I do not see a problem.

In my view, anything that schools can do to make science subjects come alive for the students is worth trying. Students need to realise the practical applications science has rather than be bored with theoretical information which seems to have no relevance to them. With luck, all students will soon look forward to sciences classes, not just the few.

USE OF ENGLISH 6

Part 1

1 C 'go against' something means to argue against it

2 B if something is 'the case', then it is true

3 D 'to do with' means 'connected to'

4 A 'goes some way to' is a collocation meaning 'partly'

5 D 'in turn' is a phrase that means 'alternately'

6 B 'went for' is a phrasal verb meaning 'chose'

7 A 'made' collocates with 'it difficult to'

8 C a linker – 'in contrast ' introduces the opposite idea

Part 2

9	what	used in place of 'the thing which'
10	otherwise/or	adverb
11	in	phrase – 'in someone's eyes'
12	which	relative pronoun
13	sense	phrase – 'a sense of humour'
14	While/Although/Though	linker
15	on	dependent preposition – 'based on'
16	for	fixed phrase meaning 'in my case'

Part 3

17	appearances	verb to plural noun
18	recognisably	verb to adverb
19	versatility	adjective to noun
20	believable	verb to adjective
21	ironic	noun to adjective
22	necessarily	adjective to adverb
23	uninteresting	verb to negative adjective
24	likable/likeable	verb to adjective

Part 4

25 sooner had I shouted than

26 must have been the sound

27 succeeded in finishing all

28 did was change my job

29 are not allowed in

30 on the grounds that

COMMON LANGUAGE ERRORS AT C1 ADVANCED: WRITING AND SPEAKING

1 1 Hardly **had he** finished the work than the boss arrived. (word order)

2 She lent him the book she had borrowed from **the** library the previous week. (article)

3 I wonder what **Sue might** be doing on Saturday evening. (question/word order)

4 The boss proposed we **work** overtime but we refused. (verb form)

5 People often **find** it difficult to accept criticism. (verb agreement)

6 She finished the work he **had started** the previous day. (tense)

7 He's never been **taught** to behave politely! (irregular verb)

8 It was a difficult task but **in** the end we completed it. (linking phrase/preposition)

2 1 I wanted to ask you where you buy your clothes.

2 The local **school's** results were excellent – it's the best school in the area.

3 Our **three-week** holiday turned out to be very expensive.

4 I think it's a shame that more **girls** don't play football.

5 Young people should take a more **responsible** attitude towards their studies.

6 Although it was an unfortunate **occurrence**, the punishment was necessary.

7 I received an email yesterday asking me a purely **rhetorical** question – pointless!

8 The man **whose** car is parked outside is my boss.

9 'It's a pretty difficult situation,' said my sister.

10 Can you tell me how often you get the chance to go to the cinema?

3 **1** **A:** The weather is strange for this time of year – what**'s** your view?

B: Yes, I ~~am~~ **agree** with you. It seems to be raining all the time.

A: Let's hope it improves soon!

2 **A:** I think that we should accept the new contract after all.

B: No, sorry, I **can't go along with that**. I think it's a terrible idea.

A: Well, we may not have much choice.

3 **A:** We could always change the appointment – it probably wouldn't be too difficult to rearrange my diary.

B: I hadn't thought **of** that. You're good at thinking outside the box!

A: It's called lateral thinking!

4 **A:** We need to talk about these ideas on the task sheet – what ~~do~~ **shall** we start with/where **shall** we start?

B: Let's consider ~~about~~ this idea first. I think it's an important issue.

A: Sorry, I'd rather discuss ~~about~~ this one first.

5 **A:** It's important to study hard before an exam.

B: You **make** a good point. I'll do my best!

A: Me too!

EXAM STRATEGIES: WRITING AND SPEAKING

Writing

1 **1** B **2** A **3** C

2 The candidate has forgotten 3.

3 **1** B **2** A **3** C

4 The candidate has forgotten 3.

Speaking

1 **1** C **2** B **3** A

2 The candidate has forgotten 3.

3 **1** B **2** A **3** C

4 The candidate has forgotten 1.

5 **1** B **2** C **3** A

6 The candidates have forgotten 2.

7 **1** C **2** B **3** A

8 The candidate has forgotten 1.

PRACTICE TEST

Reading and Use of English

Part 1

1 B 'put off' is a phrasal verb meaning 'deterred from'

2 D 'larger than life' is an expression

3 D 'get promotion' is a collocation

4 C 'on the surface' is a collocation meaning 'superficially'

5 A 'consequently' is a linker that is often followed by a comma

6 B to 'favour' someone means to give them an unfair advantage

7 D something 'carries weight' if it has influence

8 C 'turn down' is a phrasal verb meaning 'reject'

Part 2

9 part **10** it **11** what **12** not **13** apart
14 While/Besides **15** make **16** which

Part 3

17 clarify — adjective to verb

18 revitalised — adjective to adjective

19 Amusingly — verb to adverb

20 stubbornness — adjective to noun

21 debatable — verb/noun to adjective

22 unsurprising — noun to adjective

23 refreshed — adjective to adjective

24 restless — noun to adjective

Part 4

25 (just) on the point of calling

26 came as a total/complete shock to

27 original intention was to

28 had not been held up by

29 sooner had she arrived home than

30 was the strength of his feeling/feelings/was his strength of feeling

Part 5

31 C 'Unable to handle the volume of requests, at the suggestion of a friend, he started to record his lessons on video and post them on YouTube

32 D have started 'flipping' the classroom, encouraging students to watch Khan's videos at home and then tackling maths problems together in class.

33 B Khan's premises are unprepossessing. Arriving at an unmarked red door, sandwiched between a clothes shop and a Chinese restaurant, I decide I have the wrong address

34 C Curiosity is just stamped out of them. I'm convinced it's indoctrination, not a genetic thing.

35 A if a teacher's main job is lecturing to the students, it doesn't really matter how many students are in the classroom

36 B a more creative learning ground./Some students would be working at computers; others would be learning economics through board games; others would be building robots or designing mobile apps; others would be working on art or creative writing

Part 6

37 A 'almost purist, emotional detachment on the part of the observing artist (D: the curious absence of feeling at the heart of Lowry's work')

38 D 'those of individuals, as well as his haunting pictures of the sea and hillsides … are his best work (C: of his lesser-known portraits and late seascapes … similar, if not more interest)

39 C 'although it has several flaws, too many similar paintings grouped together, repetitive, boring, (A: riveting exhibition ; B: radical and exciting re-evaluation ; D: noteworthy, important to see it for yourself)

40 B and a thrilling display of how paint conveys ideas, time and place; the paintings show a self-contained world at once fascinating and convincing in its relation to the artist's own experiences. (A: it typifies the effect Lowry's work has had on our sense of what he called 'the northern industrial scene'./No other artist has painted factories and chimneys stretching far into the distance like stage sets so insistently and so recognisably)

Part 7

41 E 'posters urging the report of/jars of coffee mate on top of the fridge, etc.' refer back to 'you would never know it (not a real police building) if you looked round the building.'

42 A 'why is it so popular' refers back to 'attract an audience of 9.4 million viewers

43 D 'the women are believable and sympathetic. Rachel Bailey is …' refer back to 'good on the way women relate to each other'

44 G 'talking to the CID detective inspector' refers back to 'had met Di Taylor through a mutual friend'

45 F 'so Wainwright did just that when she created Gill Murray' refers back to 'I wanted to reflect that in the series (born detective/robust personality/deeply human)'

46 C 'as well as creating multi-faceted characters like Murray' refers back to 'imperious/funny/larky/annoying/beady/entertaining' and 'the lady from the prison service loves *Scott and Bailey* because it's very true to life' refers forward to 'this is indicative of the feedback …'

Part 8

47 C All Hattie Rickards' jewellery is made using Fairtrade precious stones from Thailand and India and eighteen-carat, Fairtrade, fair-mined gold from Colombia./the premium ecological label

48 B although she doesn't always want to sell./I find it really hard to let go/I work as a shopper rather than a seller

49 A All her pieces are made in solid silver, plated in twenty-two-carat yellow gold or black rhodium, with black diamonds and freshwater pearls

50 B Her recent O project interprets that letter in various typefaces.

51 D I don't try to do something that is for the moment. My pieces are classics in their own right, not trend-specific.

52 C The ethos behind Geo is connection and relationships, bringing tessellating or geometrical shapes together/I am passionate that people understand the symbolism behind my work

53 D Keivom draws her influences from a peripatetic childhood with her diplomat parents that took them to Africa

54 A Franklin's robust designs are instantly recognisable

55 B She combines jewellery design with other artistic pursuits such as sculptural welding and life drawing.

56 A My friend's grandmother had an amazing stag brooch with huge antlers and that's where it started

Writing

Model answers

Part 1

1 Many of us take our health for granted. Improved medicines and treatment mean that we are likely to live longer than our predecessors did, but this is only if we keep as fit and healthy as possible and adopt healthy lifestyles. To do this we need to exercise and eat well. However, most of us need some encouragement.

One form of encouragement comes through media campaigns that are aimed at persuading us to do healthy things such as reducing the amount of salt or sugar we eat and going to the gym. These campaigns can have a significant effect, especially if celebrities are involved. Some people are more likely to take notice of what a famous sportsperson or singer advises than their own family or even doctor.

However, when it comes to healthy eating, it can sometimes be difficult to know exactly what is in the food we buy. In my opinion, this is where the government should step in. The regulation of TV commercials has banned the advertising of certain foods in children's programmes, which is very good news. Other regulations controlling food labelling have forced food suppliers to give clearer details about what their products contain. Not everyone will want to read the labels, but at least, if they are there, those people who want to can find the information.

All in all, I believe that people should be responsible for their own health, but help from campaigns and the government is important in order to increase awareness of health issues, so that we are all able to make informed choices about how to lead healthier lives.

Part 2

2 Proposal

Introduction

The temporary closure of Eastfair Leisure Centre for essential repairs offers a good opportunity to make/implement improvements to other facilities and services. The purpose of this proposal is to outline where improvements could be made and recommend what action could be taken.

Changing rooms

The changing rooms are in desperate need of renovation. The flooring, tiling and lockers are in bad condition. Both floor and wall tiles have cracked, which creates a potential health risk. Many of the lockers are broken or without keys. The showers are unreliable and several of them actually leak.

Table tennis room

Most of the sports equipment available for the use of visitors is modern and in good repair. However, in the table tennis room some of the nets are ripped and some bats have lost their covering. Table tennis is a popular sport at the Centre and the room would benefit from additional tables.

Classes

Many visitors have requested that the Centre should offer dance classes in addition to the yoga and aerobics classes that it currently offers. Ballroom dancing has increased in popularity due to the TV reality shows featuring celebrity dancers.

Recommendations

I would suggest the following:

- The changing rooms need complete refurbishment to provide security and reduce health hazards.
- The shower facilities need repairing where necessary.
- Table tennis bats and nets need replacing. The current layout of the tables could be changed to allow an additional two tables.
- The Centre should advertise for a dance instructor to develop a programme of dance classes and allocate a room where such classes might take place.

Conclusion

The Centre is an important focal point for the community and implementing the above suggestions would ensure that the Centre is meeting local needs.

3 Report

Introduction

The aim of this report is to outline the differences in work routines and work places between our French and UK branches and to comment on the benefits of the work exchange I recently took part in.

Routine and Workplace

Our French branch has an earlier start to the working day with reduced time for lunch break. This means that the working day finishes much earlier than in the UK, 3.30 instead of 5.30, and the employees benefit from having a longer period of free time after work. Another benefit is that they avoid commuter congestion, as they are travelling outside the rush hour.

The workplace has a similar layout to the UK branch. It is mainly open plan. However, the French branch has a number of small rooms off the main office where one-to-one discussions can take place or private work can be done without distraction. This seems to work very well.

Benefits

I profited a great deal from this experience. Not only did my command of the French language improve, but I also learnt a lot from dealing directly with both French clients and colleagues. It taught me important things about certain work practices and etiquette.

Recommendation

I would definitely recommend this exchange for other employees of the UK branch. Apart from individual benefits for the employees concerned, it also fosters a good working relationship between the two branches.

It widens our experience of dealing with French clients and ultimately contributes to the smooth running of our business.

4 Review

I usually enjoy fast-moving, action-packed thrillers. Recently, however, I was given a book completely outside that genre but which, I must admit, kept me up all night. It's by the novelist Julian Barnes and is called *The Noise of Time*.

 The novel concerns the life of the Russian composer Shoshtakovitch and the difficulties experienced by artists who were living in Russia when Stalin was in power. The story of *The Noise of Time* is not sequential, but takes us backwards and forwards in time and deals with many different strands of his story. The result is an in-depth picture of the challenges – personal, artistic and political – that he had to face.

The Noise of Time is not full of action or 'exciting' in the normal sense of the word. It doesn't present mysteries for the reader to solve. However, it does have a fascinating jigsaw, crossword puzzle element in that we are initially presented with short extracts containing hints that are later picked up and developed, until we finally see the whole picture. The style is very readable, but the whole novel is so clever, carefully structured and balanced that it could almost be compared to one of Shoshtakovitch's own musical pieces.

I learnt a great deal from the book about the politics, society and literature of the period, and of course about the great composer himself. I was completely captivated by this book and would recommend it to anyone looking for a very well written, intelligent and interesting read.

Listening

Part 1

1 A only being able to concentrate for a short time is going to be pretty useless! Think about the number of characters you have to remember – and that's without the complexities of the plot!

2 B F: But longer series are great for character development – and writers seem to be moving towards longer books, too. They can really explore a character and engage readers, that's why they're on the up.
M: It's true that short stories aren't that popular. Going back to attention spans, you'd think if people really had difficulty concentrating, they'd choose to read those, not longer books, which is not actually the case.

3 A I feel strongly that even this can't replace the personal connection.

4 A F: I think board games fulfil our need for the face-to-face contact we used to have.
M: But you have to look at this surge in the popularity of board games in context. There's a big retro-trend going on now – you know, like, with clothes and even vinyl records! So it's also true that most keen digital games players are board game enthusiasts. It's niche, but significant.

5 C There's this idea that it's part of a long progression which began with the first written records on stone tablets and continued developing without a hitch to the present day's sophisticated level of storing data, whereas, in fact, it can actually be compared to the science of biology, which had ups and downs and many species along the way simply died off and never made it.

6 A F: So over the long term, things we'd like to pass on from now might actually be more difficult for future generations to access than, for example, finding out about a dead civilisation from actual relics.
M: We can certainly learn a lot about past civilisations simply by digging up clay tablets, but there's the possibility of an enormous gap in history covering the period from the rise of the internet to whenever we reach a point in the future where methods of archiving are fixed and accessible.

Part 2

7 achievement My friends defined success as owning possessions but though I kind of went along with that, it was the sense of achievement that I was aiming for.

8 commuter I also turned into a clock-watcher because the job wasn't really demanding and a commuter; that was the biggest downside as it took hours every day

9 joke I suspect that far from being thoughtful, my friend thought it would be a joke

10 worthwhile Far from boring, or mundane, it looked so worthwhile and, suddenly, my own job seemed pointless.

11 enthusiasm I had zero qualifications, no experience but loads of enthusiasm, which may have swung it for me at the interview.

12 smelly It gets to me if I hear visitors say the animals are cute but it's a shame they're smelly – I take pride in making sure that's not the case!

13 moods They're not pets and although they know me, they could still attack. I can identify a shift in their moods from their behaviour. That protects me.

14 cubs We try to make their lives as natural as possible – even though it's tempting, I never mollycoddle cubs or meddle with the way family groups interact among them

Part 3

15 B Of course, some of what I do's just to pay bills – like recording samples for automated announcements in stations. That's mundane, even though I don't actually have to record millions of different things!

16 C But the greatest challenge is adjusting to the fact that there isn't any extended practice beforehand which would let you create a character – it's all very quick.

17 D I often get offered the kind of work I've done before, which is fun, but stuff I don't normally get to do is most thrilling because it's scary

18 B F: Sometimes when I go into the recording studio, it just happens; but even then it has to have the ring of truth.
M: … as long as you're coming from your own experience and it's believable, you'll get your character across

19 D Then you have to do it in different ways and it might be followed by shouting. You certainly need throat sweets afterwards!

20 A F: The most popular route is going to drama school, studying improvisation, like me, and I can't fault that.
M: … getting the right kind of basic drama training is really the bottom line.

Part 4

21 C I subsequently looked it up on the website when a friend mentioned it in passing. The beautiful pictures got me hooked.

22 B When I got the chance to go climbing in the Dolomites, it seemed like something too good to miss – at least that's what my friend said

23 F I'm never happier than mucking around with engines – I've done that in my spare time all my life, and collected old cars – so that was probably why I agreed

24 G I have no real idea how I got involved other than the attraction of the idea that the winner got a large cheque, which was most appealing!

25 H I decided something was missing in my life – that it was too run of the mill, and others seemed to have so much more.

26 A The upside was the people who I'll stay in touch with for a long time to come.

27 D Unexpectedly, I revelled in honing the technique of climbing and I want to progress with that – a bit of a surprise, really.

28 C It was frightening at times but I found an inner determination I didn't know was there.

29 F there were some highly technical and scary ascents and descents, which I hadn't fully realised, so I dismounted for the parts where I lost my nerve. I actually found that a salutary life lesson

30 G We didn't win, but one thing I had to do was become proficient in weather forecasting – it's fascinating and has opened up a whole new aspect of life.

Audio scripts

Unit 1, Speaking, Activity 1

Track 01

1 How are you planning to spend next weekend?
2 What do you do to keep in touch with your friends?
3 Could you tell us about an interesting show or exhibition you've seen recently?
4 Is there a sport or hobby you did when you were younger that you've stopped doing?
5 Where do you like to spend your holidays?
6 What do you see yourself doing in four years' time?

Unit 1, Listening, Activity 2

Track 02

1 When I was young, I never imagined living alone. But at weekends I can lie in bed all day if I want to, read a book … no one tells me what to do. My fridge is empty because I don't need to cook. I've never bothered because the nearest takeaway is at the end of a phone – though I'm sure that's not good for me physically or financially! I don't have to apologise for anything I do – that's the best. It's up to me: I can leave my stuff all over the place and it's still there when I want it – no one asks me to move it.

2 I come from a large family, so privacy was at a premium in my early years. Now I love the large number of people I count as friends but I see who I like when I choose. It's completely in my hands and that's the best thing. Of course, although there are countless options open to me, it can be a bit mundane at times and then I have to do something about it – go out, see a film – I do have to make the effort to find entertainment. It's true that I can cook what I enjoy and although it may be selfish, the ability to make my own food choices is an unexpected bonus.

3 I don't see it as selfishness, though I know others do – it's probably more knowing what I like and doing it without thinking about the impact on anyone else. I'm not anti-social; in fact, I'd say the opposite – I have loads of mates I care about. But living alone means I can recharge my batteries, chill out, get myself ready for work – and I do have quite a stressful job. Of course, there can be downsides – paying all the bills on my own isn't always easy but at least I can play my music as loud as I like without getting told off!

4 Up to now I've always been surrounded by people and living on my own has been a bit of an eye-opener – though not in a bad way. At uni I shared a flat with six others – that was a real challenge! It was tough to cope with the constant untidiness and chatter. Now I love coming home and being greeted by silence – I can always fill it with music or radio programmes if I need to. I guess I do miss having someone to chat over problems with, suggest what to do, but I can always pick up the phone. I even quite enjoy doing the cleaning myself!

5 I actually like my own company – it gives me time to sort out my thoughts, get things into perspective. It's easier to do that when you're alone. That doesn't mean I don't like people – far from it – but it's like having small children: it's great when they go to bed and you can take it easy! I know I can rely on friends or family if I need help. There are loads of different forms of technology that enable me to keep in constant contact with others, though it'd be good to have someone to sort it out for me when it goes wrong! I'm no good at that sort of thing!

Unit 2, Speaking, Activity 1

Track 03

OK, I'm going to look at these two pictures – the one of the teacher and the one of the politician; at least I'm pretty sure he's a politician because it looks as if he's at an important press conference. Both pictures show people who need to communicate well in their jobs. In my opinion, both of them have to get across important information but for different reasons. The teacher is trying to explain something to young students in a science class who may be hearing about something for the first time, whereas the politician is talking to a whole group of experienced journalists and photographers; I guess it could be just before an election and he's trying to explain his position, or he could be just meeting the press after something important has happened and he has to brief them about this. The teacher has to communicate very well to be certain that the children understand the point of the experiment and also I think it goes without saying that he must make sure that the children are enjoying the lesson – that's really important for effective learning. In this picture they look as if they're having a good time. The politician, on the other hand, has to appear confident, convincing and persuasive. He has to convince the journalists about what he is saying. I don't mean to imply that politicians don't always tell the whole truth but as far as I'm concerned, they need to be quite good actors!

Unit 2, Listening, Activity 1

Track 04

1

A: I'd never been to anything quite like this before. Sure, there'd been lots of conferences at uni, some excellent, but they were academic. This one was different. I'd not had high expectations – I'd heard speakers could be anything from top-rate to mediocre but, in fact, I wasn't disappointed.

B: I thought the presentations generally were slick but their content was average – I'd heard it all before. I'd hoped they'd break new ground but it didn't happen. I got the impression they wanted to push their own products on us and I wasn't ready to be cajoled. And as for the exhibition stands, there were loads of them.

A: What I was surprised about was the practical nature of the whole thing. Maybe I'm naive but I thought some of the innovative software being promoted looked cool. I've collected loads of brochures to look at.

B: A lot of it certainly appeared to be timesaving but you know what technology is: once it goes wrong, it wastes more time than it saves. I may stick to the tried and tested stuff I know; though there were a couple of things that I'll take away with me to try.

2

A: People don't seem to converse directly anymore – it's all online! So, I went to a park in town with a table and four chairs. I put up a sign offering free conversation and I pinned up a list of possible conversation topics, like the weather, history, birds. It only took a few minutes for a young couple to sit down. They went for a topic of cars. We talked for twenty minutes about their impact on the environment. After they'd left, more people came and sat down, and I ended up chatting to a steady stream of strangers. They really appreciated the chance to interact personally.

B: Sounds cool – like you're doing your bit to save the endangered art of social conversation! My seminars on being a good communicator get much the same reaction. People feel deprived of genuine meaningful interaction. We used to value that but not anymore.

A: All we have now are superficial posts on Twitter. How can you express anything meaningful in 140 characters? I realise people want to communicate quickly and succinctly but it's pretty shallow and creates a false intimacy.

B: If you can see body language and facial expressions, you can interpret tone, which avoids misunderstandings and creates deeper relationships.

3

A: I feel privileged because what I do with patients changes their lives. You've seen the film *The King's Speech*, where the king learnt how to manage when he stammered badly …

B: That's what I like most – helping people, seeing them gain confidence and do well; that makes everything worthwhile. And it takes ages to qualify, so it's important to enjoy working with colleagues – that's crucial 'cos we can't do it alone.

A: That film didn't show everything we really do! It implied we only work with speech but, in fact, communication is more than making sure someone can produce all their sounds properly and it bothers me that people don't get that. Sometimes we help injured patients use non-verbal ways to get their point across. They might need help after having a physical problem like a stroke – they can talk but what they say doesn't make sense. Then we can make a real difference.

B: The key thing, I think, is to like people, be a good communicator and listener yourself – a people person.

A: It's impossible to do it alone – you must be involved with other professionals in the whole process so the outcome for the patient is as good as it can be.

Unit 3, Speaking, Activities 3 and 4

Track 05

A: Well, I don't like to say it but I think it's got to be money. When you leave school or college and start work, you can't do anything without money.

B: Yes, there's that, but maybe you're being a bit too harsh? Yes, I agree money is important but friendships are, too. Who do you go to when you haven't got a job or anywhere to live? Your friends.

A: I still think it's money. Money gives you the means to do everything: get a flat, go out with your friends, buy new clothes to keep up your image, even fund more education if you want to.

B: OK. We'll have to differ here, then. Let's say both money and friendships!

Unit 3, Listening Activity 1

Track 06

I = Interviewer   J = Jon   C = Clare

I: Today we're talking to Jon Simmons and Clare Harries, who both work as life coaches. Jon, tell us what a life coach actually does.

J: It's actually quite complex but, basically, people come to a life coach when they want to work on aspects of their life that are unsatisfying or when they feel their general quality of life isn't what they want. There may be different things bothering them – their weight, relationships, work and so on. My clients decide what they want to achieve and it's my job to make that happen – like a catalyst bringing about change. I don't regard my role as like that of a therapist, who goes into issues from the past in depth. Life coaching works on action in the present in order to facilitate a specific outcome later on. I provide support and encouragement so people can take control themselves.

I: Clare, what made you decide to become a life coach?

C: I'm fascinated by human potential – not just in terms of accomplishments, but happiness. I've always loved helping people and I've been through negative experiences myself – this job is all about both. I think sometimes people get stuck in a rut and if they have no one to talk to, they go round in circles. Friends and family may try to help but their advice is often based on their own insecurities and fears. What I particularly like is that coaching is about listening. People often know what the answer is deep down. I listen, ask questions and suggest practical action steps. It's underlying things like bad habits and limiting thoughts and behaviour that stop people achieving.

I: Are you ever surprised about why people come to a life coach?

C: People want positive change and growth. I know informal mentoring used to go on in the workplace and it often led to promotion. That was efficient but now people change jobs and careers very quickly. The knock-on effect is they've lost consistent and constructive feedback from people who know them well. Generally, society's quite fragmented – traditional means of support are breaking down, so people need to re-evaluate their aims themselves. Some big companies realise this, though I didn't expect to be working within one, which I actually often do.

I: Jon, what do you think is most important to understand about relationships?

J: Relationships are complex and affect every aspect of life. The basic principle of building robust and lasting relationships starts with how you feel about yourself. Self-esteem creates success and failure in everything. I've seen loads of people trying to live up to some sort of unrealistic self-image so they can fulfil the expectations of those around them. This creates emotional turmoil, stress and anxiety. The values you live by define who you are, what you do, so if you don't understand your own core values, you don't know yourself. A life coach helps people set goals and progress – just like a physical personal trainer.

I: What do you both think should be the core message of a life coach?

J: I wouldn't define happiness as being rich, having material possessions or being in love. I'd say it's more being able to use your unique talents, feel you're making a positive contribution to something larger than yourself while not thinking about what you can't do; that's pretty crucial and puts people on the road to feeling a high degree of happiness and fulfilment.

C: It's true that people are rarely able to stop unhelpful thoughts but a life coach can show them how. Such thoughts can become addictive and that means there's no progress or good use of people's unique talents. That's what I make them focus on; without it, they won't make progress.

I: What's the most rewarding part of your job?

J: I love working with individuals and small groups but I also get satisfaction from running larger seminars – that's when I feel I touch lots of lives. It's a given that things you appreciate in life contribute to your happiness. I feel very fortunate when I help people appreciate themselves and realise their own worth.

C: I love what I do and I've met loads of interesting people, but seeing clients build up their own self-assurance is probably the greatest feeling; and it's an unexpected bonus that I also get to see things in myself that I hadn't fully realised.

I: Thank you both.

Unit 4, Listening, Activities 1 and 2

Track 07

Hi, everyone – my name's Susie, and I'm here to talk about the life of a ballet dancer.

I started dancing as a child at a local dance academy but then was lucky enough to be selected for a vocational dance school. My parents wanted me to have a second string to my bow, so I also studied accountancy, not as a long-term career plan but as a kind of insurance policy. The training was physically draining, and I nearly gave up several times, but luckily I persevered.

Aspiring young dancers who get into a prestigious ballet school imagine that'll set them up for life, but they're wrong. After I graduated I was unprepared for how difficult a professional contract was to come by. There's so much competition within the industry – everyone wants to be a star! But as with any job, you start on the bottom rung of the ladder – in my case in the back row of the chorus – but I learnt so much there, especially self-discipline and where my strengths lay.

What's a ballet dancer's everyday life like? It's often routine, some say mundane, but in my opinion striving for perfection makes it rewarding. Every day begins with a class involving repetition of exercises to warm up the body. We practise in front of a mirror – that's not vanity, it's so we can spot any minor mistakes and correct them. It's all about getting everything exactly right, and this can cause some to overextend. At first I was shocked by the number of supports some dancers were told to wear in class, but fear of injury is always there.

Men find jumping and lifting puts strain on their feet, so they get bad ankles. When dancing en pointe, a woman's entire body weight is on her toes, potentially causing broken bones and bleeding. Physiotherapists deal with these issues daily, and encourage us to work hard to overcome them. One described us as 'hard as nails', another as tough, but I prefer 'determined'. In the past, if a dancer was injured, they'd just go away and rest. Now we're taught to do proper rehabilitation, which I appreciate.

I'm often asked whether ballet dancers are born or made, and genetics are important – not everyone is cut out for the life of a dancer. These days, though, it's all about science. Many people don't realise the hours we spend in a gym being monitored by computers. It's almost clinical. Sports scientists study our training methods. I learnt early on that my problem was flexibility, and improving that has been a long and painful journey.

In my dance company we rehearse two or three different ballets simultaneously. This means we have to be on top form all the time, but I love the variety. I might be a peasant, a queen or a swan, and I must make the audience believe in me. When I spend so much time focusing on technique it's easy to downplay acting, which is crucial for selling the story.

Finally, what marks out successful dancers? It's that magical spark that some call musicality, others charisma but I think it's stage presence. I'm so lucky to be able to do it.

Unit 4, Speaking, Activities 1 and 2

Track 08

A: OK, shall we start by looking at relationships?

B: Yeah, we know a bit about that one, don't we?

A: It's something everyone is looking for, isn't it? The perfect relationship. But it can be so hard.

B: That's very true. It's all about compatibility, really, and how prepared you are to work hard at the relationship.

A: My feeling is that a lot of relationships fail because people don't give and take. You need to accept the other person's faults as well as their good points.

B: Absolutely. What about succeeding in education? That's about hard work, too. You have to be disciplined and focus on your exams and stuff. Sometimes people don't balance their academic studies and social life very well, and that can mean you don't concentrate enough on your work.

A: You mean, like too many parties? Also, you have to have the right approach and the right abilities. Some people want to get a degree but they're just not cut out for that type of studying.

B: I completely agree with you. A case in point is my brother; he thought he'd like to be a teacher but when it came to writing the assignments and developing lesson plans and so on, he realised it was beyond him. He's a successful businessman now!

Unit 5, Speaking, Activities 1 and 2

Track 09

I'd like to talk about these two pictures. In my opinion the people in both pictures are experiencing a feel-good moment. It's special for all of them but, obviously, for different reasons. The people are in contrasting locations, too. One looks as if it's a cold place, in a lovely mountainous area, whereas the other is obviously hot. In both pictures the place must be very quiet but in the second I imagine the woman herself must stay quiet so as not to disturb the animals. The woman in the first picture is probably with people we can't see, but from the way she looks, I'd say she's feeling proud about achieving something difficult. She certainly looks pretty pleased with herself. And this is just a guess but this might be the first time she's ever done anything so physically difficult, so it would be a very special moment for her. In the second picture the woman looks very happy and excited. I suppose she's always wanted to go on a safari like this. I can't be sure but I imagine this is probably a special moment for her because she's never seen such amazing animals close up before.

Unit 5, Listening Activity 1

Track 10

I = Interviewer J = Janet D = Dave

I: Today I'm talking to Janet Wilson and Dave Edwards, two comedians specialising in stand-up comedy. Janet, what does a stand-up comedian do, and how did you start?

J: I go into theatres, stand on stage and tell jokes! I'm completely alone – no actors. It's pretty scary, but that's part of the appeal. I write my own material, which can be demanding, and I love the creativity of it more than the actual writing process. I've always known I wanted to perform in one way or another. At school I had a ball acting in plays – I even joined a local drama club. Even then I preferred comedy roles, though I only found out about stand-up itself when I was taken to a show for a birthday treat. It seemed a logical extension of being an actor and I got hooked pretty quickly.

I: How did your parents react when you told them what you wanted to do?

J: My dad's into technology – he's a genius with computers. I'm a bit of a geek myself but I'm not particularly talented, though I write tech jokes in my material. I guess they hoped that I'd do something safe, like computing or medicine, but my academic record put paid to that! My brother's a lawyer and my parents are really proud of him. They've never been unsupportive of me but they'd just like to see a more clearly defined career structure – and the entertainment sector doesn't give that at all. Even people who make it big aren't necessarily working all the time.

I: Dave, how do you feel when you're actually performing?

D: It can be hard remembering everything as well as being flexible and responding to the audience, which is an important part of stand-up. They can be very demanding – they've paid money to be entertained and if I don't make them laugh, I've failed. As a comedian you have to understand that and not let it get under your skin. It's happened to me. What I thought were good jokes fell on stony ground and when there's silence instead of laughter that's disconcerting. I want to spread joy, take people out of themselves, and it's pretty special when I can see I'm having that kind of effect on others. It's true that performing can be exhausting, even when everything's going well, but you're buoyed up by the audience.

I: So what do you think is most important for a successful comedian?

D: I'm happy with a good experience on stage. I'd love to win trophies, get recognised for my work, but there's more to it than that. As a creative person, I want to have a sense of progress. It's not just about comedy, it's about where you are in your life. You have to give all of yourself on stage, so you're very exposed and that has the potential to be hurtful. The bottom line is you need to be thick-skinned and confident in what you're doing but taking constructive comments on board. Take the rough with the smooth, in other words.

I: How do you both feel about the future of stand-up comedy?

J: It's definitely higher-profile than ever but there'll be more comedians trying to get work which will create extra pressure on all of us. It's a more viable career choice now – there are academic courses specialising in stand-up, so the genre could become even more specialised. I think it will always have a satirical edge to it, though.

D: It's high stakes, and understandably people get stressed. Though there may be more opportunities, it's vital to grab them with both hands because if you don't, someone else will. You must update your material constantly, but you can't let that unnerve you –you have to evolve however hard that might be.

I: Janet, how do you feel about your own future?

J: People often think comedians are misfits but I reckon that's an idea put about by comedians themselves, to make themselves sound interesting and boost audiences! I'm enjoying writing at the moment and I'd like to do more gigs. When you're over-specific about what you want to do, you risk setting yourself up for a fall if it doesn't happen. I don't make enough as a stand-up, which is something I have to address – I need to be realistic and bring in a regular wage for a while. I've got movies in my long-term sights. I've been looking at scripts, though I don't know how likely they are to materialise.

I: Thank you both for sharing those insights with us and good luck with your careers.

Unit 6, Listening, Activity 1

Track 11

1

A: People keep things that mean something to them. It may be a reminder of a special moment, a keepsake from a deceased relative, a picture of a place where something significant took place. It may be we feel these things somehow define us, but no-one else does. They mean nothing to other people.

B: I remember my aged aunt asking me if there was anything I wanted from her house. She had loads of things that meant a great deal to her. Embarrassingly, it was all stuff I'd think of as junk. But it was hard not to hurt her feelings, so I did choose something in the end.

A: Maybe the point is they make us feel part of our heritage. Certainly, that's the case with royalty, who have stuff going back hundreds of years – because it's part of their history – and they feel they have a responsibility to store it for future generations. And we all go to marvel at it in museums and galleries, so there's a point to it.

B: I reckon that each generation has its own priorities and they just don't fancy being coerced into keeping things that mean nothing to them.

2

A: Some people seem to have forgotten the key role museums play in preserving and cataloguing everything that's fundamental to our past and present – and they even provide pointers for the future. Students love them because they get a practical slant on subjects that otherwise they'd only read about. That advantage of museums shouldn't be underestimated or undervalued.

B: Be that as it may, it all comes at a cost and priorities are different nowadays. Museums may be important for those keen on history or anyone with a particular interest in a particular thing – like railways or dolls' houses. Of course, society would lose something if they weren't available but to be honest, they're a minority interest and therefore a luxury we can ill afford.

A: Museums are a highlight for tourists, who bring in revenue. They can enhance people's experiences of seeing new places and add to our understanding of how and why things have happened. We all have a responsibility to learn from the past. Obviously, not everything will appeal to everyone but that doesn't mean museums shouldn't be there.

B: People need to be trained to set them up and the payback isn't sufficient. If you think about it, technology's taken over – and it's more cost-effective than maintaining a stuffy old building!

3

A: Well, that was a bit of a slog! The story was so slow it almost stopped – it seemed to go on forever! I know that period of history was a bit complex and they had to get the facts across but they could have done better. After all the trailers and the hype, I expected better.

B: Facts? Is that what they were? I reckon most of it was fabricated; certainly, there were characters invented just to up the tension. That seems a cop-out – and worse than that, it's feeding false information to people who see it without knowing anything about what actually happened.

A: It's a film, not a history lesson – that seems a valid thing to do. Reading texts can be dry and kill interest in history. Making films at least brings it to life, though maybe not in this particular case! I'd rather see children in cinemas watching history unfold in front of them than not know anything about it. And the costumes and sense of the period were certainly on target.

B: What people see on screen is filtered through the consciousness of the director and the interpretation of the actors – it's not unbiased or objective.

A: It's sold as entertainment, not education – though in this case, it wasn't even that!

Unit 6, Speaking, Activity 2

Track 12

I'd like to look at these two pictures. The first one shows a woman on an archaeological site. She's crouching down over some notes and is either reading what she has written or checking some information. In the second picture it looks as if an athletics coach is monitoring a runner, making a note of how fast he can run. The coach is holding a stopwatch so that he can make sure the time is absolutely accurate.

Both pictures show different events being recorded but whereas the first could be an important public record of a historical finding, I imagine that the second one is a personal record so that in the future the coach and the runner can look back and check it to see how his performance has changed or improved. Regarding the accuracy of the recording, the historical information really needs to be totally reliable because the archaeologist is recording facts that people will need to know about in the future, and they will rely on the notes she makes. Although it's also vital for the athlete that the timings are spot-on because he may be aiming to break a record and so he must be completely sure exactly how fast he can run, the information is only for him and his coach, not for public record.

Unit 7, Listening, Activity 1

Track 13

I = Interviewer E = Emily J = James

I: Today I'm talking to entrepreneurs Emily Johnson and James Harris, who both started their own marketing business in their early twenties. Emily, what made you do that?

E: I didn't set out to be an entrepreneur; I kind of stumbled into it. I'd studied graphic design because I was pretty creative but when it came to finding a job, I wasn't getting anywhere. A mate said, 'You're good at marketing and selling. Why don't you try that?' So I did! Job satisfaction's more important than money. It doesn't seem like work when I'm doing something I enjoy or it feels worthwhile. Advertising fitted in with my creative side and marketing is an extension of that.

I: What's helped you most as a young entrepreneur?

E: Being a good communicator is up there – you have to sell yourself and your business. Of course, education influences who you are but it's just a grounding – experience in the business world is ultimately what counts. I did several internships for free when I was job hunting, and that type of experience is really helpful – it gears you up for the real world. It builds confidence, helps you see what the possibilities are. And I was pretty focused on making it work.

I: James, how did it feel when you actually started your own business?

J: You put yourself on the line and it's not easy to give up on security. I wasn't nervous about not cutting it, though that's the hurdle for most wannabe entrepreneurs. The way I came to terms with it was to take things one step at a time. I kind of knew there'd be ups and downs but you can't plan for how it feels when you're going through a low patch. When you're in a tight corner, you've only got yourself to fall back on and, surprisingly, I found that unpredictability thrilling. I do have to steel myself to learn from my mistakes, though.

I: So how is it for young entrepreneurs in a tough business environment?

J: Positive and negative – people admire your courage while having this stereotypical image of young people, which more often than not works against you. That's difficult, but the more you put yourself out there and people see what you can do, how determined you are, the more your name gets bandied about. Then age becomes a non-issue – people realise you've got recognition just because of your ability. That's crucial; we get clients through word of mouth and that can grow a business exponentially.

I: What do you enjoy most about running your own business, Emily?

E: You have to show the value of your business and how it benefits your client. My business is based on ideas, which makes running it more difficult than those with something concrete to sell. How do you evaluate an idea, know whether it's any good? But that's the buzz I get – seeing my ideas on a station wall, on TV. The best feeling, though, is when my work has helped a client achieve what they want. When they do well, so do I. I did think the hardest thing would be having the discipline because I needed to work nineteen-hour days. I got through it on my own but it was surprisingly easy because I loved every minute and I was doing it for myself.

I: What advice would you both give any aspiring young entrepreneur?

E: I wish I'd known how it could affect friendships – I realised I'd be giving up a big social life but I hadn't bargained on how it affected my relationships. You'd probably expect me to say, keep at it, but you have to believe that there's a point to it all and you're making a difference, so focus on that.

J: I'd say there's a world out there and conquering it is in your hands, so make yourself into something unique – don't accept second best. But your aim shouldn't be just getting rich – believe in what you're doing, make it count for something. Then it will give you more satisfaction than you can ever imagine. Oh, and enjoy it!

I: Thank you both …

Unit 8, Listening, Activity 2

Track 14

I'm Peter and I'm here to talk about my work as a travel writer. It started by chance. I'd been on several short family holidays to Europe, America, Africa; then after college I took any job I could to save money for a few days in Singapore, followed by a six-month trek around Australia on my own – just for fun, but it got me hooked. I couldn't afford to do it in style, but being independent gave me options. I could choose where I stayed or how I travelled. I quickly discovered that the bonus of travelling alone was getting close to the local culture – I hated being what tour companies describe as 'protected' or 'sheltered' but I feel is 'narrow-minded'.

After that I checked out possibilities of travelling for a living, and a friend suggested travel writing. I found writing courses promising a life of leisure, free travel and non-stop holidays after qualifying. It sounded ideal and at the time I was excited by the concept, but I was probably immature. Once I actually became a writer I discovered that like anything in life, you must work hard and have a bit of luck.

Rather than diving in at the deep end by writing books, I decided articles would be the simplest way in. Being a rookie travel writer is hard; you can only spend a short time in a city or resort but you must learn everything about it. Consequently, you rush from restaurant to hotel, attraction to scenic landmark, making copious notes to expand into something coherent. Even after I got into what I call real travel writing, it's an uncertain way to earn a living. The biggest downside is there's no salary, plus you often have to pay for expenses up front and it can be months before a book's published and you get any royalties.

It's a competitive world and every casual traveller imagines they can make a contribution. Editors are swamped with stuff sent on spec by those hoping to pass on their own unique observations, but visiting an out-of-the-way destination and writing about it is no guarantee of publication. That's why many write online blogs instead.

It offends me how travel blogs are often just a way for people to vent their frustrations about their unpleasant journey or experience. A real travel writer filters out personal details – readers want to know your reaction to a place, not whether you were ill! They have to like and trust you, and through you engage with the place itself. That's where your skill comes in – ultimately, successful communication far outweighs your enthusiasm for travel or anything else.

If you're considering becoming a travel writer, think about why you want to do it, and be prepared for hardships. Sure, you need to be curious and perceptive, with an eye for the quirky and unusual, but that's not enough. Develop your own style and, primarily, never ignore feedback wherever it comes from. Oh, and meet deadlines or you'll get a reputation for tardiness!

Unit 9, Speaking, Activities 2 and 3

Track 15

These two pictures are quite different, although they both rely on an illusion to be successful. The first one shows a person performing on a … sorry, it's gone – you know – the thing actors and dancers perform on? Anyway, it looks as if they're dancing in a classical ballet or something like that. A performance like this depends on the dancers managing to convince the audience that the world they're dancing in is real. This is quite difficult as ballet is very – what's the word? – stylised

– and because of that a lot of people just don't get it. The dancers need to have creativity – no, that's not the word I'm looking for; it's … yes, talent – they have to have talent and imagination to create an illusion that becomes believable. That's really difficult for them to do, because dancing isn't something we do in real life, but if they're successful, the audience can enter that illusion and escape into a different world where dance and music combine to tell a story.

The second picture looks like it's a sort of machine where people can practise things before they do them in real life. It creates the illusion of the real situation, and in this case the golfer can hit the ball without having to walk miles to pick it up. I can't remember the exact word for the machine, but it's, like, when people are learning how to drive. The benefit they get is from practising in a safe situation so that they can do it well later. The machine – oh, what's it called? Never mind … The machine is probably quite easy to create when you've got the right technology but in this situation it doesn't make playing golf any easier I imagine, because the golfer still has to have a lot of skill. It's vital to practise, though, and that's how he's benefiting from the illusion.

Unit 9, Listening, Activity 1

Track 16

1   I've always been an avid reader of psychology books and own many which have given me real insights and access to ideas that I often refer to. I'm involved in management training and I had a feeling that this would supplement my reading in that area and enhance my professional life. As I have no real psychology background and haven't studied it formally, it's inappropriate for me to comment on it technically but I'd imagine it would be rather simplistic for anyone wanting an in-depth specialist overview. It opens your eyes to different ways of looking at things, which can't be bad for people like me.

2   I haven't finished it yet but that's not because it's boring – rather the opposite, as I have to think carefully about each chapter and digest it. I probably wouldn't bother if it weren't part of my psychology module, though. I hadn't expected it but it's actually pretty accessible. There's a balance of technical information and fascinating details, and it's fairly readable. The examples given to support various facts are real – like, a baby's eyes have a fixed focus length that's exactly right for seeing its mother's face while it's feeding. That kind of thing's unusual in a science book but it brings it all to life.

3   Even for a complete novice, it's possible to understand and learn from this book. It wasn't on my university reading list nor had my tutor mentioned it but I came across a second-hand copy when I was browsing with a friend in a shop – it was cheap and on the flip test it looked worth reading, so I thought I'd give it a go. It gave me the impetus to track down other psychology books, which is why I reckon other people should try it. It isn't a textbook, so it's unsuitable for anyone wanting in-depth analysis. It's been written by someone who's knowledgeable and enthusiastic about his subject, which is great.

4   I studied psychology many years ago and when I saw a positive review about this book saying it was worth reading, I decided to buy it. I didn't find it at all dry or long-winded, and the lively style captivated me. I was surprised to discover just how far the field has changed and progressed in recent years and this should guarantee its appeal to ex-students like me, perhaps less to the uninformed reader with only a superficial interest. It's a field which has many facets to explore, and this brought back many memories and provided a few surprises.

5   I actually bought this for my student girlfriend but we'd been going through a bad patch and I wanted to share some of her interests to build bridges. As soon as I started reading, I was hooked. For anyone studying seriously, there are notes, suggestions for further reading and details about informative websites, which would probably be better for them than the book

itself – it's more – it's more for anyone with a passing interest in expanding their knowledge easily. Its main selling point is there's not too much jargon, which can be mind-bending and put people off. It's also related to everyday life. It's made me think about the way I deal with people!

Unit 10, Listening, Activities 1 and 2

Track 17

1   I grew up with animals – in fact, I lived on a farm – but choosing a pet for our children was a different ballgame. We did loads of research: books, internet, contacted pet owners to identify the pitfalls. It was a concern about taking care of the animal when we were away – we're inveterate travellers and I'd hate that to be curtailed – so it had to be something small. My kids are pretty thoughtless and I wondered whether it might encourage a sense of responsibility in them. Predictably, though, it's me who's ended up cleaning out the hamster's cage and making sure it's fed – it's really backfired on me. Now I'm stuck with it.

2   I wanted my kids to get the kind of pleasure I got from having a dog – though, actually, that wasn't an option as we live in a flat. They did some research into what they could have, then presented me with a choice. We're not that well off, so I was wary of anything that might run up bills by ruining furniture or needed the vet, so tropical fish were just the thing. They're fun to watch and though it's hard to believe, up to now I haven't had any problems with the kids forgetting to clean out the tank – they seem to love it.

3   I really struggle with doing exercise – it's my greatest bugbear – and as I get older, the weight seems to creep on. So when a friend suggested we got a dog so I'd have to take it for walks, it seemed worth considering, but the kids weren't keen – I think they realised they'd probably have the responsibility of doing the walking! We came to the conclusion together that we'd find an animal that would be pretty easy-care. My daughter wanted a cat and although there were costs involved, that wasn't an issue for me. And at least it walks itself, though the neighbours don't always like it!

4   The impetus came from the children – they'd been on about having a pet for ages, then when their closest friends got one, well, that caused huge arguments in our house! I didn't want the hassle some pets would cause, so I was strongly against it. But the final push stemmed from some classwork they had on birds and I felt I should support them. I'm prepared to admit now that my fears were unfounded. I feel bad about what I said because it's worked out for us. The parrot's pretty and the kids enjoy stuff like cleaning the cage – I don't have to do anything.

5   The great outdoors has always been my big thing. I've tried to instil it in the kids – not easy! They're more the 'read-about-it-on-the-tablet' types. I thought it would encourage them to get out into the countryside – a dog needs that – but it was me that ended up doing it. Not that I mind – I work from home and it gives me an excuse to get out without having to justify it. It was a failure as far as my initial plan was concerned, though. Sure, the kids love the dog and on some level they're glad he's there but they're still attached to their tablets!

Unit 10, Speaking, Activity 1

Track 18

1

A: For a marriage to succeed, I'd say you need to have a lot of common interests.

B: I agree up to a point, but I think having different hobbies can be refreshing in a way.

2

A: I think in a successful business partnership, both partners need to have different roles.

B: That may well be so, but don't you think they also need to have the same outlook and ambitions?

3

A: In a speaking test, I think it's important to have a partner who has the same sort of personality as you do.

B: I'm not entirely convinced. Suppose you get two very strong personalities together, who just keep interrupting each other all the time?

4

A: If you look at successful, famous comedy acts from the past, there's usually one partner who seems quite serious while the other one is the real funny man.

B: Isn't it sometimes the case that the serious one is really the brains behind the partnership?

5

A: To work together in a successful coalition, surely, the politicians have to have a mutual respect for each other and at least support each other in public.

B: But that is unlikely to hold true in all cases. If one member of the coalition disagrees really strongly with something, then it would be hard to stay quiet!

A: I dare say you're right but then that would risk the coalition and be against his best interests, don't you think?

Unit 10, Speaking, Activity 2

Track 19

A: Well, that's a tricky one, isn't it? As we said, I think all of them present difficulties. Which would you say is the most difficult to make succeed?

B: Yes, it's not an easy choice. There are challenges in all the types of partnerships. I imagine in the short term a coalition could well be the hardest to make succeed because usually the politicians have different principles and politics from each other. Working together must be very hard!

A: You're so right! They have to swallow their pride a bit and make compromises. But if we're thinking long term, I guess the most difficult of these has got to be a marriage!

B: Yes, there are so many pressures when two people get married, it's very easy for the marriage to fail. It's all a matter of give and take, isn't it?

A: Yes! That's the same for all partnerships, of course, but in the long run, I think it's hardest to make a marriage work well.

B: I'm with you there. Let's go for that.

Unit 11, Listening, Activity 1

Track 20

I = Interviewer   K = Karen   J = Jason

I: We're talking to Karen Simpson and Jason Todd, fashion designers promoting handmade eco-fashion. Karen, a controversial question: it's sometimes said that consumers of fashion are just obsessed with their appearance. What's your take on that?

K: Well, there are many things involved in fashion and that's why people love it – self-esteem and image, certainly, but also fun. I got into it after reading my sister's fashion magazines and yes, I was knocked out by those beautiful pictures. But I grew up in the country; my family drummed environmental responsibility into me but I realised that wasn't the case for many people. After I went

into fashion design, I wanted to promote those values, show it was possible to blend a beautiful appearance with an underlying responsible approach.

I: Jason, is it easy combining an ethical approach with fashion design?

J: There's a lot to consider. I aim to design clothes from materials that won't run down any non-renewable resources but it's important to also make sure the process of producing them doesn't cause pollution in itself. Then there's what happens when clothes are finished with – whether throwing them away harms the environment. It's not how everyone in the industry thinks and I'm not sure I got it myself at first. I want to make people look good but didn't realise how much of an uphill struggle it would be to achieve this while making them environmentally aware at the same time.

I: What would you both say about your design style? Jason?

J: I'm pretty hard-boiled as a person and I've had my fair share of setbacks. I've tried to turn those to my advantage – I expect a lot of myself and what I can achieve, and push myself creatively. My designs embody where I'm at in terms of the look I want and the materials I use, and they stand out. I'm always true to what I believe in.

K: I get inspiration from travelling, though I put my own take on what I find. I mix different traditions to make something unique and I think outside the box – like the garment that can be worn in different ways depending on how it's put on. That saves people money 'cos they buy fewer clothes! But I do have an identifiable look underlying all my designs so people know what they're getting with me.

I: Karen, what's the priority in your designs?

K: I design for someone who stands out from the crowd and isn't frightened of expressing themselves or standing up for their principles. My clothes give confidence. For some designers, the bottom line's financial and so they kowtow to the mass market – their designs don't push the envelope, they avoid risks. I show it's not impossible to be the height of fashion while sticking to my core values. And it's not just eyewash – I hate waste, so I use recycled materials – it's plain common sense, not just ecologically responsible.

I: Jason, as a creative designer, how do you feel about the practical side of production?

J: When I start designing, I get my head into colours, fabrics, the look I want. That's creative and takes ages. The final designs are often nothing like my first ideas 'cos I chop and change and get input from other people. I stick to my requirements for low-impact clothes in spite of any market pressures, but it's an evolving process. I'm pretty driven, which means I'm heavily involved in it all and I get a real kick from seeing my abstract concepts take shape.

I: Finally, how do you both see the future?

K: I guess it's obvious – people are seeing our throwaway society and realising that there is a way of getting what you want without destroying anything. That probably sounds totally idealistic but I'm hopeful. It's not plain sailing, and I know it'll be challenging– but this is not just happening in fashion, it's happening in other areas, too.

J: People sometimes describe so-called green fashion as unattractive but that perception needs addressing. I'd love to sell huge numbers of clothes but not at the expense of what I believe in, and that'll be tough. Clearly, anything handmade shows values like quality, tradition and attention to detail, though, of course, people need to accept that it means it's costly, which they don't want.

I: Karen and Jason, thanks for your time!

Unit 11, Speaking, Activity 2

Track 21

Right, I'd like to discuss these pictures – the one with the woman getting the presents and the footballers. Obviously, in both the pictures the people are feeling strongly about something but they're in very different situations and have very different feelings.

The people in the first picture are enjoying a special moment, and they all seem to be very happy because they're laughing, whereas there's no doubt that the footballers have very negative feelings. They're certainly not laughing!

The people in the first picture are very excited to see the woman happy. I think they're her family and maybe it's her birthday and they've been planning to give her a surprise for a long time. They're glad that it's turned out to be a success, and she's feeling happy that her family have been so thoughtful.

Conversely, the footballers are showing completely different emotions. They both look angry, even aggressive, and the referee is trying to stop them having a fight. Maybe the one in green and yellow kicked the other one, or perhaps tried to push him out of the way and he didn't like it. I'm convinced that it'll be difficult to calm them down, but in a competitive game like football emotions are often very intense but quite short-lived. I suppose the referee will sort everything out.

Unit 12, Listening, Activity 1

Track 22

Hi, I'm Tony and I'm here to talk about being a toy inventor. Although I never studied design or technology, I've always come up with out-of-the-box ideas. Like, while I was at school, I wrote stories for comics, cartoon captions and, most bizarrely, jokes for radio. I think I've got the knack of seeing the funny side!

Toys have always been my thing – how they're designed and put together and what's actually enjoyable about them. I get a buzz from trying to work something out – other people call it problem-solving or lateral thinking but I regard it as a puzzle. My breakthrough came about by chance, though. I was watching a game of badminton when I started thinking about different ways a shuttlecock moves. Then I thought of this table-top game where you punch it forward not with a racquet but with a glove. I wanted to make loads of money, so I looked on the net for big companies I thought might take it up.

The people at the first company were friendly and made positive comments but they were worried about finance and my idea didn't really suit their brand image. They recommended a different company, and the people there were keen to adopt my prototype and then it all kicked off. I'm now a freelance inventor but I still send my ideas to different manufacturers and there are no guarantees they'll be accepted. It's not what I'd call a secure existence!

You're all looking for unusual careers like mine, so here are some things I've learnt. Don't give up if success doesn't come immediately. I know some incredibly creative people who throw in the towel at the first rejection – I don't get that at all. If I get turned down, I revisit it immediately – come at it from a different angle.

I realise you need to bounce ideas off people who should provide some support and back-up, but more crucially, honesty – I'm certain that's vital if the feedback is to be of any practical use. Telling white lies isn't helpful.

Check out what companies specialise in. It may seem obvious but people often don't – they just go for a name they know, which could mean you start off on the wrong foot. Companies don't want you to submit the same idea several times, however much you might have amended it. They won't necessarily give advice or make suggestions but should provide feedback on why they've turned you down; if not, request it – though sometimes you may have to accept that an apparently good idea isn't going to work.

Any company will take time to assess a new idea – whether it's practicable, functional or saleable. You must be determined but there's a difference between persistence and making a nuisance of yourself. First and foremost you need patience. If they get annoyed, they'll think it's easier to work with someone else.

It's a fascinating job and in the modern world of digital games it may seem old-fashioned, but there's a market out there and it's a creative and exciting job to do. So … any questions?

Practice test, Listening Part 1

Track 23

1

A: People say we don't need much of an attention span these days but if you look at something like, say, a TV series, and there are different branches of the story to keep up with over a long period, only being able to concentrate for a short time is going to be pretty useless! Think about the number of characters you have to remember – and that's without the complexities of the plot!

B: But longer series are great for character development – and writers seem to be moving towards longer books, too. They can really explore a character and engage readers – that's why they're on the up.

A: It's true that short stories aren't that popular. Going back to attention spans, you'd think if people really had difficulty concentrating, they'd choose to read those, not longer books, which is not actually the case.

B: It's a shame they don't though. I think sometimes one page can say what a whole novel takes about 400 to do! There's irrelevant detail in a novel, too, which really irritates me.

A: Ironically, something short needs even more attention because it isn't all spelt out for us, so we need to think about it more.

2

A: We're all using digital technology more these days but it can be isolating in spite of the fact that we use it for social networking. So, when it comes to playing games, it's understandable that digital multiplayer games are featuring more and more. I feel strongly that even this can't replace the personal connection.

B: Well, we're living in an age where digital information networks get into every aspect of our lives. In a way, games are a cultural reflection of this. Playing against another person lets you try something out, play with cause and effect in a safe environment – no personal contact. In that sense, digital games are helpful.

A: People want leisure activities that let them actively interact. I think board games fulfil our need for the face-to-face contact we used to have. With board games we're doing something but also connecting with each other on a personal level, and so they're becoming popular again.

B: But you have to look at this surge in the popularity of board games in context. There's a big retro-trend going on now – you know, like, with clothes and even vinyl records! So it's also true that most keen digital games players are board game enthusiasts. It's niche, but significant.

3

A: Technology is generally used for archiving information. There's this idea that it's part of a long progression which began with the first written records on stone tablets and continued developing without a hitch to the present day's sophisticated level of storing data, whereas, in fact, it can actually be compared to the science of biology, which had ups and downs and many species along the way simply died off and never made it.

B: Archivists joke about how digital information either lasts forever or five years, whichever comes first. What they mean is, it's ridiculously intricate because formats change, operating systems get updated and the hardware running those systems becomes outdated and unusable.

A: So over the long term, things we'd like to pass on from now might actually be more difficult for future generations to access than, for example, finding out about a dead civilisation from actual relics.

B: We can certainly learn a lot about past civilisations simply by digging up clay tablets, but there's the possibility of an enormous gap in history covering the period from the rise of the internet to whenever we reach a point in the future where methods of archiving are fixed and accessible.

A: It's still important to archive, though!

Practice test, Listening Part 2

Track 24

Hi, everyone! I'm Carol, and I'm here to talk about making lifestyle changes and how I turned my life around. After university, I'd hoped to do something intellectually challenging that would also get me into the high life. My friends defined success as owning possessions but though I kind of went along with that, it was the sense of achievement that I was aiming for. Working in finance seemed ideal. But the ethical side of it all bothered me. I also turned into a clock-watcher because the job wasn't really demanding and a commuter; that was the biggest downside as it took hours every day!

One day, a friend bought me a birthday present that changed everything. It wasn't a physical present – it was an experience, which is quite a common type of present in the city. My experience was becoming a zookeeper for a day. I suspect that far from being thoughtful, my friend thought it would be a joke, but I got to see what went on behind the scenes and the complexities of looking after exotic animals. Far from boring, or mundane, it looked so worthwhile and, suddenly, my own job seemed pointless. I kept my feelings to myself – people might have thought I was crazy! But when I saw a vacancy for a zookeeper, I went for it. I had zero qualifications, no experience but loads of enthusiasm, which is what may have swung it for me at the interview.

The full training took two years and now I'm in charge of the lions, tigers and wolves. It's definitely not glamorous – you have to muck in, get dirty, work all hours in all weathers. A typical day starts with cleaning cages and checking on the welfare of the animals. It gets to me if I hear visitors say the animals are cute but it's a shame they're smelly – I take pride in making sure that's not the case!

There are strict safety standards – crucial, given the wild animals I work with! They're shut away while I'm in their cages but I check the lock on the door many times while I'm in there – I still get shivers when I first go inside. They're not pets and although they know me, they could still attack. I can identify a shift in their moods from their behaviour. That protects me.

People ask about the morality of zoos. Well, keeping animals in compounds isn't ideal, but we're protecting endangered species – a zoo could be their last refuge. We try to make their lives as natural as possible. Even though it's tempting, I never mollycoddle cubs or meddle with the way family groups interact among themselves. I'm very emotionally involved, which makes this more rewarding than anything I've done before.

I do miss city life and my colleagues but I'm healthier doing a physical job, though I never get the chance to dress up in smart clothes – my hands and nails are a real mess!

Practice test, Listening Part 3

Track 25

I = Interviewer   Ji = Jim   Je = Jenny

I: Today we're talking to two voice actors, Jim Horton and Jenny Simmons. Jim, tell us what you do and how you feel about it.

Ji: Hi! I provide voices for animated characters in films and video games. I also work in radio dramas and commercials. Sometimes it's just speaking but there can also be singing. I'm a workaholic, which means I accept pretty much everything I'm offered – my personal life takes a back seat, though I don't mind that. I'm very creative and I love variety. Of course, some of what I do's just to pay bills – like recording samples for automated announcements in stations. That's mundane, even though I don't actually have to record millions of different things! Each announcement is assembled from fragments, thank goodness.

I: Jenny, you trained as a regular actor. What was hardest for you about changing to voice-overs?

Je: I was at drama school when a director of an animated film invited me to do some stuff with him. I had to work on the technical aspects of dubbing, like synchronising, but I used my overall acting skills and followed my instincts. It's about having a clear voice in the recording studio; getting your feelings across through that alone. But the greatest challenge is adjusting to the fact that there isn't any extended practice beforehand which would let you create a character – it's all very quick. It's demanding even though it's just another aspect of theatre work.

I: How do you start working on a new project, Jim?

Ji: Generally, I get the picture of my character with a description and synopsis of the plot. I establish something I can work with and the director hones that, suggests things, maybe gets me to try something different, which can be annoying. There are only a certain number of voices anyone can do and the skill is to portray a different character even though the voice may be similar. I often get offered the kind of work I've done before, which is fun, but stuff I don't normally get to do is most thrilling because it's scary! I guess any acting's like that.

I: How do you both go about portraying a character?

Je: When I first started, I had to work at it – establish my limitations and set aims – but as I go along, I find different nuances in my voice that I can use to create different characters. Sometimes when I go into the recording studio, it just happens; but even then it has to have the ring of truth. The process can be quite organic.

Ji: There's a lot of experimenting, trying different things out, and everyone joins in with this but as long as you're coming from your own experience and it's believable, you'll get your character across. I love coming up with something surprising, though if it's rejected, I don't take it personally!

I: Jim, you work on video games - how does that compare with animated films?

Ji: They pay quite well but in many ways they're harder – there's so much crammed into a short time. There are different issues – like, if it's a fighting game, you can't fake anything, you have to really yell. The script looks completely different, too – it's more like a spreadsheet with cues. You don't get to see any animation and it's timed, so you might have to scream for exactly three seconds. That might not seem much, but you try it! Then you have to do it in different ways and it might be followed by shouting. You certainly need throat sweets afterwards!

I: What's your advice for anyone hoping to become a voice actor?

Je: The most popular route is going to drama school, studying improvisation, like me, and I can't fault that. You could find someone to help you apply for auditions. I might recommend getting an agent quite early on, to provide support, though that's a matter of preference.

Ji: You must have a natural quality in your voice that directors identify and people respond to – though you can't learn that. Voiceovers require sophisticated skills, so getting the right kind of basic drama training is really the bottom line. And, of course, don't give up – but that goes without saying.

I: Thanks, both of you!

Practice test, Listening Part 4

Track 26

1   This competition was a multi-sport race – running, kayaking, swimming and cycling, in some of Australia's most spectacular places. I'd wanted to do something similar for a while – although I'm very fit, I wanted a challenge, though I wasn't sure what. This wasn't on my radar initially, though I subsequently looked it up on the website when a friend mentioned it in passing. The beautiful pictures got me hooked. It wasn't all easy, especially as I'm not a strong swimmer and the water there's famous for sharks and rip tides – pretty scary and certainly challenging! The upside was the people, who I'll stay in touch with for a long time to come.

2   I've always been scared of heights, though I've never chosen to confront it head-on – I haven't felt the need. When I got the chance to go climbing in the Dolomites, it seemed like something too good to miss – at least that's what my friend said! The system of paths, cables and ladders in this place gave novice climbers like me the chance to get to the top of some of the peaks, and it was good being part of a group, even though there was a prize for the fastest climber. Unexpectedly, I revelled in honing the technique of climbing and I want to progress with that – a bit of a surprise, really.

3   I took part in a car rally across the desert – madness, you might say! We raced across the red sands at high speeds in searing heat – I actually lost a lot of weight, which hadn't been my intention! It was frightening at times but I found an inner determination I didn't know was there. I'm never happier than mucking around with engines – I've done that in my spare time all my life, and collected old cars – so that was probably why I agreed; oh, and I suppose, the reward – though that didn't lead anywhere – shame we came twenty-fourth!

4   I cycle to work every day, mostly because it keeps me fit, though I do enjoy it. I went in for this twenty-four-hour bike race in America. It was in a beautiful desert region that to describe as tough would be an understatement, and I have no real idea how I got involved other than the attraction of the idea that the winner got a large cheque, which was most appealing! Sleep deprivation was the main difficulty and there were some highly technical and scary ascents and descents, which I hadn't fully realised, so I dismounted for the parts where I lost my nerve. I actually found that a salutary life lesson!

5   My mate had this small light plane and offered me the chance to learn to fly it – for a financial investment, of course! I decided something was missing in my life – that it was too run of the mill, and others seemed to have so much more. I opted in, even though I was scared of heights and, at first, this was an issue. I soon got used to it and we competed in this long-distance flying race. We didn't win, but one thing I had to do was become proficient in weather forecasting – it's fascinating and has opened up a whole new aspect of life.

Practice test, Speaking Part 1

Track 27

First of all we'd like to know something about you. Where are you from?

What do you do there?

How long have you been learning English?

What do you use the internet for most?

Who are you most like in your family?

What has been your most interesting holiday so far?

What kind of career would you really like to follow?

Where do you see yourself in ten years' time?

Practice test, Speaking Part 2

Track 28

In this part of the test I'm going to give each of you three pictures. I'd like you to talk about two of them on your own for about a minute, and also to answer a question briefly about your partner's pictures.

Candidate A, it's your turn first. Here are your pictures. They show people studying in different places. I'd like you to compare two of the pictures and say why the people might have chosen to study in these different places and what difficulties they might have. All right?

Thank you. Candidate B, which place do you think presents the greatest challenge to the people studying?

Thank you. Now, Candidate B, here are your pictures. They show people taking part in different competitions. I'd like you to compare two of the pictures and say why the people might have chosen to enter these competitions and how difficult it might be to prepare for them. All right?

Thank you. Candidate A, which competition do you think would be most satisfying to win?

Thank you.

Practice test, Speaking Part 3

Track 29

Now I'd like you to talk about something together for about two minutes. Here are some things that many people want to achieve in their lives and a question for you to discuss. First you have some time to look at the task.

Now, talk to each other about why many people want to achieve these things in their lives. All right? Could you start now, please?

Thank you. Now you have about a minute to decide which achievement would make most people proud.

Thank you.

Practice test, Speaking Part 4

Track 30

Some people say that we are too materialistic nowadays. What do you think?

How much influence do you think advertising and the media have on people's aspirations?

Do you think that celebrity culture has a positive or negative effect on people? Why?

Some people say that being happy is more important than earning a lot of money. What do you think?

How important is it for people to have experience of the arts like music and theatre?

Do you think that technology improves our lives or makes it worse?

Thank you. That is the end of the test.

Pearson Education Limited
KAO TWO, KAO Park, Hockham Way,
Harlow, Essex, CM17 9SR, England
and Associated Companies throughout the world

www.pearsonELT.com/gold

© Pearson Education Limited 2019

The right of Sally Burgess and Amanda Thomas to be identified as authors
of this Work has been asserted by them in accordance with the Copyright,
Designs and Patents Act, 1988.

New Edition first published 2019

ISBN: 978-1-292-20217-4   (Gold Advanced New Edition Exam Maximiser)

ISBN: 978-1-292-20218-1   (Gold Advanced New Edition Exam Maximiser
                          with Key)

Set in Frutiger Neue LT Pro Thin
Printed in Slovakia by Neografia

Acknowledgements

We are grateful to the following for permission to reproduce
copyright material:

Text
Extract in Unit 1, page 9, from Madrid, my sweet home, *The Telegraph*,
19/09/2012 (Bohter, I.E.), © Telegraph Media Group Limited 2012;
Extract in Unit 2, page 15, from The art of conversation in the natural world,
The Telegraph, 15/06/2002 (Blundell, N.), © Telegraph Media Group
Limited 2002; Extract in Unit 4 from Secret to success: practice, not talent,
The Guardian, 04/06/2011 (Syed, M.), copyright Guardian News & Media
Ltd 2018; Extract in Unit 6, page 43, from My hoarder mum and me,
The Telegraph, 17/08/2011 (Pettie, A.), © Telegraph Media Group Limited
2011; Extract in Unit 7, page 50, from To survive on the High Street, shops
must prioritise experience and ethics, *The Telegraph*, 30/04/2016 (Portas,
M.), © Telegraph Media Group Limited 2016; Extract in Unit 8, page
56, from Confessions of a Voluntourist, *New Internationalist*, 454, July/
August 2012, pp. 58–59 (Dobrovolny, M.), reprinted by kind permission
of New Internationalist. Copyright New Internationalist. www.newint.org;
Extract in Unit 9, page 64, from How the internet is altering your mind,
The Guardian, 20/08/2010 (Harris, J.), copyright Guardian News & Media
Ltd 2018; Extract in Unit 10, page 68, from A working life: the guide dog
trainer, *The Guardian*, 16/09/2011 (King, M.), copyright Guardian News
& Media Ltd 2018; Extract in Unit 12, page 84, from Professor Brian Cox:
can science survive in our post-truth world?, *The Telegraph*, 27/03/2017
(Curtis, N.), © Telegraph Media Group Limited 2017; Extract in Practice
Test Part 5, page 98, from The man who wants to teach the worlds,
The Telegraph, 28/09/2012 (de Bertodana, H.), © Telegraph Media Group
Limited 2012; Extract in Practice Test 7, page 102, from Scott and Bailey,
The Telegraph, 24/03/2012 (Calkin, J.), © Telegraph Media Group
Limited 2012; Extract in Practice Test 8, page 103, from Shining lights,
The Telegraph, 17/12/2011 (de Rosee, S.), © Telegraph Media Group
Limited 2011.

Photos
The publisher would like to thank the following for their kind permission
to reproduce their photographs:

Alamy Stock Photo: Adrian Sherratt 56, B Christopher 63, Blend Images
62, 78, Chris Rout 67, Cultura Creative (RF) 35, David Bagnall 39, Design
Pics Inc 54, Hero Images Inc. 113, 41, Hongqi Zhang 12, Ian Shaw 56, Lev
Dolgachov 41, MBI 86, Newscom 40, Patti McConville 43, Pictorial Press
Ltd 44, Reinhard Dirscherl 41, Science Photo Library 65, Tetra Images
113, 80, Unlisted Images, Inc 56, Vadym Drobot 113, WaterFrame 14,
Wavebreak Media ltd 12, William Mullins 69, fStop Images GmbH 63,
paul weston 51; **Getty Images:** Blend Images - Chris Sattlberger 86,
Caiaimage / Sam Edwards 80, Grant Faint 35, Hans Neleman 113, Mike
Marsland / WireImage 85, Photo and Co 80, SolStock 57, UpperCut
Images 86; Shutterstock.com: Brian J. Ritchie Photography Ltd 113, Erik
Pendzich 113, Greg Blok 9, Igor Bulgarin 63, Monkey Business Images 21,
Odua Images 59, Poprotskiy Alexey 37, Pressmaster 29, Sharomka 12,
VladKK 45, michaeljung 35, r.classen 71

All other images © Pearson Education

Every effort has been made to trace the copyright holders and we
apologise in advance for any unintentional omissions. We would be
pleased to insert the appropriate acknowledgement in any subsequent
edition of this publication.

Illustrated by Oxford Designers and Illustrators